1995 Supplement

to Eighth Editions

MODERN CRIMINAL PROCEDURE
Cases — Comments — Questions

BASIC CRIMINAL PROCEDURE
Cases — Comments — Questions

and

ADVANCED CRIMINAL PROCEDURE
Cases — Comments — Questions

By

Yale Kamisar
*Clarence Darrow Distinguished University Professor of Law,
University of Michigan*

Wayne R. LaFave
*Professor Emeritus in the College of Law
and Center for Advanced Study,
University of Illinois*

Jerold H. Israel
*Alene and Allan F. Smith Professor of Law,
University of Michigan
Ed Rood Eminent Scholar in Trial Advocacy and Procedure,
University of Florida, College of Law*

AMERICAN CASEBOOK SERIES®

WEST PUBLISHING CO.
ST. PAUL, MINN., 1995

COPYRIGHT © 1994 WEST PUBLISHING CO.
COPYRIGHT © 1995 By WEST PUBLISHING CO.
610 Opperman Drive
P.O. Box 64526
St. Paul, MN 55164–0526
1–800–328–9352
All rights reserved
Printed in the United States of America

ISBN 0–314–06866–X

TEXT IS PRINTED ON 10% POST CONSUMER RECYCLED PAPER

PRINTED WITH SOY INK

Preface

This supplement contains all significant United States Supreme Court cases decided during the 1994–95 Term. This volume also contains selected provisions of the U.S. Constitution (App. A); selected federal statutory provisions, e.g., the Bail Reform Act, the Speedy Trial Act and the recently amended Wire and Electronic Communications Interception Act (App. B); the Federal Rules of Criminal Procedure (App. C); and proposed amendments to the Rules (App. D).

YALE KAMISAR
WAYNE LaFAVE
JEROLD H. ISRAEL

July, 1995

Acknowledgments

Excerpts from the following articles appear with the kind permission of the copyright holders.

Cassell, Paul G., *Miranda*'s Social Cost: An Empirical Reassessment, 90 Nw.U.L.Rev. ___ (1995). Copyright © 1995 by Paul G. Cassell. Reprinted by permission.

Livingston, Debra, Brutality in Blue: Community, Authority, and the Elusive Promise of Police Reform, 92 Mich.L.Rev. 1556 (1994). Copyright © 1994 by the Michigan Law Review. Reprinted by permission.

*

Table of Contents

	Page
PREFACE	iii
ACKNOWLEDGMENTS	v
TABLE OF CASES	xi

PART ONE

INTRODUCTION

CHAPTER 3. THE RIGHT TO COUNSEL, TRANSCRIPTS AND OTHER AIDS; POVERTY, EQUALITY AND THE ADVERSARY SYSTEM 1

1. *THE RIGHT TO APPOINTED COUNSEL AND RELATED PROBLEMS* 1
   Nichols v. United States 1

PART TWO

POLICE PRACTICES

CHAPTER 4. SOME GENERAL REFLECTIONS ON THE POLICE, THE COURTS AND THE CRIMINAL PROCESS 3

Debra Livingston—Brutality in Blue: Community, Authority, and the Elusive Promise of Police Reform 3

David A. Harris—Factors for Reasonable Suspicion: When Black and Poor Means Stopped and Frisked 5

CHAPTER 5. ARREST, SEARCH AND SEIZURE 6

1. *THE EXCLUSIONARY RULE* 6
   Arizona v. Evans 6
   Note on the sufficiency of the "constitutional tort" 9
3. *PROBABLE CAUSE* 9
4. *SEARCH WARRANTS* 10
   Wilson v. Arkansas 10
5. *WARRANTLESS ARRESTS* 10
   Powell v. Nevada 10
7. *STOP AND FRISK* 11
   David A. Harris—Factors for Reasonable Suspicion: When Black and Poor Means Stopped and Frisked 11
   David A. Harris—Frisking Every Suspect: The Withering of Terry 12

TABLE OF CONTENTS

Page

8. ADMINISTRATIVE INSPECTIONS AND REGULATORY SEARCHES: MORE ON BALANCING THE NEED AGAINST THE INVASION OF PRIVACY 13
    Veronica School District v. Acton 13

CHAPTER 7. POLICE "ENCOURAGEMENT" AND THE DEFENSE OF ENTRAPMENT 26

8. CONTINUING CONTROVERSY OVER THE ENTRAPMENT DEFENSE 26
    United States v. Gendron 26
    United States v. Hollingsworth 28

CHAPTER 8. POLICE INTERROGATION AND CONFESSIONS 33

3. THE MIRANDA "REVOLUTION" 33
    Note—England curtails the right to silence 33
    Does § 3501(c) codify a limited form of the McNabb-Mallory rule? 34
    United States v. Alvarez-Sanchez 34
    Congress's attempt to "repeal" *Miranda* 35
    Justice Scalia—Concurring in Davis v. United States 35
    Applying and Explaining *Miranda* 37
    Stansbury v. California 37
    Paul G. Cassell—*Miranda*'s Social Costs: An Emperical Reassessment 37
    Davis v. United States 40
    The Impact of *Miranda* in Practice 46
    Cassell, supra, on *Miranda*'s Social Costs 46
5. MASSIAH REVISITED; MASSIAH AND MIRANDA COMPARED AND CONTRASTED 47

CHAPTER 11. THE SCOPE OF THE EXCLUSIONARY RULES 48

2. THE "FRUIT OF THE POISONOUS TREE" 48
    The issue not reached in Wilson v. Arkansas 48
    Should courts admit physical evidence derived from coerced confessions? 48

PART THREE

THE COMMENCEMENT OF FORMAL PROCEEDINGS

CHAPTER 14. THE PRELIMINARY HEARING 50
2. THE DEFENDANT'S RIGHT TO A PRELIMINARY HEARING 50
    Albright v. Oliver 50

TABLE OF CONTENTS

Page

CHAPTER 18. THE SCOPE OF THE PROSECUTION: JOINDER AND SEVERANCE OF OFFENSES AND DEFENDANTS 53
2. *FAILURE TO JOIN RELATED OFFENSES* 53
    Department of Revenue v. Kurth Ranch 53
    Witte v. United States 54

CHAPTER 19. THE RIGHT TO A "SPEEDY TRIAL"—AND TO "SPEEDY DISPOSITION" AT OTHER STEPS IN THE CRIMINAL PROCESS 57
1. *SPEEDY TRIAL* 57
    Reed v. Farley 57

PART FOUR

THE ADVERSARY SYSTEM AND THE DETERMINATION OF GUILT OR INNOCENCE

CHAPTER 21. DISCOVERY AND DISCLOSURE 58
2. *DISCOVERY BY THE DEFENSE* 58
5. *THE PROSECUTION'S CONSTITUTIONAL DUTY TO DISCLOSE* 58
    Kyles v. Whitley 58

CHAPTER 22. COERCED, INDUCED AND NEGOTIATED GUILTY PLEAS; PROFESSIONAL RESPONSIBILITY 63
2. *REJECTED, KEPT AND BROKEN BARGAINS; UNREALIZED EXPECTATIONS* 63
    United States v. Mezzanatto 63
4. *RECEIVING THE PLEA; PLEA WITHDRAWAL* 64
    Custis v. United States 64

CHAPTER 23. TRIAL BY JURY 65
1. *RIGHT TO JURY TRIAL; WAIVER* 65
    International Union v. Bagwell 65
    United States v. Gaudin 65
2. *JURY SELECTION* 66
    J.E.B. v. Alabama ex rel. T.B. 66
    Purkett v. Elem 74
    Liteky v. United States 75

CHAPTER 25. THE CRIMINAL TRIAL 76
3. *THE DEFENDANT'S RIGHT TO REMAIN SILENT AND TO TESTIFY* 76
5. *SUBMITTING THE CASE TO THE JURY* 76

CHAPTER 26. REPROSECUTION AND THE BAN AGAINST DOUBLE JEOPARDY 77
3. *REPROSECUTION FOLLOWING A CONVICTION* 77
4. *REPROSECUTION BY A DIFFERENT SOVEREIGN* 77

PART FIVE

APPEALS, POST–CONVICTION REVIEW

CHAPTER 28. HABEAS CORPUS AND RELATED COLLATERAL REMEDIES 78
2. *ISSUES COGNIZABLE* 78
    Reed v. Farley 78
3. *CLAIMS FORECLOSED BY PROCEDURAL DEFAULTS* 79
    Schlup v. Delo 79
4. *THE GOVERNING LEGAL STANDARD* 97
    O'Neal v. McAninch 97

APPENDIX

App.		Page
A.	Selected Provisions of the United States Constitution	99
B.	Selected Federal Statutory Provisions	102
C.	Federal Rules of Criminal Procedure for the United States District Courts	160
D.	Proposed Amendments to Federal Rules of Criminal Procedure	211

Table of Cases

The principal cases are in bold type. Cases cited or discussed in the text are roman type. References are to pages. Cases cited in principal cases and within other quoted materials are not included.

Albright v. Oliver, 50
Alvarez–Sanchez, United States v., 34
Arizona v. Evans, 6

Baldasar v. Illinois, 1
Barker v. Wingo, 57
Bartkus v. People of State of Ill., 77
Batson v. Kentucky, 74
Brecht v. Abrahamson, 97

County of (see name of county)
Custis v. United States, 64

Davis v. United States, 35, 37, **40**
Department of Revenue of Montana v. Kurth Ranch, 53, 55

Evans, State v., 9

Feliciano, United States v., 11

Gaudin, United States v., 65, 76
Gendron, United States v., 26
Gerstein v. Pugh, 10

Hollingsworth, United States v., 28

International Union, United Mine Workers of America v. Bagwell, 65

Jackson v. Virginia, 90
Jacobson v. United States, 32
J.E.B. v. Alabama ex rel. T.B., 66

Kyles v. Whitley, 58

Liteky v. United States, 75

Mallory v. United States, 34

McNabb v. United States, 34
Mezzanatto, United States v., 63
Miranda v. Arizona, 34, 37, 46, 47

New Jersey v. T.L.O., 9
New York v. Harris, 10
New York v. Quarles, 48
Nichols v. United States, 1
Nix v. Williams, 49

O'Neal v. McAninch, 97

Powell v. Nevada, 10
Powell v. State of Ala., 10
Purkett v. Elem, 74

Reed v. Farley, 57, 78
Riverside, County of v. McLaughlin, 10

Schiro v. Farley, 54
Schlup v. Delo, 79
Schmerber v. California, 48
Scott v. Illinois, 1
Smith v. Illinois, 45
Stansbury v. California, 37
State v. _____ (see opposing party)
Stone v. Powell, 78

Terry v. Ohio, 12

United States v. _____ (see opposing party)

Vernonia School Dist. 47J v. Acton, 13

Whiteley v. Warden, Wyo. State Penitentiary, 9
Wilson v. Arkansas, 10, 48
Witte v. United States, 54, 55, 77

1995 Supplement
to Eighth Editions

MODERN CRIMINAL PROCEDURE
Cases — Comments — Questions

BASIC CRIMINAL PROCEDURE
Cases — Comments — Questions

and

ADVANCED CRIMINAL PROCEDURE
Cases — Comments — Questions

*

Part One

INTRODUCTION

Chapter 3

THE RIGHT TO COUNSEL, TRANSCRIPTS AND OTHER AIDS; POVERTY, EQUALITY AND THE ADVERSARY SYSTEM

SECTION 1. THE RIGHT TO APPOINTED COUNSEL AND RELATED PROBLEMS

A. THE RIGHT TO APPOINTED COUNSEL IN CRIMINAL PROCEEDINGS

8th ed. p. 80; end of Note 6, add:

In *Nichols v. United States*, ___ U.S. ___, 114 S.Ct. 1921, 128 L.Ed.2d 745 (1994), the Court, per Rehnquist, C.J., adhered to *Scott*, but overruled *Baldasar*, "agree[ing] with the dissent in *Baldasar* that a logical consequence of [*Scott*] is that an uncounseled [misdemeanor] conviction valid under *Scott* [because no prison term was imposed] may be relied upon to enhance the sentence for a subsequent offense, even though that sentence entails imprisonment." In 1983 Nichols had pled *nolo contendere* to a state misdemeanor, driving under the influence of alcohol (DUI) and paid a $250 fine. He was not represented by counsel. Seven years later, when Nichols pled guilty to a federal drug charge, this uncounseled misdemeanor conviction was used to enhance his prison sentence.[a]

a. Souter, J., concurred only in the judgment. Blackmun, J., joined by Stevens and Ginsburg, JJ., dissented, maintaining that "[i]t is more logical, and more consistent with the reasoning in *Scott*, to hold that a conviction that is invalid for imposing a sentence for the offense itself remains invalid for increasing the term of imprisonment imposed for a subsequent conviction."

Part Two
POLICE PRACTICES

Chapter 4
SOME GENERAL REFLECTIONS ON THE POLICE, THE COURTS AND THE CRIMINAL PROCESS

8th ed. p. 124; after extract from Skolnick & Fyfe's *Above the Law*, add:

Does "community policing" offer a promising means of preventing the police excesses discussed in *Above the Law*? Consider Debra Livingston, *Brutality in Blue: Community, Authority, and the Elusive Promise of Police Reform* (essay review of *Above the Law*), 92 Mich.L.Rev. 1556, 1559, 1571–72 (1994):

"On its face, *Above the Law* is about constraining bad cops from misusing their authority, not about empowering good cops to address growing community concerns with the problems of neighborhood deterioration. Yet, *Above the Law* points to a connection between the twin aspirations of police reformers to control police misconduct and to improve police effectiveness in responding to problems of crime and disorder. Perhaps the book's most intriguing aspect is the authors' belief that the very turn to community policing [a]—with its attendant

---

a. Common elements of the "community" strategy, points out Professor Livingston, are "an emphasis on the community, rather than merely on police professionalism and the law, as a source of legitimation for many police tasks; the purposeful decentralization of much police decisionmaking and the reorientation of patrol in the direction of neighborhood-based policing; a redefinition of the police role to include not only response to individual criminal incidents but also matters like promoting the common welfare, solving community-nominated problems that may contribute to crime, and, for some, aggressively maintaining civil order; and, finally, the establishment of close working relationships between police and citizens, community groups, and, sometimes, relevant social service agencies."

deemphasis on law as a basis for police legitimation, *decentralization of decisionmaking,* and *increase in connections* between beat cops and community residents—may itself be a means of limiting the occasions on which police ignore legal restraints. As concerns with both crime and disorder push the police back to center stage and as policymakers indulge in modest hopes that community-oriented policing might help assuage these concerns, the authors' assessment that returning cops to the community will also help keep them from acts of brutality is, indeed, good news. The most frustrating aspect of this thoughtful book, however, may be *Above the Law*'s less-than-full attention to the problems that police face in our communities today and to the possibility that developing better responses to these problems may itself be a precondition to realizing the open, humanistic style of policing that Skolnick and Fyfe believe will help minimize the tragic incidence of police brutality. * * *

"* * * Proponents of community policing understand that so-called wars on crime cannot be 'won,' if for no other reason than that crime is not an enemy that can be vanquished. Once we set the war-on-crime conception of the police mission aside, however, even ardent advocates of community policing admit that the jury is still out on a different, more modest concern: whether community policing can, in fact, augment public safety at all. Skolnick and Fyfe assert, powerfully, that officers who are placed on the front lines of unwinnable wars on crime become cynical, alienated, and even brutal (pp. 114–15). The authors spend less time assessing the dangers for the beat cop of a reform philosophy that may not be fully realized or that does not, as it turns out, address current concerns about crime and disorder.

"This inattention would be less noteworthy if the philosophy of community policing did not itself raise legitimate concerns relevant to the problem of police brutality. Community policing, however, both frankly bestows discretion on the beat cop and founds the propriety of his actions in part on community norms—notwithstanding how problematic the notion of *community* really is.[48] As David Bayley has noted, implications of the theory of community policing provoke concern that this theory, in practice, may 'weaken the rule of law in the sense of equal protection and evenhanded enforcement ... lessen the protection afforded by law to unpopular persons ... [and] even encourage vigilantism' by mobilizing one part of the community against another. Community policing [as Herman Goldstein has observed] implies 'that officers are to have much greater freedom and to exercise independence' and that communities are to 'have some input into decisions made about the form of police services.' But encouraging independence in the police and input from the community, as Mastrofski and Uchida note in passing in their review of *Above the Law,* may 'place street-level officers at greater

48. Skolnick and Fyfe recognize that if community "implies a commonality of interests, traditions, identities, values, and

risk to be responsive to vigilante values in "defended" neighborhoods.'[51] Moreover, with the decentralized decisionmaking that community policing implies, no one may know 'precisely how patrol officers spend their time.' In first acknowledging and then promoting the beat cop's street-level discretion, community policing theorists must also be concerned that police officers not employ that discretion for their *own* ends—lest community policing in practice lead to increased slackness and time wasting on the beat and to various forms of corruption."

8th ed., 127; after extract from Tracey Maclin's article, add:

Consider, too, David A. Harris, *Factors for Reasonable Suspicion: When Black and Poor Means Stopped and Frisked,* 69 Ind.L.J. 659, 679–81 (1994), maintaining that, because of the disproportionately high number of African Americans and Hispanic Americans living in high crime areas, "location plus evasion" stops and frisks (stops and frisks based on an individual's presence in a high crime location plus evasion of the police) have "widen[ed] the racial divide in the United States." (See also the extract from Professor Harris's article at Supp., p. 11.) But cf. Randall Kennedy, *The State, Criminal Law, and Racial Discrimination: A Comment,* 107 Harv.L.Rev. 1255, 1259 (1994): "Although the administration of criminal justice has, at times, been used as an instrument of racial oppression, the principal problem facing African–Americans in the context of criminal justice today is not over-enforcement but *under*-enforcement of the laws. The most lethal danger facing African–Americans in their day-to-day lives is not white, racist officials of the state, but private, violent criminals (typically black) who attack those most vulnerable to them without regard to racial identity."

expectations," community may simply not exist in many areas. * * *

51. Stephen D. Mastrofski & Craig D. Uchida, *Transforming the Police,* 30 J.Res. Crime & Delinq. 330, 348 (1993).

Chapter 5
ARREST, SEARCH AND SEIZURE

SECTION 1. THE EXCLUSIONARY RULE

8th ed., p. 157; before Note 6, add:

5a. *Evidence obtained by virtue of conduct of nonpolice government employee, used in criminal proceedings.* The *Burdeau* rule, grounded in the proposition that the Fourth Amendment is entirely inapplicable where there is no governmental action, must be distinguished from that recognized in ARIZONA v. EVANS, __ U.S. __, 115 S.Ct. 1185, 131 L.Ed.2d 34 (1995): that some government searches covered by the Fourth Amendment are nonetheless inappropriate occasions for use of the exclusionary rule, considering the kind of government official who was at fault. After Evans was stopped for a traffic violation, the patrol car's computer indicated he had an outstanding arrest warrant, so Evans was arrested; incident thereto, the officer found marijuana. It was later learned that this warrant (issued because of Evans' nonappearance on several traffic violations) had been quashed upon Evans' voluntary appearance in court a few weeks earlier, but that apparently the court clerk had not thereafter followed the usual procedure of notifying the sheriff's department so that the warrant could be removed from the computer records. The state supreme court concluded this amounted to a violation of the Fourth Amendment and that consequently the evidence must be suppressed, but the Supreme Court, per REHNQUIST, C.J., considering only the latter point, disagreed:

" 'The question whether the exclusionary rule's remedy is appropriate in a particular context has long been regarded as an issue separate from the question whether the Fourth Amendment rights of the party seeking to invoke the rule were violated by police conduct.' The exclusionary rule operates as a judicially created remedy designed to safeguard against future violations of Fourth Amendment rights through the rule's general deterrent effect. As with any remedial device, the rule's application has been restricted to those instances where its remedial objectives are thought most efficaciously served. Where 'the exclusionary rule does not result in appreciable deterrence, then, clearly, its use ... is unwarranted.' * * *

"Applying the reasoning of *Leon* [8th ed., p. 135] to the facts of this case, we conclude that the decision of the Arizona Supreme Court must be reversed. The Arizona Supreme Court determined that it could not 'support the distinction drawn ... between clerical errors committed by law enforcement personnel and similar mistakes by court employees,' and that 'even assuming ... that responsibility for the error rested with the justice court, it does not follow that the exclusionary rule should be inapplicable to these facts.'

"This holding is contrary to the reasoning of *Leon,* supra; *Massachusetts v. Sheppard* [8th ed., p. 149]; and *Krull* [8th ed., p. 151]. If court employees were responsible for the erroneous computer record, the exclusion of evidence at trial would not sufficiently deter future errors so as to warrant such a severe sanction. First, as we noted in *Leon,* the exclusionary rule was historically designed as a means of deterring police misconduct, not mistakes by court employees. Second, respondent offers no evidence that court employees are inclined to ignore or subvert the Fourth Amendment or that lawlessness among these actors requires application of the extreme sanction of exclusion. To the contrary, the Chief Clerk of the Justice Court testified at the suppression hearing that this type of error occurred once every three or four years.

"Finally, and most important, there is no basis for believing that application of the exclusionary rule in these circumstances will have a significant effect on court employees responsible for informing the police that a warrant has been quashed. Because court clerks are not adjuncts to the law enforcement team engaged in the often competitive enterprise of ferreting out crime, they have no stake in the outcome of particular criminal prosecutions. The threat of exclusion of evidence could not be expected to deter such individuals from failing to inform police officials that a warrant had been quashed.

"If it were indeed a court clerk who was responsible for the erroneous entry on the police computer, application of the exclusionary rule also could not be expected to alter the behavior of the arresting officer. As the trial court in this case stated: 'I think the police officer [was] bound to arrest. I think he would [have been] derelict in his duty if he failed to arrest.' The Chief Clerk of the Justice Court testified that this type of error occurred 'on[c]e every three or four years.' In fact, once the court clerks discovered the error, they immediately corrected it, and then proceeded to search their files to make sure that no similar mistakes had occurred. There is no indication that the arresting officer was not acting objectively reasonably when he relied upon the police computer record. Application of the *Leon* framework supports a categorical exception to the exclusionary rule for clerical errors of court employees.[5]"

5. The Solicitor General, as amicus curiae, argues that an analysis similar to that we apply here to court personnel also would apply in order to determine whether the evidence should be suppressed if police personnel were responsible for the error. As the State has not made any such argument here, we agree that "[t]he record in this

O'CONNOR, J., joined by Souter and Bryer, concurring, cautioned: "While the police were innocent of the court employee's mistake, they may or may not have acted reasonably in their reliance on the recordkeeping system itself. Surely it would not be reasonable for the police to rely, say, on a recordkeeping system, their own or some other agency's, that has no mechanism to ensure its accuracy over time and that routinely leads to false arrests, even years after the probable cause for any such arrest has ceased to exist (if it ever existed). * * *

"In recent years, we have witnessed the advent of powerful, computer-based recordkeeping systems that facilitate arrests in ways that have never before been possible. The police, of course, are entitled to enjoy the substantial advantages this technology confers. They may not, however, rely on it blindly. With the benefits of more efficient law enforcement mechanisms comes the burden of corresponding constitutional responsibilities."

STEVENS, J., dissenting, argued that the majority's reliance on *Leon* was "misplaced": "The reasoning in *Leon* assumed the existence of a warrant; it was, and remains, wholly inapplicable to warrantless searches and seizures. * * * The *Leon* Court's exemption of judges and magistrates from the deterrent ambit of the exclusionary rule rested, consistently with the emphasis on the warrant requirement, on those officials' constitutionally determined role in issuing warrants. Taken on its own terms, *Leon*'s logic does not extend to the time after the warrant has issued; nor does it extend to court clerks and functionaries, some of whom work in the same building with police officers and may have more regular and direct contact with police than with judges or magistrates."

GINSBURG, J., joined by Stevens, while mainly disagreeing with the majority's invocation of "the *Long* presumption" [see 8th ed., p. 61] to assert jurisdiction, made these comments on the merits: "In the Court's view, exclusion of evidence, even if capable of deterring police officer errors, cannot deter the carelessness of other governmental actors.[5] Whatever federal precedents may indicate—an issue on which I voice no opinion—the Court's conclusion is not the lesson inevitably to be drawn from logic or experience.

case ... does not adequately present that issue for the Court's consideration." Accordingly, we decline to address that question.

5. It has been suggested that an exclusionary rule cannot deter carelessness, but can affect only intentional or reckless misconduct. This suggestion runs counter to a premise underlying all of negligence law—that imposing liability for negligence, i.e., lack of due care, creates an incentive to act with greater care. That the mistake may have been made by a clerical worker does not alter the conclusion that application of the exclusionary rule has deterrent value. Just as the risk of respondeat superior liability encourages employers to supervise more closely their employees' conduct, so the risk of exclusion of evidence encourages policymakers and systems managers to monitor the performance of the systems they install and the personnel employed to operate those systems. In the words of the trial court, the mistake in Evans' case was "perhaps the negligence of the Justice Court, or the negligence of the Sheriff's office. But it is still the negligence of the State."

"In this electronic age, particularly with respect to recordkeeping, court personnel and police officers are not neatly compartmentalized actors. Instead, they serve together to carry out the State's information-gathering objectives. Whether particular records are maintained by the police or the courts should not be dispositive where a single computer database can answer all calls. Not only is it artificial to distinguish between court clerk and police clerk slips; in practice, it may be difficult to pinpoint whether one official, e.g., a court employee, or another, e.g., a police officer, caused the error to exist or to persist. Applying an exclusionary rule as the Arizona court did may well supply a powerful incentive to the State to promote the prompt updating of computer records. That was the Arizona Supreme Court's hardly unreasonable expectation. The incentive to update promptly would be diminished if court-initiated records were exempt from the rule's sway."

In *New Jersey v. T.L.O.*, 8th ed., p. 341, involving search of a student by a high school administrator, the Court reaffirmed that "the Fourth Amendment [is] applicable to the activities of civil as well as criminal authorities." However, because the search was found to be reasonable, the Court avoided expressing any opinion about the question which prompted the original grant of certiorari: whether the exclusionary rule is also applicable to searches by school authorities. In light of *Evans*, what is the answer to that question?

8th ed., p. 160; before Note 3, add:

2a. *More on the scope and sufficiency of the "constitutional tort."* Could the Supreme Court do more to ensure there exists a meaningful tort remedy for Fourth Amendment violations? Consider Bandes, *Reinventing Bivens: The Self-Executing Constitution,* 68 So.Calif.L.Rev. 289, 292 (1995), concluding that *Bivens* "stands for the principle that enforcement of the Constitution is not dependent on the assent of the political branches or of the states," so that there could (and should) be "an expanded *Bivens* doctrine which applies to federal officials and the federal government itself, for damage remedies against state officials and state government directly under the Fourteenth Amendment, and for remedies against municipal officials and government directly under the Fourteenth Amendment when section 1983 does not provide adequate relief." In any event, should tort remedies *replace* the exclusionary rule? Consider Amar, *Fourth Amendment First Principles*, 107 Harv.L.Rev. 757, 786, 798 (1994) (yes, as they were "clearly the ones presupposed by the Framers of the Fourth Amendment" and "make much more sense, *as deterrence*," because "the traditional civil model is not skewed to reward the guilty"). But compare Maclin, *When the Cure for the Fourth Amendment is Worse Than the Disease,* 68 So.Cal.L.Rev. 1 (1994); Steiker, *Second Thoughts About First Principles,* 107 Harv.L.Rev. 820 (1994).

SECTION 3. PROBABLE CAUSE

8th ed. p. 213; following *Whiteley*, add:

What is the status of *Whiteley* after *Evans*, Supp. p. 6? The defendant there relied on *Whiteley*, which the Court distinguished because it mistakenly "treated identification of a Fourth Amendment violation as synonymous with application of the exclusionary rule to evidence secured incident to that violation"?

SECTION 4. SEARCH WARRANTS

B. EXECUTION OF THE WARRANT

8th ed., p. 218; Note 2 before *Gassner*, add:

In WILSON v. ARKANSAS, ___ U.S. ___, 115 S.Ct. 1914, 131 L.Ed.2d 976 (1995), a unanimous Court, per THOMAS, J., proceeded "to resolve the conflict among the lower courts" by holding that the common law doctrine which "recognized a law enforcement officer's authority to break open the doors of a dwelling, but generally indicated that he first ought to announce his presence and authority," "forms a part of the reasonableness inquiry under the Fourth Amendment." (This conclusion, the Court noted, was consistent with its prior decisions in which "we have looked to the traditional protections against unreasonable searches and seizures afforded by the common law at the time of the framing" in evaluating the scope of the Fourth Amendment's protections.) The Court cautioned that the "Fourth Amendment's flexible requirement of reasonableness should not be read to mandate a rigid rule of announcement that ignores countervailing law enforcement interests," for "the common-law principle of announcement was never stated as an inflexible rule." However, the Court did not have occasion to define just when "law enforcement interests may also establish the reasonableness of an unannounced entry," or to consider whether the requisite circumstances were present in the instant case, as these matters had not been addressed by the lower court.

SECTION 5. WARRANTLESS ARRESTS

8th ed., p. 238; before Note 11, add:

10a. Assuming a *Gerstein* violation, what bearing should it have if the individual is later prosecuted? In *Powell v. Nevada*, ___ U.S. ___, 114 S.Ct. 1280, 128 L.Ed.2d 1 (1994), holding *McLaughlin* retroactive to that case, the Court, per Ginsburg, J., noted: "It does not necessarily follow, however, that Powell must 'be set free' or gain other relief, for several questions remain open for decision on remand," including "the appropriate remedy for a delay in determining probable cause (an issue not resolved by *McLaughlin*)." In *Powell*, an untimely probable cause determination was made four days after defendant's arrest, shortly after he gave the police an incriminating statement. In declaring that "whether a suppression remedy applies in that setting remains an unresolved question," Justice Ginsburg took note of two arguably analogous rules pointing in opposite directions: (i) that an after-the-fact judicial determination of probable cause does not make admissible evidence obtained in a search in violation of the Fourth Amendment's search warrant requirement; and (ii) that under *Harris,* 8th ed., p. 812, suppression of a statement subsequently obtained elsewhere is not required because of defendant's warrantless arrest inside premises in violation of the Fourth Amendment.

SECTION 7. STOP AND FRISK

C. Grounds for Temporary Seizure for Investigation

8th ed., p. 327, before Note 6, add:

5a. Are there grounds for the stops made on the following facts, essentially those in *United States v. Feliciano,* 45 F.3d 1070 (7th Cir. 1995)? An officer on patrol near a train station at midnight saw *F* and *M* walking in an area of a parking lot where there were no cars and which led to the river embankment. *M* then approached *K,* who was standing near the tracks with a suitcase, spoke with him for a while, and then left, rejoined *F,* and departed the scene in a direction opposite of that *K* then headed. The officer approached *K,* who told the officer that *M* had tried to lure him to the embankment to help an injured friend, but that *K* had refused. *K* explained that he had also seen *F* earlier and thus knew he was not injured; *K* surmised that the two had been planning to mug him. The officer asked his backup officer to stop *F* and *M*. The backup officer, who recognized *F* as a gang member recently released from prison, where *F* had served time for robbery, then stopped *F* and *M* as they walked toward their homes through the apparently deserted downtown area.

8th ed., p. 327; end of Note 6, add:

Compare also David A. Harris, *Factors for Reasonable Suspicion: When Black and Poor Means Stopped and Frisked,* 69 Ind.L.J. 659, 674, 687 (1994), noting there are many lower court cases holding that "presence in a high crime location" plus "evasion" are together "enough to sustain a *Terry* stop," and proposing that instead "the law should require that something more than a location of high crime or drug activity and evasion of the police be present, something clearly indicative of criminality. For example, gestures known to be characteristic of drug activity, such as using particular hand signals to indicate the availability of contraband, in addition to location and evasion, could be enough. For a frisk, the law should require not just possible drug possession or trafficking, but an indication that the suspect is armed.

"Such a rule would not necessarily require a rethinking of *Sokolow* [8th ed., p. 325]. While all of the defendant's actions in *Sokolow* are consistent with innocence, no activity in *Sokolow* is both innocent *and* necessary, in the sense that being at one's home or place of work is necessary. Additionally, to the extent that both the 'location plus evasion' cases and *Sokolow* are about clusters of innocent activity, *Sokolow* contains more than two such activities.

"The rule proposed here would have at least two salutary effects. First, existing law that protects, separately, the rights to be in a place and to refuse to respond to police stops without reasonable suspicion would be respected and kept vital. * * * Second, it would remove from the courts a set of cases, and from the police arsenal a group of techniques, that clearly have a disproportionate impact on the poor, and on racial and ethnic minorities."

8th ed., p. 327; before Note 7, add:

6a. Assuming grounds for a *Terry* stop but not grounds for arrest, is it (sometimes) (ever) permissible for the police to enter private premises in an effort to find the person to be detained? In the O.J. Simpson case, for example, is the police conduct in scaling the wall of the compound more understandable on the ground that Simpson was *not* a suspect and the police were attempting to see if anyone within was injured (the basis on which that conduct was upheld in court), or on the ground that Simpson *was* a suspect then sought for questioning by the police?[a]

F. Protective Search

8th ed., p. 333; before Note 2, add:

1a. Consider David A. Harris, *Frisking Every Suspect: The Withering of* Terry, 28 U.C. Davis L.Rev. 1, 5, 43–44 (1994): "Perhaps as a result of the high-visibility use of frisks as a contemporary crime control device, or because of general public antipathy to crime, lower courts have stretched the law governing frisks to the point that the Supreme Court might find it unrecognizable. Lower courts have consistently expanded the *types of offenses* always considered violent regardless of the individual circumstances. At the same time, lower courts have also found that certain *types of persons and situations* always pose a danger of armed violence to police. When confronted with these offenses, persons, or situations, police may *automatically* frisk, whether or not any individualized circumstances point to danger. Soon, *anyone* stopped by police may have to undergo a physical search at the officer's discretion, however benign the circumstances of the encounter or the conduct of the 'suspect.' * * *

" * * * African–Americans and Hispanic–Americans pay a higher personal price for contemporary stop and frisk practices than whites do. Cases from courts around the country already permit *Terry* stops of individuals based on nothing more than their presence in a high-crime or drug-involved location, and allegedly evasive behavior toward the police. Minority group members are more likely than majority race individuals to live and work in such areas. Moreover, the police often use race as a proxy for criminality in deciding whether to stop a putative suspect. Given all of this, the automatic frisk cases—especially those that allow frisks based on the character of the neighborhood—paint an ugly pic-

---

a. See LaFave, *Over the Wall: A New Theory Regarding Entry of the Simpson Compound,* 1994 Westlaw 562135.

ture: *Minority group members can be not only stopped, but subjected to a frisk without any evidence that they are armed or dangerous, just because they are present in the neighborhoods in which they work and live."*

SECTION 8. ADMINISTRATIVE INSPECTIONS AND REGULATORY SEARCHES: MORE ON BALANCING THE NEED AGAINST THE INVASION OF PRIVACY

8th ed., p. 342; end of Note 6, add:

The Court's latest foray into this area, while also not a criminal case, provides an excellent vehicle for considering the respective merits of the reasonable suspicion and standardized procedures approaches:

VERNONIA SCHOOL DISTRICT 47J v. ACTON
___ U.S. ___, 115 S.Ct. ___, ___ L.Ed.2d ___ (1995).

JUSTICE SCALIA delivered the opinion of the Court.

The Student Athlete Drug Policy adopted by School District 47J in the town of Vernonia, Oregon, authorizes random urinalysis drug testing of students who participate in the District's school athletics programs. We granted certiorari to decide whether this violates the Fourth and Fourteenth Amendments to the United States Constitution.

Petitioner Vernonia School District 47J (District) operates one high school and three grade schools in the logging community of Vernonia, Oregon. As elsewhere in small-town America, school sports play a prominent role in the town's life, and student athletes are admired in their schools and in the community.

Drugs had not been a major problem in Vernonia schools. In the mid-to-late 1980's, however, teachers and administrators observed a sharp increase in drug use. Students began to speak out about their attraction to the drug culture, and to boast that there was nothing the school could do about it. Along with more drugs came more disciplinary problems. Between 1988 and 1989 the number of disciplinary referrals in Vernonia schools rose to more than twice the number reported in the early 1980's, and several students were suspended. Students became increasingly rude during class; outbursts of profane language became common.

Not only were student athletes included among the drug users but, as the District Court found, athletes were the leaders of the drug culture. This caused the District's administrators particular concern, since drug use increases the risk of sports-related injury. Expert testimony at the trial confirmed the deleterious effects of drugs on motivation, memory, judgment, reaction, coordination, and performance. The high school football and wrestling coach witnessed a severe sternum injury suffered by a wrestler, and various omissions of safety procedures and misexecutions by football players, all attributable in his belief to the effects of drug use.

Initially, the District responded to the drug problem by offering special classes, speakers, and presentations designed to deter drug use. It even brought in a specially trained dog to detect drugs, but the drug problem persisted. According to the District Court:

"[T]he administration was at its wits end and ... a large segment of the student body, particularly those involved in interscholastic athletics, was in a state of rebellion. Disciplinary problems had reached 'epidemic proportions.' The coincidence of an almost three-fold increase in classroom disruptions and disciplinary reports along with the staff's direct observations of students using drugs or glamorizing drug and alcohol use led the administration to the inescapable conclusion that the rebellion was being fueled by alcohol and drug abuse as well as the student's misperceptions about the drug culture."

At that point, District officials began considering a drug-testing program. They held a parent "input night" to discuss the proposed Student Athlete Drug Policy (Policy), and the parents in attendance gave their unanimous approval. The school board approved the Policy for implementation in the fall of 1989. Its expressed purpose is to prevent student athletes from using drugs, to protect their health and safety, and to provide drug users with assistance programs.

The Policy applies to all students participating in interscholastic athletics. Students wishing to play sports must sign a form consenting to the testing and must obtain the written consent of their parents. Athletes are tested at the beginning of the season for their sport. In addition, once each week of the season the names of the athletes are placed in a "pool" from which a student, with the supervision of two adults, blindly draws the names of 10% of the athletes for random testing. Those selected are notified and tested that same day, if possible.

The student to be tested completes a specimen control form which bears an assigned number. Prescription medications that the student is taking must be identified by providing a copy of the prescription or a doctor's authorization. The student then enters an empty locker room accompanied by an adult monitor of the same sex. Each boy selected produces a sample at a urinal, remaining fully clothed with his back to the monitor, who stands approximately 12 to 15 feet behind the student. Monitors may (though do not always) watch the student while he produces the sample, and they listen for normal sounds of urination. Girls produce samples in an enclosed bathroom stall, so that they can be heard but not observed. After the sample is produced, it is given to the monitor, who checks it for temperature and tampering and then transfers it to a vial.

The samples are sent to an independent laboratory, which routinely tests them for amphetamines, cocaine, and marijuana. Other drugs, such as LSD, may be screened at the request of the District, but the identity of a particular student does not determine which drugs will be tested. The laboratory's procedures are 99.94% accurate. The District follows strict procedures regarding the chain of custody and access to test results. The laboratory does not know the identity of the students whose samples it tests. It is authorized to mail written test reports only to the superintendent and to provide test results to District personnel by telephone only after the requesting official recites a code confirming his authority. Only the superintendent, principals, vice-principals, and athletic directors have access to test results, and the results are not kept for more than one year.

If a sample tests positive, a second test is administered as soon as possible to confirm the result. If the second test is negative, no further action is taken. If the second test is positive, the athlete's parents are notified, and the school principal convenes a meeting with the student and his parents, at which the student is given the option of (1) participating for six weeks in an assistance program that includes weekly urinalysis, or (2) suffering suspension from athletics for the remainder of the current season and the next athletic season. The student is then retested prior to the start of the next athletic season for which he or she is eligible. The Policy states that a second offense results in automatic imposition of option (2); a third offense in suspension for the remainder of the current season and the next two athletic seasons.

In the fall of 1991, respondent James Acton, then a seventh-grader, signed up to play football at one of the District's grade schools. He was denied participation, however, because he and his parents refused to sign the testing consent forms. The Actons filed suit, seeking declaratory and injunctive relief from enforcement of the Policy on the grounds that it violated the Fourth and Fourteenth Amendments * * *. After a bench trial, the District Court entered an order denying the claims on the merits and dismissing the action. The United States Court of Appeals for the Ninth Circuit reversed, holding that the Policy violated both the Fourth and Fourteenth Amendments * * *. We granted certiorari.

The Fourth Amendment to the United States Constitution provides that the Federal Government shall not violate "[t]he right of the people to be secure in their persons, houses, papers, and effects, against unreasonable searches and seizures...." We have held that the Fourteenth Amendment extends this constitutional guarantee to searches and seizures by state officers, including public school officials, *New Jersey v. T.L.O.*, [8th ed., p. 341]. In *Skinner v. Railway Labor Executives' Assn.*, [8th ed., p. 342], we held that state-compelled collection and testing of urine, such as that required by the Student Athlete Drug Policy, constitutes a "search" subject to the demands of the Fourth Amendment. See also *Treasury Employees v. Von Raab*, [8th ed., p. 342].

As the text of the Fourth Amendment indicates, the ultimate measure of the constitutionality of a governmental search is "reasonableness." At least in a case such as this, where there was no clear practice, either approving or disapproving the type of search at issue, at the time the constitutional provision was enacted, whether a particular search meets the reasonableness standard " 'is judged by balancing its intrusion on the individual's Fourth Amendment interests against its promotion of legitimate governmental interests.' " Where a search is undertaken by law enforcement officials to discover evidence of criminal wrongdoing, this Court has said that reasonableness generally requires the obtaining of a judicial warrant. Warrants cannot be issued, of course, without the showing of probable cause required by the Warrant Clause. But a warrant is not required to establish the reasonableness of all government searches; and when a warrant is not required (and the Warrant Clause therefore not applicable), probable cause is not invariably required either. A search unsupported by probable cause can be constitutional, we have said, "when special needs, beyond the normal need for law enforcement, make the warrant and probable-cause requirement impracticable." *Griffin v. Wisconsin,* [8th ed., p. 341].

We have found such "special needs" to exist in the public-school context. There, the warrant requirement "would unduly interfere with the maintenance of the swift and informal disciplinary procedures [that are] needed," and "strict adherence to the requirement that searches be based upon probable cause" would undercut "the substantial need of teachers and administrators for freedom to maintain order in the schools." *T.L.O.* The school search we approved in *T.L.O.*, while not based on probable cause, was based on individualized suspicion of wrongdoing. As we explicitly acknowledged, however, " 'the Fourth Amendment imposes no irreducible requirement of such suspicion.' " We have upheld suspicionless searches and seizures to conduct drug testing of railroad personnel involved in train accidents, see *Skinner;* to conduct random drug testing of federal customs officers who carry arms or are involved in drug interdiction, see *Von Raab;* and to maintain automobile checkpoints looking for illegal immigrants and contraband and drunk drivers.

The first factor to be considered is the nature of the privacy interest upon which the search here at issue intrudes. The Fourth Amendment does not protect all subjective expectations of privacy, but only those that society recognizes as "legitimate." What expectations are legitimate varies, of course, with context, depending, for example, upon whether the individual asserting the privacy interest is at home, at work, in a car, or in a public park. In addition, the legitimacy of certain privacy expectations vis-à-vis the State may depend upon the individual's legal relationship with the State. For example, in *Griffin* we held that, although a "probationer's home, like anyone else's, is protected by the Fourth Amendmen[t]," the supervisory relationship between probationer and State justifies "a degree of impingement upon [a probationer's] privacy that would not be constitutional if applied to the public at large." Central, in our view, to the present case is the fact that the subjects of the Policy are (1) children, who (2) have been committed to the temporary custody of the State as schoolmaster.

Traditionally at common law, and still today, unemancipated minors lack some of the most fundamental rights of self-determination—including even the right of liberty in its narrow sense, i.e., the right to come and go at will. They are subject, even as to their physical freedom, to the control of their parents or guardians. When parents place minor children in private schools for their education, the teachers and administrators of those schools stand in loco parentis over the children entrusted to them. * * *

In *T.L.O.* we rejected the notion that public schools, like private schools, exercise only parental power over their students, which of course is not subject to constitutional constraints. Such a view of things, we said, "is not entirely 'consonant with compulsory education laws,'" * * *. But while denying that the State's power over schoolchildren is formally no more than the delegated power of their parents, *T.L.O.* did not deny, but indeed emphasized, that the nature of that power is custodial and tutelary, permitting a degree of supervision and control that could not be exercised over free adults. "[A] proper educational environment requires close supervision of schoolchildren, as well as the enforcement of rules against conduct that would be perfectly permissible if undertaken by an adult." * * * Thus, while children assuredly do not "shed their constitutional rights . . . at the schoolhouse gate," the nature of those rights is what is appropriate for children in school. * * *

Fourth Amendment rights * * * are different in public schools than elsewhere; the "reasonableness" inquiry cannot disregard the schools' custodial and tutelary responsibility for children. For their own good and that of their classmates, public school children are routinely required to submit to various physical examinations, and to be vaccinated against various diseases. * * * Particularly with regard to medical examinations and procedures, therefore, "students within the school environment have a lesser expectation of privacy than members of the population generally."

Legitimate privacy expectations are even less with regard to student athletes. School sports are not for the bashful. They require "suiting up" before each practice or event, and showering and changing afterwards. Public school locker rooms, the usual sites for these activities, are not notable for the privacy they afford. The locker rooms in Vernonia are typical: no individual dressing rooms are provided; shower heads are lined up along a wall, unseparated by any sort of partition or curtain; not even all the toilet stalls have doors.

There is an additional respect in which school athletes have a reduced expectation of privacy. By choosing to "go out for the team," they voluntarily subject themselves to a degree of regulation even higher than that imposed on students generally. In Vernonia's public schools, they must submit to a preseason physical exam (James testified that his included the giving of a urine sample), they must acquire adequate insurance coverage or sign an insurance waiver, maintain a minimum grade point average, and comply with any "rules of conduct, dress, training hours and related matters as may be established for each sport by the head coach and athletic director with the principal's approval." Somewhat like adults who choose to participate in a "closely regulated industry," students who voluntarily participate in school athletics have reason to expect intrusions upon normal rights and privileges, including privacy.

Having considered the scope of the legitimate expectation of privacy at issue here, we turn next to the character of the intrusion that is complained of. We recognized in *Skinner* that collecting the samples for urinalysis intrudes upon "an excretory function traditionally shielded by great privacy." We noted, however, that the degree of intrusion depends upon the manner in which production of the urine sample is monitored. Under the District's Policy, male students produce samples at a urinal along a wall. They remain fully clothed and are only observed from behind, if at all. Female students produce samples in an enclosed stall, with a female monitor standing outside listening only for sounds of tampering. These conditions are nearly identical to those typically encountered in public restrooms, which men, women, and especially school children use daily. Under such conditions, the privacy interests compromised by the process of obtaining the urine sample are in our view negligible.

The other privacy-invasive aspect of urinalysis is, of course, the information it discloses concerning the state of the subject's body, and the materials he has ingested. In this regard it is significant that the tests at issue here look only for drugs, and not for whether the student is, for example, epileptic, pregnant, or diabetic. Moreover, the drugs for which the samples are screened are standard, and do not vary according to the identity of the student. And finally, the results of the tests are disclosed only to a limited class of school personnel who have a need to know; and they are not turned over to law enforcement authorities or used for any internal disciplinary function. * * *

Finally, we turn to consider the nature and immediacy of the governmental concern at issue here, and the efficacy of this means for meeting it. In both *Skinner* and *Von Raab,* we characterized the government interest motivating the search as "compelling." *Skinner* (interest in preventing railway accidents); *Von Raab* (interest in insuring fitness of customs officials to interdict drugs and handle firearms). * * * It is a mistake, however, to think that the phrase "compelling state interest," in the Fourth Amendment context, describes a fixed, minimum quantum of governmental concern, so that one can dispose of a case by answering in isolation the question: Is there a compelling state interest here? Rather, the phrase describes an interest which appears important enough to justify the particular search at hand, in light of other factors which show the search to be relatively intrusive upon a genuine expectation of privacy. Whether that relatively high degree of government concern is necessary in this case or not, we think it is met.

That the nature of the concern is important—indeed, perhaps compelling—can hardly be doubted. Deterring drug use by our Nation's schoolchildren is at least as important as enhancing efficient enforcement of the Nation's laws against the importation of drugs, which was the governmental concern in *Von Raab,* or deterring drug use by engineers and trainmen, which was the governmental concern in *Skinner.* School years are the time when the physical, psychological, and addictive effects of drugs are most severe. * * * And of course the effects of a drug-infested school are visited not just upon the users, but upon the entire student body and faculty, as the educational process is disrupted. In the present case, moreover, the necessity for the State to act is magnified by the fact that this evil is being visited not just upon individuals at large, but upon children for whom it has undertaken a special responsibility of care and direction. Finally, it must not be lost sight of that this program is directed more narrowly to drug use by school athletes, where the risk of immediate physical harm to the drug user or those with whom he is playing his sport is particularly high. Apart from psychological effects, which include impairment of judgment, slow reaction time, and a lessening of the perception of pain, the particular drugs screened by the District's Policy have been demonstrated to pose substantial physical risks to athletes. * * *

As for the immediacy of the District's concerns: We are not inclined to question—indeed, we could not possibly find clearly erroneous—the District Court's conclusion that "a large segment of the student body, particularly those involved in interscholastic athletics, was in a state of rebellion," that "[d]isciplinary actions had reached 'epidemic proportions,'" and that "the rebellion was being fueled by alcohol and drug abuse as well as by the student's misperceptions about the drug culture." That is an immediate crisis of greater proportions than existed in *Skinner,* where we upheld the Government's drug testing program based on findings of drug use by railroad employees nationwide, without proof that a problem existed on the particular railroads whose employees were subject to the test. And of much greater proportions than existed in *Von Raab,* where there was no documented history of drug use by any customs officials.

As to the efficacy of this means for addressing the problem: It seems to us self-evident that a drug problem largely fueled by the "role model" effect of athletes' drug use, and of particular danger to athletes, is effectively addressed by making sure that athletes do not use drugs. Respondents argue that a "less intrusive means to the same end" was available, namely, "drug testing on suspicion of drug use." We have repeatedly refused to declare that only the "least intrusive" search practicable can be reasonable under the Fourth Amendment. Respondents' alternative entails substantial difficulties—if it is indeed practicable at all. It may be impracticable, for one thing, simply because the parents who are willing to accept random drug testing for athletes are not willing to accept accusatory drug testing for all students, which transforms the process into a badge of shame. Respondents' proposal brings the risk that teachers will impose testing arbitrarily upon troublesome but not drug-likely students. It generates the expense of defending lawsuits that charge such arbitrary imposition, or that simply demand greater process before accusatory drug testing is imposed. And not least of all, it adds to the ever-expanding diversionary duties of schoolteachers the new function of spotting and bringing to account drug abuse, a task for which they are ill prepared, and which is not readily compatible with their vocation. In many respects, we think, testing based on "suspicion" of drug use would not be better, but worse.

Taking into account all the factors we have considered above—the decreased expectation of privacy, the relative unobtrusiveness of the search, and the severity of the need met by the search—we conclude Vernonia's Policy is reasonable and hence constitutional.

We caution against the assumption that suspicionless drug testing will readily pass constitutional muster in other contexts. The most significant element in this case is the first we discussed: that the Policy was undertaken in furtherance of the government's responsibilities, under a public school system, as guardian and tutor of children entrusted to its care. Just as when the government conducts a search in its capacity as employer (a warrantless search of an absent employee's desk to obtain an urgently needed file, for example), the relevant question is whether that intrusion upon privacy is one that a reasonable employer might engage in, so also when the government acts as guardian and tutor the relevant question is whether the search is one that a reasonable guardian and tutor might undertake. Given the findings of need made by the District Court, we conclude that in the present case it is.

We may note that the primary guardians of Vernonia's schoolchildren appear to agree. The record shows no objection to this districtwide program by any parents other than the couple before us here—even though, as we have described, a public meeting was held to obtain parents' views. We find insufficient basis to contradict the judgment of Vernonia's parents, its school board, and the District Court, as to what was reasonably in the interest of these children under the circumstances.
* * *

JUSTICE GINSBURG, concurring. * * * I comprehend the Court's opinion as reserving the question whether the District, on no more than the showing made here, constitutionally could impose routine drug testing not only on those seeking to engage with others in team sports, but on all students required to attend school.

JUSTICE O'CONNOR, with whom JUSTICE STEVENS and JUSTICE SOUTER join, dissenting.

The population of our Nation's public schools, grades 7 through 12, numbers around 18 million. By the reasoning of today's decision, the millions of these students who participate in interscholastic sports, an overwhelming majority of whom have given school officials no reason whatsoever to suspect they use drugs at school, are open to an intrusive bodily search.

In justifying this result, the Court dispenses with a requirement of individualized suspicion on considered policy grounds. * * * In making these policy arguments, of course, the Court sidesteps powerful, countervailing privacy concerns. Blanket searches, because they can involve "thousands or millions" of searches, "pos[e] a greater threat to liberty" than do suspicion-based ones, which "affec[t] one person at a time." Searches based on individualized suspicion also afford potential targets considerable control over whether they will, in fact, be searched because a person can avoid such a search by not acting in an objectively suspicious way. And given that the surest way to avoid acting suspiciously is to avoid the underlying wrongdoing, the costs of such a regime, one would think, are minimal.

But whether a blanket search is "better" than a regime based on individualized suspicion is not a debate in which we should engage. In my view, it is not open to judges or government officials to decide on policy grounds which is better and which is worse. For most of our constitutional history, mass, suspicionless searches have been generally considered per se unreasonable within the meaning of the Fourth Amendment. And we have allowed exceptions in recent years only where it has been clear that a suspicion-based regime would be ineffectual. Because that is not the case here, I dissent. * * *

The *Carroll* [*v. United States,* 8th ed., p. 276] Court's view that blanket searches are "intolerable and unreasonable" is well-grounded in history. As recently confirmed in one of the most exhaustive analyses of the original meaning of the Fourth Amendment ever undertaken, what the Framers of the Fourth Amendment most strongly opposed, with limited exceptions wholly inapplicable here, were general searches—that is, searches by general warrant, by writ of assistance, by broad statute, or by any other similar authority. * * *

More important, there is no indication in the historical materials that the Framers' opposition to general searches stemmed solely from the fact that they allowed officials to single out individuals for arbitrary reasons, and thus that officials could render them reasonable simply by making sure to extend their search to every house in a given area or to every person in a given group. * * *

Perhaps most telling of all, as reflected in the text of the Warrant Clause, the particular way the Framers chose to curb the abuses of general warrants—and by implication, all general searches—was not to impose a novel "evenhandedness" requirement; it was to retain the individualized suspicion requirement contained in the typical general warrant, but to make that requirement meaningful and enforceable, for instance, by raising the required level of individualized suspicion to objective probable cause. * * *

The view that mass, suspicionless searches, however evenhanded, are generally unreasonable remains inviolate in the criminal law enforcement context. * * *

Thus, it remains the law that the police cannot, say, subject to drug testing every person entering or leaving a certain drug-ridden neighborhood in order to find evidence of crime. And this is true even though it is hard to think of a more compelling government interest than the need to fight the scourge of drugs on our streets and in our neighborhoods. Nor could it be otherwise, for if being evenhanded were enough to justify evaluating a search regime under an open-ended balancing test, the Warrant Clause, which presupposes that there is some category of searches for which individualized suspicion is non-negotiable, would be a dead letter.

Outside the criminal context, however, in response to the exigencies of modern life, our cases have upheld several evenhanded blanket searches, including some that are more than minimally intrusive, after balancing the invasion of privacy against the government's strong need. Most of these cases, of course, are distinguishable insofar as they involved searches either not of a personally intrusive nature, such as searches of closely regulated businesses, see, e.g., *New York v. Burger,* [8th ed., p. 340], or arising in unique contexts such as prisons * * *.

In any event, in many of the cases that can be distinguished on the grounds suggested above and, more important, in all of the cases that cannot, see, e.g., *Skinner* (blanket drug testing scheme); *Von Raab* (same); cf. *Camara v. Municipal Court,* [8th ed., p. 339] (area-wide searches of private residences), we upheld the suspicionless search only after first recognizing the Fourth Amendment's longstanding preference for a suspicion-based search regime, and then pointing to sound reasons why such a regime would likely be ineffectual under the unusual circumstances presented. In *Skinner,* for example, we stated outright that " 'some quantum of individualized suspicion' " is "usually required" under the Fourth Amendment, and we built the requirement into the test we announced: "In limited circumstances, where the privacy interests implicated by the search are minimal, and where an important governmental interest furthered by the intrusion would be placed in jeopardy by a requirement of individualized suspicion, a search may be reasonable despite the absence of such suspicion." The obvious negative implication of this reasoning is that, if such an individualized suspicion requirement would not place the government's objectives in jeopardy, the requirement should not be forsaken.

Accordingly, we upheld the suspicionless regime at issue in *Skinner* on the firm understanding that a requirement of individualized suspicion for testing train operators for drug or alcohol impairment following serious train accidents would be unworkable because "the scene of a serious rail accident is chaotic." (Of course, it could be plausibly argued that the fact that testing occurred only after train operators were involved in serious train accidents amounted to an individualized suspicion requirement in all but name, in light of the record evidence of a strong link between serious train accidents and drug and alcohol use.) We have performed a similar inquiry in the other cases as well. * * *

Moreover, an individualized suspicion requirement was often impractical in these cases because they involved situations in which even one undetected instance of wrongdoing could have injurious consequences for a great number of people. See, e.g., *Camara* (even one safety code violation can cause "fires and epidemics [that] ravage large urban areas"); *Skinner,* supra (even one drug- or alcohol-impaired train operator can lead to the "disastrous consequences" of a train wreck, such as "great human loss"); *Von Raab* (even one customs official caught up in drugs can, by virtue of impairment, susceptibility to bribes, or indifference, result in the noninterdiction of a "sizable drug shipmen[t]," which eventually injures the lives of thousands, or to a breach of "national security").

The instant case stands in marked contrast. One searches today's majority opinion in vain for recognition that history and precedent establish that individualized suspicion is "usually required" under the Fourth Amendment (regardless of whether a warrant and probable cause are also required) and that, in the area of intrusive personal searches, the only recognized exception is for situations in which a suspicion-based scheme would be likely ineffectual. * * *

But having misconstrued the fundamental role of the individualized suspicion requirement in Fourth Amendment analysis, the Court never seriously engages the practicality of such a requirement in the instant case. And that failure is crucial because nowhere is it less clear that an individualized suspicion requirement would be ineffectual than in the school context. In most schools, the entire pool of potential search targets—students—is under constant supervision by teachers and administrators and coaches, be it in classrooms, hallways, or locker rooms.

The record here indicates that the Vernonia schools are no exception. The great irony of this case is that most (though not all) of the evidence the District introduced to justify its suspicionless drug-testing program consisted of first- or second-hand stories of particular, identifiable students acting in ways that plainly gave rise to reasonable suspicion of in-school drug use—and thus that would have justified a drug-related search under our *T.L.O.* decision. Small groups of students, for example, were observed by a teacher "passing joints back and forth" across the street at a restaurant before school and during school hours. Another group was caught skipping school and using drugs at one of the students' houses. Several students actually admitted their drug use to school officials (some of them being caught with marijuana pipes). One student presented himself to his teacher as "clearly obviously inebriated" and had to be sent home. Still another was observed dancing and singing at the top of his voice in the back of the classroom; when the teacher asked what was going on, he replied, "Well, I'm just high on life." To take a final example, on a certain road trip, the school wrestling coach smelled marijuana smoke in a hotel room occupied by four wrestlers, an observation that (after some questioning) would probably have given him reasonable suspicion to test one or all of them.

In light of all this evidence of drug use by particular students, there is a substantial basis for concluding that a vigorous regime of suspicion-based testing (for which the District appears already to have rules in place) would have gone a long way toward solving Vernonia's school drug problem while preserving the Fourth Amendment rights of James Acton and others like him. And were there any doubt about such a conclusion, it is removed by indications in the record that suspicion-based testing could have been supplemented by an equally vigorous campaign to have Vernonia's parents encourage their children to submit to the District's voluntary drug testing program. In these circumstances, the Fourth Amendment dictates that a mass, suspicionless search regime is categorically unreasonable. * * *

The principal counterargument to all this, central to the Court's opinion, is that the Fourth Amendment is more lenient with respect to school searches. That is no doubt correct, for, as the Court explains, schools have traditionally had special guardian-like responsibilities for children that necessitate a degree of constitutional leeway. This principle explains the considerable Fourth Amendment leeway we gave school officials in *T.L.O.* In that case, we held that children at school do not enjoy two of the Fourth Amendment's traditional categorical protections against unreasonable searches and seizures: the warrant requirement and the probable cause requirement. * * *

The instant case, however, asks whether the Fourth Amendment is even more lenient than that, i.e., whether it is so lenient that students may be deprived of the Fourth Amendment's only remaining, and most basic, categorical protection: its strong preference for an individualized suspicion requirement, with its accompanying antipathy toward personally intrusive, blanket searches of mostly innocent people. [T]he answer must plainly be no.

I find unpersuasive the Court's reliance on the widespread practice of physical examinations and vaccinations, which are both blanket searches of a sort. [A] suspicion requirement for vaccinations is not merely impractical; it is nonsensical, for vaccinations are not searches for anything in particular and so there is nothing about which to be suspicious. * * * As for physical examinations, the practicability of a suspicion requirement is highly doubtful because the conditions for which these physical exams ordinarily search, such as latent heart conditions, do not manifest themselves in observable behavior the way school drug use does.

I do not believe that suspicionless drug testing is justified on these facts. But even if I agreed that some such testing were reasonable here, I see two other Fourth Amendment flaws in the District's program. First, and most serious, there is virtually no evidence in the record of a drug problem at the Washington Grade School, which includes the 7th and 8th grades, and which Acton attended when this litigation began. * * *

Second, even as to the high school, I find unreasonable the school's choice of student athletes as the class to subject to suspicionless testing—a choice that appears to have been driven more by a belief in what would pass constitutional muster, than by a belief in what was required to meet the District's principal disciplinary concern. Reading the full record in this case, it seems quite obvious that the true driving force behind the District's adoption of its drug testing program was the need to combat the rise in drug-related disorder and disruption in its classrooms and around campus. * * * And the record in this case surely demonstrates there was a drug-related discipline problem in Vernonia of " 'epidemic proportions.' " The evidence of a drug-related sports injury problem at Vernonia, by contrast, was considerably weaker.

On this record, then, it seems to me that the far more reasonable choice would have been to focus on the class of students found to have violated published school rules against severe disruption in class and around campus, disruption that had a strong nexus to drug use, as the District established at trial. Such a choice would share two of the virtues of a suspicion-based regime: testing dramatically fewer students, tens as against hundreds, and giving students control, through their behavior, over the likelihood that they would be tested. Moreover, there would be a reduced concern for the accusatory nature of the search, because the Court's feared "badge of shame," would already exist, due to the antecedent accusation and finding of severe disruption. In a lesser known aspect of *Skinner,* we upheld an analogous testing scheme with little hesitation. See *Skinner* (describing " 'Authorization to Test for Cause' " scheme, according to which train operators would be tested "in the event of certain specific rule violations, including noncompliance with a signal and excessive speeding").

It cannot be too often stated that the greatest threats to our constitutional freedoms come in times of crisis. But we must also stay mindful that not all government responses to such times are hysterical overreactions; some crises are quite real, and when they are, they serve precisely as the compelling state interest that we have said may justify a measured intrusion on constitutional rights. The only way for judges to mediate these conflicting impulses is to do what they should do anyway: stay close to the record in each case that appears before them, and make their judgments based on that alone. Having reviewed the record here, I cannot avoid the conclusion that the District's suspicionless policy of testing all student-athletes sweeps too broadly, and too imprecisely, to be reasonable under the Fourth Amendment.

Chapter 7

POLICE "ENCOURAGEMENT" AND THE DEFENSE OF ENTRAPMENT

SECTION 3. CONTINUING CONTROVERSY OVER THE ENTRAPMENT DEFENSE

8th ed., p. 439; add new Note:

6. *More on the meaning of Jacobson.* In UNITED STATES v. GENDRON, 18 F.3d 955 (1st Cir.1994), in the course of holding that defendant was not entrapped into receiving child pornography, Chief Judge (now Supreme Court Justice) BREYER observed:

"The Supreme Court has described [the entrapment] defense as resting upon an assumption that Congress, when enacting criminal statutes, does not intend the statute to apply to violations arising out of (1) the government's *'abuse'* of its crime 'detection' and law 'enforcement' efforts by 'instigat[ing]' the criminal behavior and 'lur[ing]' to commit the crime (2) persons who are *'otherwise innocent.'* Sorrells (emphasis added). Consequently, the entrapment doctrine forbids punishment of an *'otherwise innocent'* person whose 'alleged offense' is 'the *product of the creative activity'* of government officials. Id. (emphasis added).

"As the Supreme Court has recently stated: 'When the Government's quest for conviction leads to the apprehension of an *otherwise law-abiding citizen* who, *if left to his own devices,* likely would never have been afoul of the law, the courts should intervene.' *Jacobson v. United States* (emphasis added). Since the Court has repeatedly expressed concern about *both* government 'abuse' of its enforcement powers (or the like) *and* the 'otherwise law-abiding citizen' (or the like), it is not surprising that the defense has two parts, one that focuses upon government 'inducement' and the other upon the defendant's 'predisposition.'

"[The Supreme Court] saw in the entrapment defense not so much a sanction used to control police conduct, but rather a protection of the ordinary law-abiding citizen against government overreaching. Consequently, it saw no need to permit a defendant to take advantage of that defense unless he himself was such a citizen. The upshot is that we must find out just who that 'innocent person' is. Who is the *'otherwise law-abiding citizen'* who would not 'otherwise' have committed the crime?

"The question's difficulty lies in the word 'otherwise.' That word requires us to abstract from present circumstances. We cannot simply ask whether, without the government's present activity, the defendant would likely have committed the crime *when* he did. After all, without the government's having presented *that* opportunity, the defendant, no matter how 'predisposed,' would likely not have acted *then.* Nor can we simply ask whether the defendant would have acted similarly at some other time *had he faced similar circumstances,* since his present behavior virtually compels an affirmative answer to the question phrased in this way.

"The right way to ask the question, it seems to us, is to abstract from—to assume away—the present circumstances *insofar as they reveal government overreaching.* That is to say, we should ask how the defendant likely would have reacted to an *ordinary* opportunity to commit the crime. *See Jacobson,* n. 2. By using the word 'ordinary,' we mean an opportunity that lacked those special features of the government's conduct that made of it an 'inducement,' or an 'overreaching.' Was the defendant 'predisposed' to respond affirmatively to a *proper,* not to an *improper,* lure? * * *

"Finally, this way of phrasing the question prevents one from concluding automatically, simply from the fact that the defendant committed the crime, that he was 'predisposed' to commit it. At the same time, if the answer to the question so phrased is affirmative, the defendant would seem to be the sort of person (and his conduct in this instance is the sort of conduct) that the criminal statute intends to punish. He is, in other words, someone who would likely commit the crime under the circumstances and for the reasons normally associated with that crime, and who therefore poses the sort of threat to society that the statute seeks to control, and which the government, through the 'sting,' seeks to stop.

"We turn now to *Jacobson* * * *. In three respects [government agents] did more than provide an ordinary opportunity to buy child pornography: First, the solicitations reflected a psychologically 'graduated' set of responses to Jacobson's own noncriminal responses, beginning with innocent lures and progressing to frank offers. The government started with a 'sexual attitude questionnaire,' which elicited a general interest in 'pre-teen sex'; it followed with letters containing general, nonexplicit references implying a possibility of child pornography; it then sent Jacobson more personal correspondence; and, finally (but after Jacobson had discontinued the correspondence), it sent him child pornography catalogues. Second, the government's soliciting letters sometimes depicted their senders as 'free speech' lobbying organizations and fighters for the 'right to read what we desire'; they asked Jacobson to 'fight against censorship and the infringement of individual rights.' Third, the government's effort to provide an 'opportunity' to buy child pornography stretched out over two and a half years. Taken together, one might find in these three sets of circumstances—the graduated response, the long time period, the appeal to a proper (free speech) motive—a substantial risk of inducing an ordinary law-abiding person to commit the crime. Indeed, the government conceded in *Jacobson* that its methods amounted, for entrapment purposes, to an improper 'inducement.' Id. at n. 2.

"*Jacobson's* importance, however, concerns the 'predisposition' part of the entrapment defense. The Court held that the evidence, as a matter of law, required acquittal because a reasonable jury would have had to doubt Jacobson's predisposition. The evidence of predisposition consisted of two facts: (1) that before the government became involved Jacobson was on a private bookstore's mailing list for dubious photos; and (2) that he responded affirmatively to the government's solicitations. The first fact, the Court wrote, showed little about a predisposition to act *un*lawfully because ordering the photos was lawful at the time. The second, placing orders, could not show how Jacobson would have acted had the solicitation lacked the three elements we just mentioned, namely, the improper appeals to anti-censorship motives, the graduated response, and the lengthy time frame. The government therefore failed to show 'predisposition' (beyond a reasonable doubt). That means (as we understand it) that the government's evidence did not show how Jacobson would have acted had he been faced with an ordinary 'opportunity' to commit the crime rather than a special 'inducement.'

"[The evidence in this case,] taken together, reveals a defendant who met an initial opportunity to buy child pornography with enthusiasm, who responded to each further government initiative with a purchase order, and who, unlike Jacobson, showed no particular interest in an anti-censorship campaign. This evidence * * * permits a jury to find (beyond a reasonable doubt) that Gendron would have responded affirmatively to the most ordinary of opportunities, and, hence, was 'predisposed' to commit the crime. We therefore find the jury's entrapment decision lawful."

Compare UNITED STATES v. HOLLINGSWORTH, 27 F.3d 1196 (7th Cir.1994) (en banc). In the course of holding that the defendants, Pickard (a dentist) and Hollingsworth (a farmer), had been entrapped as a matter of law into engaging in a money laundering scheme in violation of federal law, a 6–5 majority, per POSNER, C.J., observed:

"[Until] the Supreme Court's recent decision in *Jacobson,* the courts of appeals had been drifting toward the view [that] the defense of entrapment must fail in any case in which the defendant is 'willing,' in the sense of being psychologically prepared, to commit the crime for which he is being prosecuted, even if it is plain that he would not have been engaged in criminal activity unless inveigled or assisted by the government. This drift in thinking reflected the semantic pull of the term 'predisposition,' the central element of the defense of entrapment as articulated in the modern cases. The word is suggestive of pure willingness; and it is the suggestion picked up by [various cases]. But the suggestion cannot in our view be squared with *Jacobson*. * * * Despite his lack of reluctance, emphasized by Justice O'Connor in her dissenting opinion, the Supreme Court reversed Jacobson's conviction, holding that he had been entrapped as a matter of law.

"[The] facts of *Jacobson* were unquestionably peculiar, and the government's tactics * * * bizarre and distasteful. Nevertheless, had the Court in *Jacobson* believed that the legal concept of predisposition is exhausted in the demonstrated willingness of the defendant to commit the crime without threats or promises by the government, then Jacobson was predisposed, in which event the Court's reversal of his conviction would be difficult to explain. The government did not offer Jacobson any inducements to buy pornographic magazines or threaten him with harm if he failed to buy them. It was not as if the government had had to badger Jacobson for 26 months in order to overcome his resistance to committing a crime. He *never* resisted.

" * * * [W]e are naturally reluctant to suppose that [*Jacobson*] is limited to the precise facts before the Court, or to ignore the Court's definition of entrapment, which concludes the analysis portion of the opinion and is not found in previous opinions, as 'the apprehension of an otherwise law-abiding citizen who, if left to his own devices, likely would have never run afoul of the law.' That was Jacobson. However impure his thoughts, he was law abiding. A farmer in Nebraska, his access to child pornography was limited. As far as the government was aware, over the period of more than two years in which it was playing cat and mouse with him he did not receive any other solicitations to buy pornography. So, had he been 'left to his own devices,' in all likelihood he would 'have never run afoul of the law.' If the same can be said of [the defendants in this case,] Pickard and Hollingsworth, they too are entitled to be acquitted. * * *

"Recently the First Circuit, struggling as are we to understand the scope of *Jacobson,* suggested that all it stands for is that the government may not, in trying to induce the target of a sting to commit a crime, confront him with circumstances that are different from the ordinary or typical circumstances of a private inducement. *Gendron.* The [First Circuit] thought that the government's attempt to persuade Jacobson that he had a First Amendment right to consume child pornography had departed from typicality. We are not so sure. Just as the gun industry likes to wrap itself in the mantle of the Second Amendment, so the pornography industry likes to wrap itself in the mantle of the First Amendment. But however that may be, the government made no effort in *this* case to show that a real customer for money laundering would have responded to an advertisement to sell a Grenadan bank * * *.

"We put the following hypothetical case to the government's lawyer at the reargument. Suppose the government went to someone and asked him whether he would like to make money as a counterfeiter, and the reply was, 'Sure, but I don't know anything about counterfeiting.' Suppose the government then bought him a printer, paper, and ink, showed him how to make the counterfeit money, hired a staff for him, and got everything set up so that all he had to do was press a button to print the money; and then offered him $10,000 for some quantity of counterfeit bills. The government's lawyer acknowledged that the counterfeiter would have a strong case that he had been entrapped, even though he was perfectly willing to commit the crime once the government planted the suggestion and showed him how and the government neither threatened him nor offered him an overwhelming inducement.[a]

"We do not suggest that *Jacobson* adds a new element to the entrapment defense—'readiness' or 'ability' or 'dangerousness' on top of inducement and, most important, predisposition. [Rather,] the Court clarified the meaning of predisposition. Predisposition is not a purely mental state, the state of being willing to swallow the government's bait. It has positional as well as dispositional force. The dictionary definitions of the word include 'tendency' as well as 'inclination.' The defendant must be so situated by reason of previous training or experience or occupation or acquaintances that it is likely that if the government had not induced him to commit the crime some criminal would have done so; only then does a sting or other arranged crime take a dangerous person out of circulation. A public official is in a position to take bribes; a drug addict to deal drugs; a gun dealer to engage in illegal gun sales. For these and other traditional targets of stings all that must be shown to establish predisposition and thus defeat the defense of entrapment is willingness to violate the law without extraordinary inducements; ability can be presumed. It is different when the defendant is not in a position without the government's help to become involved in illegal activity. * * *

"There is no evidence that before 'Hinch' began his campaign to inveigle them into a money-laundering scheme either Pickard or Hollingsworth had contemplated engaging in such behavior. [When] the opportunity to become *crooked* international financiers beckoned, they were willing enough, though less willing than Jacobson had been to violate the federal law against purchasing child pornography through the mails—Jacobson never evinced reluctance, even though he had received no financial inducements. Pickard and Hollingsworth had no prayer of becoming money launderers without the government's aid. Their solicitations for financial business had produced a tiny investor, but no customers. Their corporation was running out of money when they placed the ad in *USA Today* for the Grenadan banking license. No one responded to the ad, except [undercover customs agent] 'Hinch.' Suppose he hadn't responded. What would Pickard and Hollingsworth have

---

a. Did the government's lawyer concede too much?

done next? Whatever it takes to become an international money launderer, they did not have it. Had Hinch not answered the ad, Pickard would soon have folded his financial venture.

"[The] point is not that Pickard and Hollingsworth were *incapable* of engaging in the act of money laundering. Obviously they were capable of the act. All that was involved in the act was wiring money to a bank account designated by the government agent. Anyone can wire money. But to get into the international money-laundering business you need underworld contacts, financial acumen or assets, access to foreign banks or bankers, or other assets. Pickard and Hollingsworth had none. * * * Even if they had wanted to go into money laundering before they met Hinch—and there is no evidence that they did—the likelihood that they could have done so was remote. They were objectively harmless.

"We do not wish to be understood as holding that lack of *present* means to commit a crime is alone enough to establish entrapment if the government supplies the means. Only in punishing speech is the government limited to preventing clear and present dangers. Suppose that before Hinch chanced on the scene (for *Jacobson* makes clear [that] a predisposition *created* by the government cannot be used to defeat a defense of entrapment), Pickard had decided to smuggle arms to Cuba but didn't know where to buy a suitable boat. On a hunch, a government agent sidles up to Pickard and gives him the address of a boat dealer; and Pickard is arrested after taking possession of the boat and setting sail, and is charged with attempted smuggling. That would be a case in which the defendant had the idea for the crime all worked out and lacked merely the present means to commit it, and if the government had not supplied them someone else very well might have. It would be a case in which the government had merely furnished the opportunity to commit the crime to someone already predisposed to commit it. [A] person who is likely to commit a particular type of crime without being induced to do so by government agents, although he would not have committed it when he did but for that inducement, is a menace to society and a proper target of law enforcement. The likelihood that he has committed this type of crime in the past or will do so in the future is great, and by arranging for him to commit it now, in circumstances that enable the government to apprehend and convict him, the government punishes or prevents real criminal activity. The government's inducement affects the timing of the offense; it does not create the offense by exploiting the susceptibility of a weak-minded person. The defense of entrapment reflects the view that the proper use of the criminal law in a society such as ours is to prevent harmful conduct for the protection of the law abiding, rather than to purify thoughts and perfect character.

"Our two would-be international financiers were at the end of their tether, making it highly unlikely that if Hinch had not providentially appeared someone else would have guided them into money laundering. No real criminal would do business with such tyros. Or so it appears;

perhaps the government could have shown that a Grenadan banking license has no other use but money laundering and that sooner or later Pickard and Hollingsworth would have gotten into money laundering even without the government's aid. No attempt was made to show this; and we remind that the government's acknowledged burden is to prove beyond a reasonable doubt that a defendant who raises a colorable defense of entrapment, as Pickard plainly did, has not in fact been entrapped." [b]

[b]. In three separate dissents, Judges Coffey, Easterbrook and Ripple voiced strong disagreement with the majority's interpretation of *Jacobson*.

Chapter 8
POLICE INTERROGATION AND CONFESSIONS

SECTION 1. SOME DIFFERENT PERSPECTIVES

8th ed., p. 452, at the end of the extract from Professor Grano's book, add new fn. b:

b. For an essay review of Professor Grano's book, a review that, inter alia, discusses the arguments for and against overruling *Miranda*, see George C. Thomas, III, *An Assault on the Temple of Miranda*, 85 J.Crim.L. & Criminology 807 (1995).

SECTION 3. THE *MIRANDA* "REVOLUTION"

8th ed., p. 489; end of fn. 57 to *Miranda*, add:

[Ed. Note—*England curtails the right to silence.* In the fall of 1994, the British Parliament adopted various restrictions on the right to silence, effective March 1, 1995. These restrictions were similar to those Parliament had imposed on Northern Ireland in 1988. The new law permits judges and jurors to draw adverse inferences when, during interrogation, suspects do not tell the police any fact subsequently relied upon in their defense at trial if, under the circumstances, the suspects would have been "reasonably expected" to mention that fact to the police. (This section corresponds to a provision of the Northern Ireland Order which, according to the government, was designed to end terrorists' use of the "ambush defense," whereby terrorists would remain silent during interrogation and thus prevent the prosecution from preparing a rebuttal to subsequent defense claims.)

[The new law also permits judges and jurors to draw adverse inferences when suspects fail to respond to police questions about any suspicious objects, substances, or marks which are found on their persons or clothing or when suspects do not explain to the police why they were present at a place at or about the time of the crime for which they were arrested. Finally, if the defendant fails to testify at trial, the new law permits the jury to draw such adverse inferences "as appear proper"—including the "common sense" inference that there is no explanation for the evidence produced against the defendant and that the defendant is guilty. See generally, Mark Berger, *Of Policy, Politics, and Parliament: The Legislative Rewriting of the British Right to Silence*, 22 Am.J.Crim.L. 391 (1995); Gregory W. O'Reilly, *England Limits the Right to Silence and Moves Toward an Inquisitional System of Justice*, 85 J.Crim.L. & C. 402 (1994).

[For the view that silence during police interrogation does not cause police to drop charges or prosecutors to dismiss cases or courts to acquit defendants; that using adverse inferences will not induce suspects to talk to the police or to reveal their defenses; that there is no indication that in the past a defendant's right to silence has been frequently invoked at trial; and that adverse inferences about a defendant's failure to testify at trial will not foster testimony by defendants, see O'Reilly, supra, at 431–42.]

8th ed., p. 501; after text of § 3501(c), add:

Does § 3501(c) codify a limited form of the McNabb–Mallory rule or repudiate the rule in its entirety? Does § 3501(c) apply at all to statements made by a person who is being held by local authorities solely on state charges? Consider *United States v. Alvarez–Sanchez,* ___ U.S. ___, 114 S.Ct. 1599, 128 L.Ed.2d 319 (1994), which arose as follows:

While executing a warrant to search respondent's residence for heroin, Los Angeles law enforcement officers discovered not only narcotics, but counterfeit Federal Reserve Notes. Respondent was arrested and booked on state felony narcotics charges on Friday afternoon and spent the weekend in police custody. On Monday morning Los Angeles authorities informed the U.S. Secret Service of the counterfeit currency they had found. Several hours later two Secret Service agents arrived at the Sheriff's Department and interviewed respondent. After waiving his *Miranda* rights, respondent admitted that he had known that the currency was counterfeit. Shortly thereafter, the Secret Service agents arrested respondent and took him to their field office for booking.

Respondent moved to suppress the statements he had made to the secret service agents on the ground that the delay between his arrest on state charges and his presentment on the federal charge rendered his confession inadmissible under § 3501(c). The District Court denied his motion. Respondent was subsequently convicted after a jury trial at which the statements were admitted into evidence. But the U.S. Court of Appeals overturned the conviction, reasoning that, by negative implication, § 3501(c) must in some circumstances allow suppression of a confession made more than six hours after arrest solely on the basis of pre-presentment delay, "regardless of the voluntariness of the confession." The Supreme Court, per Thomas, J., reversed.

The Ninth Circuit was of the view that § 3501(c) codified a limited form of the *McNabb–Mallory* rule and thus required the suppression of a confession made before presentment but after the expiration of the six-hour "safe harbor" period. The Government contended, on the other hand, that § 3501 repudiated the *McNabb–Mallory* rule in its entirety and that the admissibility of a confession obtained beyond the six-hour period is controlled by § 3501(a), which provides that voluntary confessions "shall be admitted in evidence." The Court saw no need to resolve this dispute because "the terms of § 3501(c) were never triggered in this case":

"[T]here can be no 'delay' in bringing a person before a federal magistrate until, at a minimum, there is some obligation to bring the person before such a judicial officer in the first place. Plainly, a duty to present a person to a federal magistrate does not arise until the person has been arrested for a *federal* offense. [Until then] there is no duty, obligation, or reason to bring [the person] before a judicial officer 'empowered to commit persons charged with offenses against the laws of the United States,' and therefore, no 'delay' under § 3501(c) can occur.

"* * * This is true even if the arresting officers (who, when the arrest is for a violation of state law, almost certainly will be agents of the State or one of its subdivisions) believe or have cause to believe that the person also may have violated federal law. Such a belief, which may not be uncommon given that many activities are criminalized under both state and federal law, does not alter the underlying basis for the arrest and subsequent custody. As long as a person is arrested and held only on state charges by state or local authorities, the provisions of § 3501(c) are not triggered."

The Court declined to discuss the effect of § 3501(c), if any, in "the situation that would arise if state or local authorities, acting in collusion with federal officers, were to arrest and detain someone in order to allow the federal agents to interrogate him in violation of his right to a prompt federal presentment." For there was "no evidence" that such collusion had taken place in this case.[a]

8th ed., p. 502; after the discussion, at pp. 501–02, of the validity of § 3501—Congress's attempt to "repeal" Miranda—and the reluctance of the Department of Justice to invoke this statutory provision, add:

Consider the views of Justice SCALIA, concurring in DAVIS v. UNITED STATES (1994) (discussed at Supp., p. 40):

"[Section 3501] declares that 'a confession ... *shall be admissible in evidence if it is voluntarily given*,' and that the issue of voluntariness shall be determined on the basis of "*all* the circumstances surrounding the giving of the confession, *including* ... whether or not [the] defendant was advised or knew that he was not required to make any statement ...[;] ... whether or not [the] defendant had been advised prior to questioning of his right to the assistance of counsel; [and] whether or not [the] defendant was without the assistance of counsel when questioned....' §§ 3501(a), (b) (emphases added). It continues (lest the import be doubtful): "The presence or absence of any of the above-mentioned factors ... need not be conclusive on the issue of voluntariness of the confession." § 3501(b). Legal analysis of the admissibility of a confession without reference to these provisions is equivalent to legal analysis of the admissibility of hearsay without consulting the Rules of Evidence; it is an unreal exercise. Yet [that] is precisely what the United States has undertaken in this case. It did not raise § 3501(a) below and asserted that it is 'not at issue' here.*

"This is not the first case in which the United States has declined to invoke § 3501 before us—nor even the first case in which that failure has been called to its attention. In fact, with limited exceptions the provision has been studiously avoided by every Administration, not only

---

a. Ginsburg, J., joined by Blackmun, J., wrote a concurring opinion. Stevens, J., wrote a separate opinion concurring only in the judgment.

* [The] Court today bases its refusal to consider § 3501 not upon the fact that the provision is inapplicable, but upon the fact that the Government failed to argue it—and it is *that* refusal which my present statement addresses.

in this Court but in the lower courts, since its enactment more than 25 years ago. * * *

"I agree with the Court that it is *proper,* given the Government's failure to raise the point, to render judgment without taking account of § 3501. But the refusal to consider arguments not raised is a sound prudential practice, rather than a statutory or constitutional mandate, and there are times when prudence dictates the contrary. [As] far as I am concerned, such a time will have arrived when a case that comes within the terms of this statute is next presented to us.

"For most of this century, voluntariness *vel non* was the touchstone of admissibility of confessions. Section 3501 of Title 18 *seems* to provide for that standard in federal criminal prosecutions today. I say 'seems' because I do not wish to prejudge any issue of law. I am entirely open to the argument that § 3501 does not mean what it appears to say; that it is inapplicable for some other reason; or even that it is unconstitutional. But I will no longer be open to the argument that this Court should continue to ignore the commands of § 3501 simply because the Executive declines to insist that we observe them.

"The Executive has the power (whether or not it has the right) effectively to nullify some provisions of law by the mere failure to prosecute—the exercise of so-called prosecutorial discretion. And it has the power (whether or not it has the right) to avoid application of § 3501 by simply declining to introduce into evidence confessions admissible under its terms. But once a prosecution has been commenced and a confession introduced, the Executive assuredly has neither the power nor the right to determine what objections to admissibility of the confession are valid in law. Section 3501 is a provision of law directed *to the courts,* reflecting the people's assessment of the proper balance to be struck between concern for persons interrogated in custody and the needs of effective law enforcement. We shirk our duty if we systematically disregard that statutory command simply because the Justice Department systematically declines to remind us of it.

"The United States' repeated refusal to invoke § 3501, combined with the courts' traditional (albeit merely prudential) refusal to consider arguments not raised, has caused the federal judiciary to confront a host of *'Miranda'* issues that might be entirely irrelevant under federal law. * * * Worse still, it may have produced—during an era of intense national concern about the problem of run-away crime—the acquittal and the nonprosecution of many dangerous felons, enabling them to continue their depredations upon our citizens. There is no excuse for this. Perhaps (though I do not immediately see why) the Justice Department has good basis for believing that allowing prosecutions to be defeated on grounds that could be avoided by invocation of § 3501 is consistent with the Executive's obligation to 'take Care that the Laws be faithfully executed,' U.S. Const., Art. II, § 3. That is not the point. The point is whether *our* continuing refusal to *consider* § 3501 is consistent with the Third Branch's obligation to decide according to the law. I think it is not."

8th ed., p. 506; add to the Note on prophylactic rules and the "legitimacy" of Miranda:

Consider the views of Justice Scalia, set forth at Supp., p. 35, concurring in *Davis v. United States.*

8th ed., p. 515; add to Note 4:

4. *"Custody" vs. "focus."* In *Stansbury v. California*, ___ U.S. ___, 114 S.Ct. 1526, 128 L.Ed.2d 293 (1994) (per curiam), the Court held, "not for the first time, that an officer's subjective and undisclosed view concerning whether the person being interrogated is a suspect is irrelevant to the assessment whether the person is in custody."

Stansbury, one of two suspects in the disappearance and possible murder of a young girl, agreed to answer some questions and accompanied an officer to the stationhouse. There he was questioned without being given *Miranda* warnings. Because the trial court concluded that the officer's "mind" was on the other suspect until Stansbury revealed certain information, statements Stansbury made before that time were admitted into evidence. The state supreme court affirmed, viewing "whether the investigation has focused on the subject" one of the important considerations "in deciding the custody issue." In reversing, the U.S. Supreme Court emphasized that "[s]ave as they are communicated or otherwise manifested to the person being questioned, an officer's evolving but unarticulated suspicions do not affect the objective circumstances of an interrogation or interview, and thus cannot affect the *Miranda* custody inquiry."

8th ed., p. 542; add to Note 10:

10. *Meeting the "heavy burden" of demonstrating waiver: should written records and sound recordings be required?*

Although some commentators have argued that the police should comply with *both* the *Miranda* rules *and* an electronic recording requirement, in the article extracted below Professor Cassell maintains that a recording requirement should be viewed as an *alternative* to *Miranda*.

PAUL G. CASSELL—*MIRANDA*'S SOCIAL COSTS: AN EMPIRICAL REASSESSMENT

90 Nw.U.L.Rev. ___ (1995).

Miranda's defenders have argued that any change in the decision's requirements would "roll back the clock" to an outmoded day and age. But time has passed these Warren Court warriors by—they are, in effect, advocating a 1966 solution to the problem of preventing coerced confessions when the 1990s offer superior solutions. Consider, then, videotaping of interrogations as an alternative to *Miranda*. * * *

Videotaping interrogations would be at least as effective as *Miranda* in preventing police coercion. The *Miranda* regime appears to have had little effect on what police misconduct exists. In contrast, videotaping, when it has been used, has often reduced claims of police coercion and probably real coercion as well. To be sure, police conceivably could alter tapes or deploy force off-camera. But if you were facing a police officer with a rubber hose, would you prefer a world in which he was required to mumble the *Miranda* warnings and have you waive your rights, all as reported by him in later testimony? Or a world in which the interrogation is videorecorded and the burden is on law enforcement to explain if it is not; where date and time are recorded on the videotape; where your physical appearance and demeanor during the interrogation are permanently recorded? Videotaping is the clear winner. Not surprisingly, those who are most concerned about police brutality have seen videotaping as a means of control.

Recording confessions also promises to be effective in preventing not only physical coercion but also in detecting, if not preventing, other fine points of coercion as well. In this regard, it is interesting that some of the most detailed assessments of voluntariness have come in cases of recorded interrogations, which permitted judges to parse implicit promises and threats made to obtain an admission. Recording also allows a review of police overbearing that might not be revealed in dry testimony. Taping is thus the only means of eliminating "swearing contests" about what went on in the interrogation room.

Videotaping also promises to offer more effective protection against the more esoteric problem of false confessions induced by non-coercive police questioning. A complete record of the proceedings promises to be the most effective means of identifying such cases. * * *

While recording maintains, and in many ways exceeds, *Miranda*'s supposed benefits of deterring coercion and preventing false confessions, it has the advantage over *Miranda* of not significantly impeding law enforcement. In 1992 the National Institute of Justice (NIJ) published a nationwide survey of representative samples of police agencies about videotaping interrogations. The survey found that about one-sixth of all police and sheriffs' departments in the United States videotaped at least some confessions. The survey found that 59.8% of the agencies believed that they obtained more incriminating information from suspects, 26.9% the same amount, while 13.2% thought they obtained less. Also, 8.6% thought suspects were more willing to talk to police, 63.1% thought there was no difference, while 28.3% reported suspects less willing to talk. Videotaping also had many other benefits, such as improving police interrogation practices, rendering confessions more convincing, facilitating their introduction into evidence, assisting prosecutors in negotiating more acceptable plea bargains and obtaining guilty pleas, and helping in securing convictions. * * *

Recent and substantial experience with a mandatory recording requirement in Britain suggests that a mandatory recording requirement would not significantly harm police efforts to obtain confessions. In 1988, a Code of Practice took effect that generally required that police tape record interviews with suspects. A 1993 review of the requirement by the Royal Commission on Criminal Justice reported that "[b]y general consent, tape recording in the police station has proved to be a strikingly successful innovation providing better safeguards for the suspect and the police officer alike." No significant adverse effect on obtaining confessions has been observed in the empirical studies specifically focusing on taping, and in fact police obtain more confessions and information about other offenses when interrogations are taped. According to one survey, 91% of police officers approve of the practice with 65% reporting "very favorable" views about it. * * *

Miranda's defenders might be prepared to concede that videotaping has many advantages but argue that police should comply with both *Miranda* and videotaping requirements. But such an approach singlemindedly pursues the goal of eliminating coerced confessions without considering the countervailing costs identified in this Article. The Court has described *Miranda* as "a carefully crafted balance designed to fully protect *both* the defendants' and society's interests." [598] An approach that strikes a reasonable balance between maximizing benefits and minimizing costs would be to require taping to prevent police coercion while at the same time relaxing the features of the *Miranda* regime that extract the greatest costs in terms of lost confessions. The existing empirical literature allows us to identify the particularly harmful features of *Miranda*. These features can then be modified, while the other protections remain in place. In particular, the requirement of giving a warning to suspects can be retained without significantly lowering the confession rate, while the waiver and questioning cutoff rules should be eliminated, as they cause the bulk of *Miranda*'s harms. * * *

In light of the effectiveness of videotaping and the specific features of *Miranda* that create its costs, what might a replacement for *Miranda* look like? Suspects could continue to be advised of their rights, as follows:

(1) You do not have to say anything.

(2) Anything you do say may be used as evidence.

(3) You have the right to be represented by a lawyer when we bring you before a judge.

(4) If you cannot afford a lawyer, the judge will appoint one for you without charge.

(5) We are required to bring you before a judge without unnecessary delay.

While adding a new, fifth warning that is not required by *Miranda,* the modified warnings would dispense with the *Miranda* offer of counsel, identified as a particularly harmful aspect of *Miranda* and, in any event, a right that has proven to be purely theoretical since police always terminate questioning rather than finding a lawyer. Also to be dis-

598. Moran v. Burbine, 495 U.S. 412, 433 n. 4 (1986) * * *.

pensed with would be the requirement that police obtain an affirmative waiver of rights from suspects, another particularly harmful feature of *Miranda*. However, police could continue to ask suspects whether they understood the rights communicated to them, since nothing in the empirical literature identifies this aspect of *Miranda* as being particularly harmful. Finally to be eliminated would be the requirement that police immediately terminate an interview whenever the suspect requests an end to the interview or a chance to see counsel. These features have been identified as harming the confession rate.

While these changes would eliminate most of *Miranda*'s costs, the additional safeguard of taping confessions could be added on top of existing requirements without adversely affecting confession rates. Videotaping would be required for custodial interrogation in the stationhouse; audiotaping would be required for custodial interrogation in the field (as is currently done in Alaska). * * *

One final point should be made in favor of this proposal. Since police are still required to give modified warnings and since they will be videotaped while conducting interrogations, police will not gain the mistaken impression that any judicial supervision of the interrogation process has ended.

8th ed., p. 563; add to Note 16(b):

16(b). *What constitutes an effective invocation of the right to counsel for purposes of Edwards.* See *Davis v. United States,* immediately below.

8th ed., p. 563; add to Note 17:

17. *The assumption that direct and assertive speech should be the norm.* In DAVIS v. UNITED STATES, ___ U.S. ___, 114 S.Ct. 2350, 129 L.Ed.2d 362 (1994), Justice O'CONNOR, speaking for five members of the Court, in effect rejected the position taken by Professor Ainsworth that (a) the courts should not place a premium on suspects making direct, assertive, unqualified invocations of the right to counsel and (b) all arguable references to counsel should be treated as valid invocations of the right. The *Davis* case arose as follows:

Davis, a member of the U.S. Navy, was suspected of murdering another sailor. When interviewed by agents of the Naval Investigative Service (NIS) at the NIS office, he initially waived his *Miranda* rights. About an hour and a half into the interview, he said: "Maybe I should talk to a lawyer." At this point, according to the uncontradicted testimony of one of the agents, "we made it very clear [that] we weren't going to pursue the matter unless we have it clarified is he asking for a lawyer or is he just making a comment about a lawyer" and Davis replied, "No, I'm not asking for a lawyer" and then said, "No, I don't want a lawyer."

After a short break, the agents then reminded Davis of his *Miranda* rights and the interview continued for another hour—until Davis said, "I think I want a lawyer before I say anything." At this point, questioning ceased.

A military judge admitted Davis's statements and he was convicted of murder. The U.S. Court of Appeals affirmed the conviction—as did the U.S. Supreme Court:

"The applicability of the ' "rigid" prophylactic rule' of *Edwards* requires courts to 'determine whether the accused *actually invoked* his right to counsel.' *Smith v. Illinois* (emphasis added). To avoid difficulties of proof and to provide guidance to officers conducting interrogations, this is an objective inquiry. Invocation of the *Miranda* right to counsel 'requires, at a minimum, some statement that can reasonably be construed to be an expression of a desire for the assistance of an attorney.' But if a suspect makes a reference to an attorney that is ambiguous or equivocal in that a reasonable officer in light of the circumstances would have understood only that the suspect *might* be invoking the right to counsel, our precedents do not require the cessation of questioning. * * *

"Rather, the suspect must unambiguously request counsel. As we have observed, 'a statement either is such an assertion of the right to counsel or it is not.' *Smith v. Illinois*. Although a suspect need not 'speak with the discrimination of an Oxford don' (Souter, J., concurring in judgment), he must articulate his desire to have counsel present sufficiently clearly that a reasonable police officer in the circumstances would understand the statement to be a request for an attorney. If the statement fails to meet the requisite level of clarity, *Edwards* does not require that the officers stop questioning the suspect. * * *

"We decline petitioner's invitation to extend *Edwards* and require law enforcement officers to cease questioning immediately upon the making of an ambiguous or equivocal reference to an attorney. See *Arizona v. Roberson,* (Kennedy, J., dissenting) ('the rule of *Edwards* is our rule, not a constitutional command; and it is our obligation to justify its expansion'). The rationale underlying *Edwards* is that the police must respect a suspect's wishes regarding his right to have an attorney present during custodial interrogation. But when the officers conducting the questioning reasonably do not know whether or not the suspect wants a lawyer, a rule requiring the immediate cessation of questioning 'would transform the *Miranda* safeguards into wholly irrational obstacles to legitimate police investigative activity,' because it would needlessly prevent the police from questioning a suspect in the absence of counsel even if the suspect did not wish to have a lawyer present. Nothing in *Edwards* requires the provision of counsel to a suspect who consents to answer questions without the assistance of a lawyer. * * *

"We recognize that requiring a clear assertion of the right to counsel might disadvantage some suspects who—because of fear, intimidation, lack of linguistic skills, or a variety of other reasons—will not clearly articulate their right to counsel although they actually want to have a lawyer present. But the primary protection afforded suspects subject to custodial interrogation is the *Miranda* warnings themselves. '[F]ull comprehension of the rights to remain silent and request an attorney [is] sufficient to dispel whatever coercion is inherent in the interrogation process.' *Moran v. Burbine*. A suspect who knowingly and voluntarily waives his right to counsel after having that right explained to him has indicated his willingness to deal with the police unassisted. Although *Edwards* provides an additional protection—if a suspect subsequently requests an attorney, questioning must cease—it is one that must be affirmatively invoked by the suspect.

"In considering how a suspect must invoke the right to counsel, we must consider the other side of the *Miranda* equation: the need for effective law enforcement. Although the courts ensure compliance with the *Miranda* requirements through the exclusionary rule, it is police officers who must actually decide whether or not they can question a suspect. The *Edwards* rule—questioning must cease if the suspect asks for a lawyer—provides a bright line that can be applied by officers in the real world of investigation and interrogation without unduly hampering the gathering of information. But if we were to require questioning to cease if a suspect makes a statement that *might* be a request for an attorney, this clarity and ease of application would be lost. Police officers would be forced to make difficult judgment calls about whether the suspect in fact wants a lawyer even though he hasn't said so, with the threat of suppression if they guess wrong. We therefore hold that, after a knowing and voluntary waiver of the *Miranda* rights, law enforcement officers may continue questioning until and unless the suspect clearly requests an attorney.

"Of course, when a suspect makes an ambiguous or equivocal statement it will often be good police practice for the interviewing officers to clarify whether or not he actually wants an attorney. That was the procedure followed by the NIS agents in this case. Clarifying questions help protect the rights of the suspect by ensuring that he gets an attorney if he wants one, and will minimize the chance of a confession being suppressed due to subsequent judicial second-guessing as to the meaning of the suspect's statement regarding counsel. But we decline to adopt a rule requiring officers to ask clarifying questions. If the suspect's statement is not an unambiguous or unequivocal request for counsel, the officers have no obligation to stop questioning him.

"To recapitulate: We held in *Miranda* that a suspect is entitled to the assistance of counsel during custodial interrogation even though the Constitution does not provide for such assistance. We held in *Edwards* that if the suspect invokes the right to counsel at any time, the police must immediately cease questioning him until an attorney is present. But we are unwilling to create a third layer of prophylaxis to prevent police questioning when the suspect *might* want a lawyer. Unless the suspect actually requests an attorney, questioning may continue."[a]

    a. The Court noted that "the Government has not sought to rely in this case on § 3501 [and] we therefore decline the invitation of some *amici* to consider it. Al-

Justice SOUTER, joined by Blackmun, Stevens and Ginsburg, JJ., wrote a separate opinion. Although he concurred in the judgment affirming Davis's conviction, "resting partly on evidence of statements given after agents ascertained that he did not wish to deal with them through counsel," Justice Souter could not join the majority's "further conclusion that if the investigators here had been so inclined, they were at liberty to disregard Davis's reference to a lawyer entirely, in accordance with a general rule that interrogators have no legal obligation to discover what a custodial subject meant by an ambiguous statement that could reasonably be understood to express a desire to consult a lawyer":

"Our own precedent, the reasonable judgments of the majority of the many courts already to have addressed the issue before us, and the advocacy of a considerable body of law enforcement officials are to the contrary. All argue against the Court's approach today, which draws a sharp line between interrogated suspects who 'clearly' assert their right to counsel and those who say something that may, but may not, express a desire for counsel's presence, the former suspects being assured that questioning will not resume without counsel present, the latter being left to fend for themselves. The concerns of fairness and practicality that have long anchored our *Miranda* case law point to a different response: when law enforcement officials 'reasonably do not know whether or not the suspect wants a lawyer,' they should stop their interrogation and ask him to make his choice clear.

"While the question we address today is an open one, its answer requires coherence with nearly three decades of case law addressing the relationship between police and criminal suspects in custodial interrogation. Throughout that period, two precepts have commanded broad assent: that the *Miranda* safeguards exist 'to assure that *the individual's right to choose* between speech and silence remains unfettered throughout the interrogation process,' and that the justification for *Miranda* rules, intended to operate in the real world, 'must be consistent [with] practical realities.' *Arizona v. Roberson* (Kennedy, J., dissenting). A rule barring government agents from further interrogation until they determine whether a suspect's ambiguous statement was meant as a request for counsel fulfills both ambitions. It assures that a suspect's choice whether or not to deal with police through counsel will be 'scrupulously honored' and it faces both the real-world reasons why misunderstandings arise between suspect and interrogator and the real-world limitations on the capacity of police and trial courts to apply fine distinctions and intricate rules.

though we will consider arguments raised only in an *amicus* brief, we are reluctant to do so when the issue is one of first impression involving the interpretation of a federal statute on which the Department of Justice expressly declines to take a position." Justice Scalia wrote a concurring opinion, set forth in the Supp. at p. 35, discussing the applicability of § 3501 to *Miranda* issues and concluding that the Court's continuing refusal to consider § 3501 was inconsistent with "the Third Branch's obligation to decide according to the law."

"Tested against the same two principles, the approach the Court adopts does not fare so well. First, as the majority expressly acknowledges, criminal suspects who may (in *Miranda*'s words) be 'thrust into an unfamiliar atmosphere and run through menacing police interrogation procedures,' would seem an odd group to single out for the Court's demand of heightened linguistic care. A substantial percentage of them lack anything like a confident command of the English language, many are 'woefully ignorant,' and many more will be sufficiently intimidated by the interrogation process or overwhelmed by the uncertainty of their predicament that the ability to speak assertively will abandon them.[4] Indeed, the awareness of just these realities has, in the past, dissuaded the Court from placing any burden of clarity upon individuals in custody, but has led it instead to require that requests for counsel be 'give[n] a broad, rather than a narrow, interpretation' and that courts 'indulge every reasonable presumption,' *Johnson v. Zerbst,* that a suspect has not waived his right to counsel under *Miranda.*

"[Nor] may the standard governing waivers as expressed in these statements be deflected away by drawing a distinction between initial waivers of *Miranda* rights and subsequent decisions to reinvoke them, on the theory that so long as the burden to demonstrate waiver rests on the government, it is only fair to make the suspect shoulder a burden of showing a clear subsequent assertion. *Miranda* itself discredited the legitimacy of any such distinction. The opinion described the object of the warning as being to assure 'a continuous opportunity to exercise [the right of silence].' '[C]ontinuous opportunity' suggests an unvarying one, governed by a common standard of effectiveness.

"[The] Court defends as tolerable the certainty that some poorly expressed requests for counsel will be disregarded on the ground that *Miranda* warnings suffice to alleviate the inherent coercion of the custodial interrogation. But, 'a once-stated warning, delivered by those who will conduct the interrogation cannot itself suffice' to 'assure that [the] right to choose between silence and speech remains unfettered throughout the interrogation process.' Nor does the Court's defense reflect a sound reading of the case it relies on, *Moran v. Burbine.* * * * While *Moran* held that a subject's knowing and voluntary waiver of the right to counsel is not undermined by the fact that police prevented an unsummoned lawyer from making contact with him, it contains no suggestion that *Miranda* affords as ready a tolerance for police conduct frustrating the suspect's subjectively held (if ambiguously expressed) desire for counsel. * * *

"Indeed, it is easy, amidst the discussion of layers of protection, to lose sight of a real risk in the majority's approach, going close to the core

---

4. Social science confirms what common sense would suggest, that individuals who feel intimidated or powerless are more likely to speak in equivocal or nonstandard terms when no ambiguity or equivocation is meant. Suspects in police interrogation are strong candidates for these effects. Even while resort by the police to the 'third degree' has abated since *Miranda,* the basic forms of psychological pressure applied by police appear to have changed less. * * *

of what the Court has held that the Fifth Amendment provides. The experience of the timid or verbally inept suspect (whose existence the Court acknowledges) may not always closely follow that of the defendant in *Edwards* (whose purported waiver of his right to counsel, made after having invoked the right, was held ineffective, lest police be tempted to 'badge[r]' others like him.) Indeed, it may be more like that of the defendant in *Escobedo*, whose sense of dilemma was heightened by his interrogators' denial of his requests to talk to a lawyer. When a suspect understands his (expressed) wishes to have been ignored (and by hypothesis, he has said something that an objective listener could 'reasonably,' although not necessarily, take to be a request), in contravention of the 'rights' just read to him by his interrogator, he may well see further objection as futile and confession (true or not) as the only way to end his interrogation.

"Nor is it enough to say [as the majority does] that a 'statement either is [an] assertion of the right to counsel or it is not' [quoting *Smith v. Illinois*]. In *Smith*, we neither denied the possibility that a reference to counsel could be ambiguous nor suggested that particular statements should be considered in isolation. While it might be fair to say that every statement is meant either to express a desire to deal with police through counsel or not, this fact does not dictate the rule that interrogators who hear a statement consistent with either possibility may presume the latter and forge ahead; on the contrary, clarification is the intuitively sensible course.

"The other justifications offered for the 'requisite level of clarity' rule are that, whatever its costs, it will further society's strong interest in 'effective law enforcement', and maintain the 'ease of application' that has long been a concern of our *Miranda* jurisprudence. With respect to the first point, the margin of difference between the clarification approach advocated here and the one the Court adopts is defined by the class of cases in which a suspect, if asked, would make it plain that he meant to request counsel (at which point questioning would cease). While these lost confessions do extract a real price from society, it is one that *Miranda* itself determined should be borne.

"[As] for practical application, while every approach, including the majority's, will involve some 'difficult judgment calls,'[7] the rule argued for here would relieve the officer of any responsibility for guessing 'whether the suspect in fact wants a lawyer even though he hasn't said

---

7. In the abstract, nothing may seem more clear than a "clear statement" rule, but in police stations and trial courts the question, "how clear is clear?" is not so readily answered. When a suspect says, "uh, yeah, I'd like to do that" after being told he has a right to a lawyer, has he "clearly asserted" his right? Compare *Smith v. Illinois (per curiam)* (statement was " 'neither indecisive nor ambiguous' ") with [Justice Rehnquist's dissent in that case]. * * * (questioning clarity). * * *

As a practical matter, of course, the primary arbiters of "clarity" will be the interrogators themselves, who tend as well to be courts' preferred source in determining the precise words a suspect used. And when an inculpatory statement has been obtained as a result of an unrecorded, incommunicado interrogation, these officers rarely lose "swearing matches" against criminal defendants at suppression hearings.

so.' To the contrary, it would assure that the 'judgment call' will be made by the party most competent to resolve the ambiguity, who our case law has always assumed should make it: the individual suspect.

"Although I am convinced that the Court has taken the wrong path, I am not persuaded by [Davis's] contention, that even ambiguous statements require an end to all police questioning. [While] it is plainly wrong, for example, to continue interrogation when the suspect wants it to stop (and so indicates), the strong bias in favor of individual choice may also be disserved by stopping questioning when a suspect wants it to continue (but where his statement might be understood otherwise). [The] costs to society of losing confessions would, moreover, be especially hard to bear where the suspect, if asked for his choice, would have chosen to continue. One need not sign the majority's opinion here to agree that resort to the rule [Davis] argues for should be had only if experience shows that less drastic means of safeguarding suspects' constitutional rights are not up to the job * * *.

"Our cases are best respected by a rule that when a suspect under custodial interrogation makes an ambiguous statement that might reasonably be understood as expressing a wish that a lawyer be summoned (and questioning cease), interrogators' questions should be confined to verifying whether the individual meant to ask for a lawyer. While there is reason to expect that trial courts will apply today's ruling sensibly (without requiring criminal suspects to speak with the discrimination of an Oxford don) and that interrogators will continue to follow what the Court rightly calls 'good police practice' (compelled up to now by a substantial body of state and Circuit law), I believe that the case law under *Miranda* does not allow them to do otherwise."

THE IMPACT OF *MIRANDA* IN PRACTICE

8th ed., p. 600; after discussion of *Miranda*'s effects, add:

In *Miranda's Social Costs: An Empirical Reassessment*, 90 Nw. U.L.Rev. ___ (1995) (forthcoming), Professor Paul G. Cassell contends that despite the "conventional academic wisdom" to the contrary, "*Miranda* has significantly harmed law enforcement efforts in this country." *Miranda*'s effects, maintains Professor Cassell, "should be measured not by looking at suppression motions that are filed after police have obtained a confession, but rather by examining how many confessions police never obtain because of *Miranda*."

According to Cassell, the existing empirical data supports "the tentative estimate" that *Miranda* has led to "lost cases" against 3.8 percent of all criminal suspects.[a] "While defenders of *Miranda* may

---

a. Professor Cassell recognizes that "in the empirical debate over the costs of the search and seizure exclusionary rule, defenders of the rule have made the plausible argument that the concept of a 'cost' is simply inappropriate" because "a case that is lost, either because the police did not unreasonably search or because the results of such a search were later suppressed, is simply the logical consequence of the Fourth Amendment." However, continues Cassell: "Whatever force such an argument may

argue that a 3.8% 'cost' is acceptable given *Miranda*'s benefits, critics will respond that the apparently small percentage figure multiplied across the run of criminal cases reflects a large number of criminals."

For 1993, the most recent year for which statistics are available, the Uniform Crime Reports (UCR) Crime Index reports 754,110 arrests for violent crimes and slightly over two million arrests for property crimes. "Multiplying the *Miranda* cost figure (3.8%) by the UCR index arrest figures suggests that in 1993 *Miranda* produced roughly 28,000 lost cases against suspects for index violent crimes and 79,000 lost cases against suspects for index property crimes." According to Cassell, the available data suggests that *Miranda* results in plea bargains to reduced charges in almost the same number of cases.[b]

ANOTHER LOOK AT *MIRANDA*: " 'TWAS A FAMOUS VICTORY"

8th ed., p. 608, end of fn. g to David Simon's *Homicide*, add:

Does *Davis v. United States,* Supp., p. 40, vindicate the detective's view of the *Miranda–Edwards* rule?

SECTION 5. *MASSIAH* REVISITED; *MASSIAH* AND *MIRANDA* COMPARED AND CONTRASTED

A. The Revivification of *Massiah*

8th ed., p. 642; add to Note on the "no-contact" rule:

A rule proposed by Attorney General Janet Reno to govern communications by governmental attorneys with persons represented by counsel has become a final rule, 59 Fed.Reg. 39910 (1994) (codified at 28 C.F.R. pt. 77). For the full text of the rule with accompanying supplemental information, see 55 Crim.L.Rep. 2269 (Aug. 10, 1994).

---

might have in the exclusionary rule context, it has little force as an argument against tabulating *Miranda*'s costs. [For they] are costs generated by a set of regulations on police not required by the Constitution and for which reasonable alternatives exist."

b. Professor Cassell goes on to say that alternatives such as videotaping of police interrogations can "more effectively prevent coercion while reducing harms to society." See the extracts from his article at Supp., p. 37.

Chapter 11
THE SCOPE OF THE EXCLUSIONARY RULES

SECTION 2. THE "FRUIT OF THE POISONOUS TREE"

B. THE "INEVITABLE DISCOVERY" DOCTRINE: THE SEQUEL TO *BREWER V. WILLIAMS*

8th ed., p. 823; add new Note:

5. *The issue not reached in Wilson v. Arkansas.* In *Wilson v. Arkansas,* Supp., p. 10, the Court declined to reach an argument put forward as an alternative ground for affirming denial of defendant's suppression motion: "that exclusion is not a constitutionally compelled remedy where the unreasonableness of a search stems from the failure of announcement. Analogizing to the 'independent source' doctrine applied in *Segura* [8th ed., p. 814], and the 'inevitable discovery' rule adopted in *Nix v. Williams,* respondent and its amici argue that any evidence seized after an unreasonable, unannounced entry is causally disconnected from the constitutional violation and that exclusion goes beyond the goal of precluding any benefit to the government flowing from the constitutional violation."

Assuming that the Court had reached this issue, what (would) (should) the result be?

C. IS A CONFESSION OBTAINED IN VIOLATION OF *MIRANDA* A "POISONOUS TREE"?

8th ed., p. 832; add new Note:

6. *The physical fruits of coerced confessions.* Should courts admit physical evidence derived from coerced confessions? Is this a logical extension of the sharp distinction the Court drew in *Schmerber v. California* (8th ed., p. 45) between words and physical evidence? Did Justice O'Connor point the way in *Quarles* (8th ed., p. 823)? Could the

same result also be reached by simply expanding the inevitable discovery doctrine adopted in *Nix v. Williams* (8th ed., p. 818), i.e., by simply presuming that the fruits of a coerced confession could or would always have come to light anyway? Compare Akhil Reed Amar and Renée B. Lettow, *Fifth Amendment First Principles: The Self–Incrimination Clause,* 93 Mich.L.Rev. 857 (1995) (yes) *with* Yale Kamisar, *On the Fruits of Miranda Violations, Coerced Confessions and Compelled Testimony,* 93 Mich.L.Rev. 929 (1995) (no).

Part Three
THE COMMENCEMENT OF FORMAL PROCEEDINGS

Chapter 14
THE PRELIMINARY HEARING

SECTION 2. THE DEFENDANT'S RIGHT TO A PRELIMINARY HEARING

8th ed., p. 960; end of Note 1 add:

In *Albright v. Oliver,* ___ U.S. ___, 114 S.Ct. 807, 127 L.Ed.2d 114 (1994), the Court addressed the question of whether substantive due process affords protection against initiation of prosecution without probable cause. The Court majority (7–2) sustained the dismissal of a federal civil rights action (filed under 42 U.S.C. § 1983), concluding that the complaint did not set forth an actionable claim under the single constitutional theory advanced there. The complaint alleged that a police detective, relying solely upon information supplied by a clearly unreliable informant, had filed charges against the plaintiff, alleging that he sold a substance that simulated an illegal drug, and had then obtained an arrest warrant based on those charges. Upon learning of the issuance of the warrant, the plaintiff surrendered to the detective and was subsequently released after posting bond. At a preliminary hearing, the detective testified as to the alleged sale and the plaintiff was bound over for trial. The charge was later dismissed at a pretrial hearing on the ground that it did not state an offense under state law.

Chief Justice Rehnquist, in a plurality opinion joined by Justices O'Connor, Scalia, and Ginsburg, stressed that petitioner had framed his claim solely as a substantive due process claim, and had not relied on either procedural due process or the Fourth Amendment. Dismissal was therefore required under previous precedent holding that where a particular Amendment "provides an explicit textual source of constitutional protection," then "that Amendment, not the more generalized notion of 'substantive due process' must be the guide for analyzing [that claim]." The Fourth Amendment, the Chief Justice noted, specifically addresses pretrial deprivations of liberty, and they "go hand in hand with criminal prosecutions, see *Gerstein v. Pugh*." Also the Court had noted in *Gerstein* and *Lem Woon* that "the accused is not entitled to judicial oversight or review of the decision to prosecute." Accordingly, any claim here would have to be based on the Fourth Amendment rather than "substantive due process, with its 'scarce and open-ended guideposts.' " [a]

Justice Kennedy joined by Justice Thomas, concurred in the judgment. Justice Kennedy concluded that the plaintiff's due process claim focused not on his arrest, but on his malicious prosecution on baseless charges, which presented a separate issue. Nonetheless, dismissal was still required since due process does not "include a standard for the initiation of prosecution." This was evidenced by the common law, which while it provided for "grand jury indictment and speedy trial, * * * did not provide a specific evidentiary standard applicable to a pretrial hearing on the merits of the charges or subject to later review by the courts. See *United States v. Williams* [8th ed., p. 1013]; *Costello v. United States* [8th ed., p. 1004]." Moreover, insofar as the common law of torts might reflect some notion of due process protection against malicious prosecution, prior precedent established that a state actor's "random and unauthorized" deprivation of such an interest could not be challenged under 42 U.S.C. § 1983 so long as the state provides "an adequate post-deprivation remedy" (here found in the state's tort remedy). Also concurring in the judgment, Justice Souter concluded that none of the injuries cited by plaintiff as flowing from his prosecution without probable cause went to a substantial liberty interest that stood apart from the custodial deprivations establishing a potential Fourth Amendment claim. He left open the possibility that due process could come into play in an "exceptional case * * * where some quantum of harm occurs in the interim after groundless criminal charges are filed but before any Fourth Amendment seizure."

In dissent, Justice Stevens, joined by Justice Blackmun, argued that freedom from prosecution except upon probable cause is a deeply-rooted substantive liberty interest protected by Fourteenth Amendment due process. At stake are a range of consequences, producing " 'a wrenching disruption of everyday life,' regardless of whether the initiation of

---

a. Although joining the plurality opinion, Justices Scalia and Ginsburg each wrote separate concurring opinions. Justice Scalia noted that he thought it "unlikely that the procedures constitutionally 'due' with regard to an arrest consist of anything more than what the Fourth Amendment specifies, but petitioner has in any case not invoked 'procedural' due process." Justice Ginsburg cited various elements of the case—the issuance of an arrest warrant, the petitioner's voluntary submission based on the warrant, his subsequent release subject to bail restrictions, and preliminary hearing testimony by the detective which "served to maintain and reinforce" any "Fourth Amendment violation"—that supported "viewing this case through a Fourth Amendment lens."

criminal prosecution prompts an arrest." While *Hurtado* held that due process does not require states to proceed by grand jury indictment, it had allowed the states to do so "only if the substance of the probable cause requirement remains adequately protected." Here, the state had established procedures to ensure that probable cause was present, but, as evidenced by cases such as *Mooney v. Holohan,* involving the prosecution's knowing use of perjured testimony (see 8th ed., Note 1, p. 1297), a "state compliance with facially valid procedures" should not invariably "meet the demands of due process, without regard to the substance of the resulting probable cause determination."

Chapter 18

THE SCOPE OF THE PROSECUTION: JOINDER AND SEVERANCE OF OFFENSES AND DEFENDANTS

SECTION 2. FAILURE TO JOIN RELATED OFFENSES

8th ed., p. 1101; after Note 3, add:

4. In DEPARTMENT OF REVENUE v. KURTH RANCH, ___ U.S. ___, 114 S.Ct. 1937, 128 L.Ed.2d 767 (1994), police raided the Kurths' farm, arrested them and confiscated and destroyed their marijuana plants. After the Kurths pleaded guilty to drug charges, the state revenue department attempted, in a separate proceeding, to collect a state tax imposed on the possession and storage of dangerous drugs. The Supreme Court, in a 5–4 decision, held, per STEVENS, J., that this tax "is fairly characterized as punishment" for the same offense and "therefore must be imposed during the first prosecution or not at all." The Court explained that while most taxes are *not* deemed punishment for double jeopardy purposes, the instant situation was different because of the "obvious deterrent purpose" and the "high rate of taxation" ("more than eight times the drug's market value"), together with another "unusual feature," i.e., that the "tax is conditioned on the commission of a crime," "is exacted only after the taxpayer has been arrested for the precise conduct that gives rise to the tax obligation in the first place," and "is levied on goods that the taxpayer neither owns nor possesses when the tax is imposed."

An Associated Press story dated May 23, 1995, notes a very significant consequence of *Kurth Ranch:* "In a legal development alarming those who crusade against drunken driving, courts are permitting DWI defendants to walk away from criminal prosecution if their licenses are already suspended, on grounds further punishment would constitute double jeopardy.

"Trial court judges in at least a dozen states * * * have already dismissed drunken-driving charges in such instances. The argument has cropped up in most of the 37 states that currently suspend or revoke licenses before prosecuting drunken drivers."

8th ed., pp. 1105–06; end of fn. e, add:

But in *Schiro v. Farley*, ___ U.S. ___, 114 S.Ct. 783, 127 L.Ed.2d 47 (1994), the Court held that the "failure to return a verdict does not have collateral estoppel effect * * * unless the record establishes that the issue was actually and necessarily decided in the defendant's favor." In that case, defendant's trial for a single killing resulted in the jury being given ten possible verdicts, including three murder counts ("knowingly" killing, rape felony-murder, deviate conduct felony-murder), voluntary and involuntary manslaughter, guilty but mentally ill, not guilty by reason of insanity, and not guilty. Because the jury returned a guilty verdict as to rape felony murder and left the other verdict sheets blank, defendant claimed the state was collaterally estopped from now showing intentional killing as an aggravated factor supporting a death sentence. The Court disagreed, concluding that because the jury (i) was not instructed to return more than one verdict but (ii) was instructed that intent was required for each variety of murder, defendant had "not met his 'burden ... to demonstrate that the issue whose relitigation he seeks to foreclose was actually decided' in his favor."

8th ed., p. 1109; following Note 6, add:

7. *Sentencing guidelines and multiple prosecutions for related offenses.* In *Witte v. United States*, ___ U.S. ___, 115 S.Ct. 2199, ___ L.Ed.2d ___ (1995), the Supreme Court considered the bearing of federal guideline sentencing upon separate prosecutions for offenses that are distinct offenses under *Blockburger* but involve the same criminal enterprise. Defendant there entered into a conspiracy in June 1990 to participate in the transportation of large amounts of marijuana and cocaine from Central America. One of the participants in the planned operation was an undercover agent, who later arranged for the arrest of several of the participants in Mexico as they were about to ship cocaine to the United States. In January 1991, the defendant agreed with the undercover agent to purchase and distribute a shipment of marijuana, using equipment purchased for distributing the 1990 shipment that never arrived. Defendant was arrested after receiving that marijuana. He subsequently was charged with attempted possession with intent to distribute, based solely upon the planned distribution of the 1991 shipment, and he entered a guilty plea to that charge. The statutorily authorized penalty for that offense was 5–40 years in prison.

Under the federal sentencing guidelines, the sentencing court is directed to take account of all "relevant conduct" in which the defendant was engaged. As applied to narcotics offenses, the relevant conduct provision holds the defendant "accountable for all quantities of contraband with which he was directly involved, and in the case of jointly undertaken criminal activity, all reasonably foreseeable quantities of contraband that were within the scope of criminal activity that he jointly undertook." In defendant's case, this meant consideration of the marijuana and cocaine that was to have been received under the failed 1990 plan, as well as the amount to be received in January 1991, as those shipments were part of "the same continuing conspiracy." The quantities involved in the anticipated Central America shipments added considerably to the offense-level score of 40, which produced (with adjustments for defendant's cooperation) the defendant's ultimate sentence of 144 months. Defendant was subsequently prosecuted for conspiring to import cocaine based upon the arrangements entered into in 1990. He moved to dismiss that charge on the ground that punishing him for that offense would violate the double jeopardy prohibition against multiple punishments as he had already been punished for the anticipated cocaine shipment in the calculation of his 144 month sentence.

Rejecting defendant's double jeopardy contention, the Supreme Court majority (per O'Connor, J.) held that consideration of the 1990 relevant conduct in setting the sentence for the 1991 offense did not constitute punishment for the criminal activity involved in that earlier conduct. Sentencing courts, in setting the sentence for the offense of conviction, traditionally have been allowed to consider a broad range of behavior, "including past criminal behavior, even if no conviction resulted from that behavior. *Nichols v. United States* [Supp. p. 1]." Such behavior guides the court in assessing defendant's range of culpability and thereby determining precisely where his sentence should fall within the range legislatively authorized for the offense of conviction. The sentence imposed consequently constitutes punishment only for the offense of conviction. Indeed, on the same principle, the Court had repeatedly upheld recidivist statutes, reasoning that the enhanced punishment "imposed for the later offenses is not to be viewed as either a new jeopardy or additional penalty for the earlier crimes."

The Court majority rejected the contention of Justice Stevens in dissent that the Guidelines altered the above analysis because they treated relevant conduct not as reflecting upon the character of the offender, but as a measure of the character of the offense. It noted that while relevant conduct "may relate to the severity of the particular crime, the commission of multiple offenses in the same course of conduct also necessarily provides important evidence that the character of the offender requires special punishment." The "offender is still punished only for the fact that the present offense was carried out in a manner that warrants increased punishment, not for a different offense." Concurring in the judgment, Justice Scalia, joined by Justice Thomas, suggested that the majority's analysis rested upon "perceiv[ed] lines that do not really exist," and the proper approach was to recognize, contrary to recent precedent (e.g., *Department of Revenue v. Kurth Ranch*, Supp. p. 53), that the double jeopardy clause simply does not prohibit multiple punishment for the same offense.

The Court majority in *Witte* also spoke to the appropriate interpretation of the Guidelines. This portion of the opinion was not joined by two members of the six justice majority (the Chief Justice and Justice Kennedy), but was joined by Justice Stevens. It noted that the Guidelines include significant safeguards that would protect Witte against having the length of his second sentence multiplied by duplicative consideration of the same criminal conduct already considered as "relevant conduct" for the marijuana sentence. These included a provision for concurrent sentencing where a charged offense was fully considered in a prior sentence. Moreover, even if the Sentencing Commission had not formalized such protective standards for multiple convictions, district courts retain enough flexibility under the Guideline provisions on variances to take into account the fact that conduct underlying the offense at issue has previously been treated as relevant conduct in the sentencing for another offense.

Consider also, Elizabeth Lear, *Contemplating the Successive Prosecution Phenomenon in the Federal System,* 85 J.Crim.L. & Criminology 625 (1995) (concluding that "while the Guidelines may eliminate some incentives for [a second] prosecution in the Federal system, substantial pressures favoring piecemeal litigation remain").

Chapter 19

THE RIGHT TO A "SPEEDY TRIAL"—AND TO "SPEEDY DISPOSITION" AT OTHER STEPS IN THE CRIMINAL PROCESS

SECTION 1. SPEEDY TRIAL

8th ed., p. 1130; before Note 2, add:

1a. *Barker "rebalanced"?* Was the *Barker* test "revised" in *Reed v. Farley*, ___ U.S. ___, 114 S.Ct. 2291, 129 L.Ed.2d 277 (1994) (also discussed at Supp., p. 78)? The Court there held that a state court's failure to observe the 120–day time-for-trial rule of the Interstate Agreement on Detainers was not cognizable on federal habeas corpus when, as there, the defendant registered no objection to the trial date when it was set and suffered no prejudice from the delay. In responding to Reed's argument the result should be otherwise because the IAD's speedy trial provision "effectuates" the Sixth Amendment speedy trial guarantee, the Court asserted, citing *Barker:* "A showing of prejudice is required to establish a violation of the Sixth Amendment Speedy Trial Clause, and that necessary ingredient is entirely missing here."

Part Four

THE ADVERSARY SYSTEM AND THE DETERMINATION OF GUILT OR INNOCENCE

Chapter 21

DISCOVERY AND DISCLOSURE

SECTION 2. DISCOVERY BY THE DEFENSE

8th ed., p. 1252; add to Note 4:

The third edition of the A.B.A. Standards defines a "written statement" as including: "the substance of a statement of any kind made by that person that is embodied or summarized in any writing or recording, whether or not specifically signed or adopted by that person. The term is intended to include statements contained in police or investigative reports, but does not include attorney work product." A.B.A. Standards for Criminal Justice: Discovery (3rd ed., 1994).

SECTION 5. THE PROSECUTION'S CONSTITUTIONAL DUTY TO DISCLOSE

8th ed., p. 1506; following Note 1, add:

1(a). *Materiality.* In KYLES v. WHITLEY, ___ U.S. ___, 115 S.Ct. 1555, 131 L.Ed.2d 490 (1995), a closely divided Court (5–4) found a *Brady* violation in a state capital murder conviction challenged in the federal courts on habeas review. The prosecution's evidence at trial consisted largely of eyewitness identification by four persons who had been at the scene of the killing in a grocery store parking lot (three of those witnesses having previously picked out defendant from a photo lineup) and physical evidence that linked the defendant to the crime (in particular, the victim's purse, found in the rubbish behind the defendant's house, and the murder weapon, found behind the defendant's kitchen stove). The defense contended (as it had in an earlier trial resulting in a hung jury) that the eyewitnesses were mistaken and that the physical evidence had been planted by an acquaintance ("Beanie") who had instigated the police investigation of defendant and had urged the police to search his apartment and trash. Before trial, defense counsel had filed what was described as "a lengthy motion for disclosure by the state of any exculpatory or impeachment evidence" but the prosecution had "responded that there was 'no exculpatory evidence of any nature.'" Following defendant's conviction and sentence to death, it was discovered that the prosecution had failed to disclose various evidentiary items known to the police. The non-disclosed items included: (1) the initial eyewitness statements taken by police, which offered conflicting descriptions of the murderer, some inconsistent with the defendant's height, age, and hair style (and arguably closer to fitting Beanie); (2) police records establishing Beanie's initial call to the police, his inconsistent statements to the police, and his suggestion that the police search the rubbish; (3) evidence linking Beanie to other crimes committed at the same grocery store and to an unrelated murder; and (4) a computer print-out of the license numbers of the cars police found in the parking lot on the night of the murder (which did not include defendant's car, although it was the police theory that the killer had left his car in the lot after driving off with the victim's car and the jury had been shown a "grainy enlargement" of a crime scene photograph that supposedly had defendant's car in the background).

The Supreme Court majority (per SOUTER, J.) initially discussed "four aspects of materiality under *Bagley*" that guided its assessment of materiality in this case. Following that discussion, which is quoted below, the majority analyzed the nondisclosed evidence as it related to the proof at trial and concluded that the potential cumulative effect of the nondisclosed evidence established a *Brady* violation. The dissent (per SCALIA, J.) initially questioned whether certiorari should have been granted in the case, arguing that there was no dispute as to governing legal principles, but only as to the application of those principles to the facts of this particular case. Turning to those facts, the dissent concluded that there had been no *Brady* violation, as the state had presented a "massive core of evidence" establishing defendant's guilt and "the effect that *Brady* materials would have had in chipping away at the edges of the State's case can only be called immaterial."

While the *Kyles* ruling rested in the end on a fact-intensive analysis that has limited precedential value (especially in light of Court's close division as to that analysis), the opinion for the Court is noteworthy for its initial discussion of general character of "materiality" under *Bagley*. The majority stated in this regard:

"Four aspects of materiality under *Bagley* bear emphasis. Although the constitutional duty is triggered by the potential impact of favorable but undisclosed evidence, a showing of materiality does not require demonstration by a preponderance that disclosure of the suppressed evidence would have resulted ultimately in the defendant's acquittal (whether based on the presence of reasonable doubt or acceptance of an explanation for the crime that does not inculpate the defendant). * * * *Bagley*'s touchstone of materiality is a 'reasonable probability' of a different result, and the adjective is important. The question is not whether the defendant would more likely than not have received a different verdict with the evidence, but whether in its absence he received a fair trial, understood as a trial resulting in a verdict worthy of confidence. A 'reasonable probability' of a different result is accordingly shown when the Government's evidentiary suppression 'undermines confidence in the outcome of the trial.' *Bagley*.

"The second aspect of *Bagley* materiality bearing emphasis here is that it is not a sufficiency of evidence test. A defendant need not demonstrate that after discounting the inculpatory evidence in light of the undisclosed evidence, there would not have been enough left to convict. The possibility of an acquittal on a criminal charge does not imply an insufficient evidentiary basis to convict. One does not show a *Brady* violation by demonstrating that some of the inculpatory evidence should have been excluded, but by showing that the favorable evidence could reasonably be taken to put the whole case in such a different light as to undermine confidence in the verdict.

"Third, we note that, contrary to the assumption made by the Court of Appeals, once a reviewing court applying *Bagley* has found constitutional error there is no need for further harmless-error review. Assuming *arguendo* that a harmless error enquiry were to apply, a *Bagley* error could not be treated as harmless, since 'a reasonable probability that, had the evidence been disclosed to the defense, the result of the proceeding would have been different,' *Bagley*, necessarily entails the conclusion that the suppression must have had ' "substantial and injurious effect or influence in determining the jury's verdict," ' *Brecht v. Abrahamson* [8th ed., p. 1684] * * *.

"The fourth and final aspect of *Bagley* materiality to be stressed here is its definition in terms of suppressed evidence considered collectively, not item-by-item. As Justice Blackmun emphasized in the portion of his opinion written for the Court, the Constitution is not violated every time the government fails or chooses not to disclose evidence that might prove helpful to the defense. We have never held that the Constitution demands an open file policy (however such a policy might work out in practice), and the rule in *Bagley* (and, hence, in *Brady*) requires less of the prosecution than the ABA Standards for Criminal Justice, which call generally for prosecutorial disclosures of any evidence tending to exculpate or mitigate. * * *

"While the definition of *Bagley* materiality in terms of the cumulative effect of suppression must accordingly be seen as leaving the government with a degree of discretion, it must also be understood as imposing a corresponding burden. On the one side, showing that the prosecution knew of an item of favorable evidence unknown to the defense does not amount to a *Brady* violation, without more. But the prosecution, which alone can know what is undisclosed, must be assigned the consequent responsibility to gauge the likely net effect of all such evidence and make disclosure when the point of 'reasonable probability' is reached. This in turn means that the individual prosecutor has a duty to learn of any favorable evidence known to the others acting on the government's behalf in the case, including the police. But whether the prosecutor succeeds or fails in meeting this obligation (whether, that is, a failure to disclose is in good faith or bad faith, see *Brady*), the prosecution's responsibility for failing to disclose known, favorable evidence rising to a material level of importance is inescapable.

"The State of Louisiana would prefer an even more lenient rule. It pleads that some of the favorable evidence in issue here was not disclosed even to the prosecutor until after trial, and it suggested below that it should not be held accountable under *Bagley* and *Brady* for evidence known only to police investigators and not to the prosecutor. To accommodate the State in this manner would, however, amount to a serious change of course from the *Brady* line of cases. In the State's favor it may be said that no one doubts that police investigators sometimes fail to inform a prosecutor of all they know. But neither is there any serious doubt that 'procedures and regulations can be established to carry [the prosecutor's] burden and to insure communication of all relevant information on each case to every lawyer who deals with it.' *Giglio v. United States* [8th ed., p. 1289, fn. b]. Since, then, the prosecutor has the means to discharge the government's *Brady* responsibility if he will, any argument for excusing a prosecutor from disclosing what he does not happen to know about boils down to a plea to substitute the police for the prosecutor, and even for the courts themselves, as the final arbiters of the government's obligation to ensure fair trials.

"Short of doing that, we were asked at oral argument to raise the threshold of materiality because the *Bagley* standard 'makes it difficult . . . to know' from the 'perspective [of the prosecutor at] trial . . . exactly what might become important later on.' The State asks for 'a certain amount of leeway in making a judgment call' as to the disclosure of any given piece of evidence. * * * Uncertainty about the degree of further 'leeway' that might satisfy the State's request for a 'certain amount' of it is the least of the reasons to deny the request. At bottom, what the State fails to recognize is that, with or without more leeway, the prosecution cannot be subject to any disclosure obligation without at some point having the responsibility to determine when it must act. Indeed, even if due process were thought to be violated by every failure to disclose an item of exculpatory or impeachment evidence (leaving harmless error as the government's only fallback), the prosecutor would still be forced to make judgment calls about what would count as favorable evidence, owing to the very fact that the character of a piece of evidence as favorable will often turn on the context of the existing or potential evidentiary record. Since the prosecutor would have to exercise some judgment even if the State were subject to this most stringent disclosure obligation, it is hard to find merit in the State's complaint over the responsibility for judgment under the existing system, which does not tax the prosecutor with error for any failure to disclose, absent a further showing of materiality. Unless, indeed, the adversary system of prosecution is to descend to a gladiatorial level unmitigated by any prosecutorial obligation for the sake of truth, the government simply cannot avoid responsibility for knowing when the suppression of evidence has come to portend such an effect on a trial's outcome as to destroy confidence in its result.

"This means, naturally, that a prosecutor anxious about tacking too close to the wind will disclose a favorable piece of evidence. * * * This is as it should be. Such disclosure will serve to justify trust in the prosecutor as 'the representative ... of a sovereignty ... whose interest ... in a criminal prosecution is not that it shall win a case, but that justice shall be done.' *Berger v. United States*. And it will tend to preserve the criminal trial, as distinct from the prosecutor's private deliberations, as the chosen forum for ascertaining the truth about criminal accusations. * * * The prudence of the careful prosecutor should not therefore be discouraged."

Chapter 22

COERCED, INDUCED AND NEGOTIATED GUILTY PLEAS; PROFESSIONAL RESPONSIBILITY

SECTION 2. REJECTED, KEPT AND BROKEN BARGAINS; UNREALIZED EXPECTATIONS

8th ed., p. 1325; following first paragraph of Note 8, add:

In UNITED STATES v. MEZZANATTO, ___ U.S. ___, 115 S.Ct. 797, 130 L.Ed.2d 697 (1995), when defendant and his attorney met with the prosecutor for plea discussions, the prosecutor conditioned the discussions on defendant agreeing that any statements he made could be used to impeach any contradictory testimony defendant might give if the case went to trial. Defendant, after consulting his lawyer, agreed to those terms. The case later did go to trial and such impeachment occurred, but defendant's conviction was overturned on appeal on the ground that the agreement was unenforceable. The Supreme Court, per THOMAS, J., disagreed, reasoning that defendant had not shown "that the plea-statement Rules [a] depart from the presumption of waivability" which exists as to "legal rights generally, and evidentiary provisions specifically": (1) defendant's claim that the Rules "guarantee fair procedure" and thus cannot be waived is in error, for the "admission of plea statements for impeachment purposes *enhances* the truth-seeking function of trials and will result in more accurate verdicts"; (2) defendant's claim that waiver is inconsistent with the Rules' goal of encouraging voluntary settlement is in error, as "it simply makes no sense to conclude that mutual settlement will be encouraged by precluding negotiation over an issue that may be particularly important to one of the parties to the transaction"; and (3) defendant's claim that waivers should be forbidden because they invite prosecutorial overreaching is in error, as "the appropriate response to [such] predictions of abuse is to permit case-by-case inquiries into whether waiver agreements are the product of fraud or coercion." [b]

a. The reference is to Fed.R.Crim.P. 11(e)(6) and virtually identical Fed.R.Evid. 410.

b. Three concurring Justices speculated "that a waiver to use such statements in the case-in-chief would more severely undermine a defendant's incentive to negotiate, and thereby inhibit plea bargaining." Two dissenters concluded the record showed Congress found that "conditions of unrestrained candor are the most effective means of encouraging plea discussions" and thus meant to bar waiver.

SECTION 3. PROFESSIONAL RESPONSIBILITY: THE ROLE OF PROSECUTOR AND DEFENSE COUNSEL

8th ed., p. 1349; end of footnote, add:

With regard to this "no-contact" rule, reconsider Note 5, 8th ed., p. 641.

SECTION 4. RECEIVING THE PLEA; PLEA WITHDRAWAL

F. Significance of Noncompliance With Requirements for Receiving Guilty Plea

8th ed., p. 1378; new fn. end of second sentence of Note 6:

a. As for the possibility of permitting *no* challenge of prior guilty pleas during sentencing following a later conviction, consider *Custis v. United States*, ___ U.S. ___, 114 S.Ct. 1732, 128 L.Ed.2d 517 (1994). The Court there held that it is constitutionally permissible to bar, as in the Armed Career Criminal Act, 18 U.S.C. § 924(e), virtually all collateral attacks upon prior state convictions being used for sentence enhancement in a federal trial. While a defendant may raise the "unique constitutional defect" of "failure to appoint counsel for an indigent defendant," challenge of other constitutional defects, such as an invalid guilty plea, may constitutionally be barred entirely in this setting. "Ease of administration" and the "interest in promoting the finality of judgments" (said to "bear extra weight in cases in which the prior convictions, such as the ones challenged by Custis, are based on guilty pleas") were the considerations relied upon by the *Custis* Court in support of that conclusion.

Chapter 23
TRIAL BY JURY

SECTION 1. RIGHT TO JURY TRIAL; WAIVER

8th ed., p. 1390; end of second line of last paragraph, add fn. aa:

aa. The distinction between a criminal contempt and a civil contempt, as to which there is no right to jury trial, is often difficult to draw. In *International Union, UMW v. Bagwell,* ___ U.S. ___, 114 S.Ct. 2552, 129 L.Ed.2d 642 (1994), a state court enjoined the union from conducting unlawful strike-related activities against certain mining companies, later fined the union for its disobedience and announced the union would be fined for any future breaches according to a specified fine schedule, and still later levied fines against the union totalling over $64,000,000. The state supreme court held these fines were civil and thus could be imposed without jury trial, but a unanimous Supreme Court reversed. The Court, per Blackmun, J., stressed these points: (1) While a contempt fine is civil if it merely compensates the complainant for losses sustained, such was not the case here, as the complainants neither requested compensation nor presented evidence regarding their injuries. (2) While traditionally a contempt fine has been considered civil if it forced a defendant into compliance with a court order, this does *not* mean (a) that the fines here were civil because there was a prospective fine schedule, for the "union's ability to avoid the contempt fines was indistinguishable from the ability of any ordinary citizen to avoid a criminal sanction by confirming his behavior to the law"; or (b) that the fines are criminal where they prohibit conduct but not when they mandate affirmative action, as often "injunctive provisions containing essentially the same command can be phrased either in mandatory or prohibitory terms." (3) While direct contempts in the presence of the court are subject to immediate summary adjudication without jury trial, the union's conduct did not occur in the court's presence. (4) Civil contempt without jury trial is appropriate for certain indirect contempts, "such as failure to comply with document discovery, [which] impedes the court's ability to adjudicate the proceedings before it," but the union's conduct was also not of that variety. (5) Because the state court "levied contempt fines for widespread, ongoing, out-of-court violations of a complex injunction," and thereby "effectively policed petitioner's compliance with an entire code of conduct that the court itself had imposed," resulting in fines which "unquestionably" were not at the petty offense level, the contempt must be deemed criminal, as in "such circumstances disinterested factfinding and even-handed adjudication were essential," and thus "petitioners were entitled to a criminal jury trial."

8th ed., p. 1397; replace Note 6:

6. *Fact or Law.* In United States v. Gaudin, ___ U.S. ___, 115 S.Ct. ___, ___ L.Ed.2d ___, 1995 WL 360212 (1995), the defendant was charged under 18 U.S.C. § 1001 with having made false statements on federal loan documents. Although "materiality" is an element of the offense, at the close of the evidence the trial judge instructed the jury: "The issue of materiality ... is not submitted to you for your decision but rather is a

matter for the decision of the court. You are instructed that the statements charged in the indictment are material statements." A unanimous Court, per Scalia, J., in affirming the court of appeals' reversal of defendant's conviction, relied on the Fifth Amendment due process clause and the Sixth Amendment right to jury trial, which "require criminal convictions to rest upon a jury determination that the defendant is guilty of every element of the crime with which he is charged." Although the government argued that this principle "actually applies to *only the factual components* of the essential elements," the Court disagreed. Specifically, the Court reasoned that though it is for the judge to "instruct the jury on the law and to insist that the jury follow his instructions," "the jury's constitutional responsibility is not merely to determine the facts, but to apply the law to those facts and draw the ultimate conclusion of guilt or innocence."

SECTION 2. JURY SELECTION

8th ed., p. 1408; end of Note 3, add:

Questions From the Jury Pool on Privacy, N.Y. Times, May 13, 1994, p. B9, col. 1, reports that a prospective juror was sentenced to a three-day jail term for contempt of court for answering "not applicable" to 12 questions in a 100-question questionnaire posed to prospective jurors in a murder case. She gave that answer "to queries about her income, her religion, her political affiliation and books and TV shows she enjoys, among other questions." What should the result be on her appeal of the contempt citation? This article notes: "But prosecutors and criminal defense lawyers alike contend that a prospective juror's right to privacy must yield to the imperatives of a fair trial, particularly in a murder case. Questions that appear entirely irrelevant to a member of a jury pool, they say, may nonetheless help lawyers develop a well-rounded profile."

8th ed., p. 1431; following Note 7, add:

J.E.B. v. ALABAMA EX REL. T.B.
___ U.S. ___, 114 S.Ct. 1419, 128 L.Ed.2d 89 (1994).

Justice BLACKMUN delivered the opinion of the Court. * * *

On behalf of relator T.B., the mother of a minor child, respondent State of Alabama filed a complaint for paternity and child support against petitioner J.E.B. in the District Court of Jackson County, Alabama. On October 21, 1991, the matter was called for trial and jury selection began. The trial court assembled a panel of 36 potential jurors, 12 males and 24 females. After the court excused three jurors for cause, only 10 of the remaining 33 jurors were male. The State then used 9 of its 10 peremptory strikes to remove male jurors; petitioner used all but one of his strikes to remove female jurors. As a result, all the selected jurors were female.

Before the jury was empaneled, petitioner objected to the State's peremptory challenges on the ground that they were exercised against male jurors solely on the basis of gender, in violation of the Equal Protection Clause of the Fourteenth Amendment. * * * The court rejected petitioner's claim and empaneled the all-female jury. The jury found petitioner to be the father of the child and the court entered an order directing him to pay child support. On post-judgment motion, the court reaffirmed its ruling that *Batson* does not extend to gender-based peremptory challenges.

We granted certiorari to resolve a question that has created a conflict of authority—whether the Equal Protection Clause forbids peremptory challenges on the basis of gender as well as on the basis of race. Today we reaffirm what, by now, should be axiomatic: Intentional discrimination on the basis of gender by state actors violates the Equal Protection Clause, particularly where, as here, the discrimination serves to ratify and perpetuate invidious, archaic, and overbroad stereotypes about the relative abilities of men and women.

Discrimination on the basis of gender in the exercise of peremptory challenges is a relatively recent phenomenon. Gender-based peremptory strikes were hardly practicable for most of our country's existence, since, until the 19th century, women were completely excluded from jury service. So well-entrenched was this exclusion of women that in 1880 this Court, while finding that the exclusion of African–American men from juries violated the Fourteenth Amendment, expressed no doubt that a State "may confine the selection [of jurors] to males." *Strauder v. West Virginia,* 100 U.S. 303, 310, 25 L.Ed. 664.

Many States continued to exclude women from jury service well into the present century, despite the fact that women attained suffrage upon ratification of the Nineteenth Amendment in 1920. States that did permit women to serve on juries often erected other barriers, such as registration requirements and automatic exemptions, designed to deter women from exercising their right to jury service.

The prohibition of women on juries was derived from the English common law which, according to Blackstone, rightfully excluded women from juries under "the doctrine of *propter defectum sexus,* literally, the 'defect of sex.'" In this country, supporters of the exclusion of women from juries tended to couch their objections in terms of the ostensible need to protect women from the ugliness and depravity of trials. Women were thought to be too fragile and virginal to withstand the polluted courtroom atmosphere. * * *

Taylor [*v. Louisiana,* 8th ed., p. 1400] relied on Sixth Amendment principles, but the opinion's approach is consistent with the heightened equal protection scrutiny afforded gender-based classifications. Since *Reed v. Reed,* 404 U.S. 71, 92 S.Ct. 251, 30 L.Ed.2d 225 (1971), this Court consistently has subjected gender-based classifications to heightened scrutiny in recognition of the real danger that government policies that professedly are based on reasonable considerations in fact may be reflective of "archaic and overbroad" generalizations about gender, or based on "outdated misconceptions concerning the role of females in the home rather than in the 'marketplace and world of ideas.'"

Despite the heightened scrutiny afforded distinctions based on gender, respondent argues that gender discrimination in the selection of the petit jury should be permitted, though discrimination on the basis of race is not. Respondent suggests that "gender discrimination in this country ... has never reached the level of discrimination" against African–Americans, and therefore gender discrimination, unlike racial discrimination, is tolerable in the courtroom. While the prejudicial attitudes toward women in this country have not been identical to those held toward racial minorities, the similarities between the experiences of racial minorities and women, in some contexts, "overpower those differences." As a plurality of this Court observed in *Frontiero v. Richardson*, 411 U.S. 677, 93 S.Ct. 1764, 36 L.Ed.2d 583 (1973):

> "[T]hroughout much of the 19th century the position of women in our society was, in many respects, comparable to that of blacks under the pre-Civil War slave codes. Neither slaves nor women could hold office, serve on juries, or bring suit in their own names, and married women traditionally were denied the legal capacity to hold or convey property or to serve as legal guardians of their own children.... And although blacks were guaranteed the right to vote in 1870, women were denied even that right—which is itself 'preservative of other basic civil and political rights'—until adoption of the Nineteenth Amendment half a century later."

Certainly, with respect to jury service, African–Americans and women share a history of total exclusion, a history which came to an end for women many years after the embarrassing chapter in our history came to an end for African–Americans.

We need not determine, however, whether women or racial minorities have suffered more at the hands of discriminatory state actors during the decades of our Nation's history. It is necessary only to acknowledge that "our Nation has had a long and unfortunate history of sex discrimination," a history which warrants the heightened scrutiny we afford all gender-based classifications today. Under our equal protection jurisprudence, gender-based classifications require "an exceedingly persuasive justification" in order to survive constitutional scrutiny. Thus, the only question is whether discrimination on the basis of gender in jury selection substantially furthers the State's legitimate interest in achieving a fair and impartial trial. In making this assessment, we do not weigh the value of peremptory challenges as an institution against our asserted commitment to eradicate invidious discrimination from the courtroom. Instead, we consider whether peremptory challenges based on gender stereotypes provide substantial aid to a litigant's effort to secure a fair and impartial jury.

Far from proffering an exceptionally persuasive justification for its gender-based peremptory challenges, respondent maintains that its decision to strike virtually all the males from the jury in this case "may reasonably have been based upon the perception, supported by history, that men otherwise totally qualified to serve upon a jury might be more sympathetic and receptive to the arguments of a man alleged in a paternity action to be the father of an out-of-wedlock child, while women equally qualified to serve upon a jury might be more sympathetic and receptive to the arguments of the complaining witness who bore the child." [9]

We shall not accept as a defense to gender-based peremptory challenges "the very stereotype the law condemns." Respondent's rationale, not unlike those regularly expressed for gender-based strikes, is reminiscent of the arguments advanced to justify the total exclusion of women from juries. Respondent offers virtually no support for the conclusion that gender alone is an accurate predictor of juror's attitudes; yet it urges this Court to condone the same stereotypes that justified the wholesale exclusion of women from juries and the ballot box.[11] Respondent seems to assume that gross generalizations that would be deemed impermissible if made on the basis of race are somehow permissible when made on the basis of gender.

Discrimination in jury selection, whether based on race or on gender, causes harm to the litigants, the community, and the individual jurors who are wrongfully excluded from participation in the judicial process. The litigants are harmed by the risk that the prejudice which motivated the discriminatory selection of the jury will infect the entire proceedings. The community is harmed by the State's participation in the perpetuation of invidious group stereotypes and the inevitable loss of confidence in our judicial system that state-sanctioned discrimination in the courtroom engenders. When state actors exercise peremptory challenges in reliance on gender stereotypes, they ratify and reinforce prejudicial views of the relative abilities of men and women. Because these stereotypes have wreaked injustice in so many other spheres of our

---

9. Respondent cites one study in support of its quasi-empirical claim that women and men may have different attitudes about certain issues justifying the use of gender as a proxy for bias. See R. Hastie, S. Penrod & N. Pennington, Inside the Jury 140 (1983). The authors conclude: "Neither student nor citizen judgments for typical criminal case material have revealed differences between male and female verdict preferences. * * * The picture differs [only] for rape cases, where female jurors appear to be somewhat more conviction-prone than male jurors". The majority of studies suggest that gender plays no identifiable role in jurors' attitudes. See, e.g., V. Hans & N. Vidmar, Judging the Jury 76 (1986) ("[I]n the majority of studies there are no significant differences in the way men and women perceive and react to trials; yet a few studies find women more defense-oriented, while still others show women more favorable to the prosecutor").

Even in 1956, before women had a constitutional right to serve on juries, some commentators warned against using gender as a proxy for bias. See 1 F. Busch, Law and Tactics in Jury Trials § 143, p. 207 (1949) ("In this age of general and specialized education, availed of generally by both men and women, it would appear unsound to base a peremptory challenge in any case upon the sole ground of sex....").

11. Even if a measure of truth can be found in some of the gender stereotypes used to justify gender-based peremptory challenges, that fact alone cannot support discrimination on the basis of gender in jury selection. We have made abundantly clear in past cases that gender classifications that rest on impermissible stereotypes violate the Equal Protection Clause, even when some statistical support can be conjured up for the generalization. * * *

country's public life, active discrimination by litigants on the basis of gender during jury selection "invites cynicism respecting the jury's neutrality and its obligation to adhere to the law." The potential for cynicism is particularly acute in cases where gender-related issues are prominent, such as cases involving rape, sexual harassment, or paternity. Discriminatory use of peremptory challenges may create the impression that the judicial system has acquiesced in suppressing full participation by one gender or that the "deck has been stacked" in favor of one side.

In recent cases we have emphasized that individual jurors themselves have a right to nondiscriminatory jury selection procedures. Contrary to respondent's suggestion, this right extends to both men and women. All persons, when granted the opportunity to serve on a jury, have the right not to be excluded summarily because of discriminatory and stereotypical presumptions that reflect and reinforce patterns of historical discrimination.[13] Striking individual jurors on the assumption that they hold particular views simply because of their gender is "practically a brand upon them, affixed by law, an assertion of their inferiority." It denigrates the dignity of the excluded juror, and, for a woman, reinvokes a history of exclusion from political participation.[14] The message it sends to all those in the courtroom, and all those who may later learn of the discriminatory act, is that certain individuals, for no reason other than gender, are presumed unqualified by state actors to decide important questions upon which reasonable persons could disagree.

Our conclusion that litigants may not strike potential jurors solely on the basis of gender does not imply the elimination of all peremptory challenges. Neither does it conflict with a State's legitimate interest in using such challenges in its effort to secure a fair and impartial jury. Parties still may remove jurors whom they feel might be less acceptable than others on the panel; gender simply may not serve as a proxy for bias. Parties may also exercise their peremptory challenges to remove from the venire any group or class of individuals normally subject to "rational basis" review. Even strikes based on characteristics that are

---

13. It is irrelevant that women, unlike African–Americans, are not a numerical minority and therefore are likely to remain on the jury if each side uses its peremptory challenges in an equally discriminatory fashion. Because the right to nondiscriminatory jury selection procedures belongs to the potential jurors, as well as to the litigants, the possibility that members of both genders will get on the jury despite the intentional discrimination is beside the point. The exclusion of even one juror for impermissible reasons harms that juror and undermines public confidence in the fairness of the system.

14. The popular refrain is that all peremptory challenges are based on stereotypes of some kind, expressing various intuitive and frequently erroneous biases. But where peremptory challenges are made on the basis of group characteristics other than race or gender (like occupation, for example), they do not reinforce the same stereotypes about the group's competence or predispositions that have been used to prevent them from voting, participating on juries, pursuing their chosen professions, or otherwise contributing to civic life.

disproportionately associated with one gender could be appropriate, absent a showing of pretext.[16] * * *

Failing to provide jurors the same protection against gender discrimination as race discrimination could frustrate the purpose of *Batson* itself. Because gender and race are overlapping categories, gender can be used as a pretext for racial discrimination. Allowing parties to remove racial minorities from the jury not because of their race, but because of their gender, contravenes well-established equal protection principles and could insulate effectively racial discrimination from judicial scrutiny.

Justice O'CONNOR, concurring.

I agree with the Court that the Equal Protection Clause prohibits the government from excluding a person from jury service on account of that person's gender. * * *. I therefore join the Court's opinion in this case. But today's important blow against gender discrimination is not costless. I write separately to discuss some of these costs, and to express my belief that today's holding should be limited to the government's use of gender-based peremptory strikes.

Batson v. Kentucky itself was a significant intrusion into the jury selection process. *Batson* mini-hearings are now routine in state and federal trial courts, and *Batson* appeals have proliferated as well. Demographics indicate that today's holding may have an even greater impact than did *Batson* itself. In further constitutionalizing jury selection procedures, the Court increases the number of cases in which jury selection—once a sideshow—will become part of the main event.

For this same reason, today's decision further erodes the role of the peremptory challenge. * * *

* * * Our belief that experienced lawyers will often correctly intuit which jurors are likely to be the least sympathetic, and our understanding that the lawyer will often be unable to explain the intuition, are the very reason we cherish the peremptory challenge. But, as we add, layer by layer, additional constitutional restraints on the use of the peremptory, we force lawyers to articulate what we know is often inarticulable.

In so doing we make the peremptory challenge less discretionary and more like a challenge for cause. We also increase the possibility that biased jurors will be allowed onto the jury, because sometimes a lawyer will be unable to provide an acceptable gender-neutral explanation even though the lawyer is in fact correct that the juror is unsympathetic. Similarly, in jurisdictions where lawyers exercise their strikes in open court, lawyers may be deterred from using their peremptories, out of the fear that if they are unable to justify the strike the court will seat a juror who knows that the striking party thought him unfit. Because I believe

---

16. For example, challenging all persons who have had military experience would disproportionately affect men at this time, while challenging all persons employed as nurses would disproportionately affect women. Without a showing of pretext, however, these challenges may well not be unconstitutional, since they are not gender- or race-based.

the peremptory remains an important litigator's tool and a fundamental part of the process of selecting impartial juries, our increasing limitation of it gives me pause.

Nor is the value of the peremptory challenge to the litigant diminished when the peremptory is exercised in a gender-based manner. We know that like race, gender matters. A plethora of studies make clear that in rape cases, for example, female jurors are somewhat more likely to vote to convict than male jurors. Moreover, though there have been no similarly definitive studies regarding, for example, sexual harassment, child custody, or spousal or child abuse, one need not be a sexist to share the intuition that in certain cases a person's gender and resulting life experience will be relevant to his or her view of the case.

Today's decision severely limits a litigant's ability to act on this intuition, for the import of our holding is that any correlation between a juror's gender and attitudes is irrelevant as a matter of constitutional law. But to say that gender makes no difference as a matter of law is not to say that gender makes no difference as a matter of fact. * * * In extending *Batson* to gender we have added an additional burden to the state and federal trial process, taken a step closer to eliminating the peremptory challenge, and diminished the ability of litigants to act on sometimes accurate gender-based assumptions about juror attitudes. * * *

Accordingly, I adhere to my position that the Equal Protection Clause does not limit the exercise of peremptory challenges by private civil litigants and criminal defendants. This case itself presents no state action dilemma, for here the State of Alabama itself filed the paternity suit on behalf of petitioner. But what of the next case? Will we, in the name of fighting gender discrimination, hold that the battered wife—on trial for wounding her abusive husband—is a state actor? Will we preclude her from using her peremptory challenges to ensure that the jury of her peers contains as many women members as possible? I assume we will, but I hope we will not.

Chief Justice REHNQUIST, dissenting.

* * * Unlike the Court, I think the State has shown that jury strikes on the basis of gender "substantially further" the State's legitimate interest in achieving a fair and impartial trial through the venerable practice of peremptory challenges. The two sexes differ, both biologically and, to a diminishing extent, in experience. It is not merely "stereotyping" to say that these differences may produce a difference in outlook which is brought to the jury room. Accordingly, use of peremptory challenges on the basis of sex is generally not the sort of derogatory and invidious act which peremptory challenges directed at black jurors may be. * * *

Justice SCALIA, with whom the CHIEF JUSTICE and Justice THOMAS join, dissenting. * * *

The core of the Court's reasoning is that peremptory challenges on the basis of any group characteristic subject to heightened scrutiny are inconsistent with the guarantee of the Equal Protection Clause. That conclusion can be reached only by focusing unrealistically upon individual exercises of the peremptory challenge, and ignoring the totality of the practice. Since all groups are subject to the peremptory challenge (and will be made the object of it, depending upon the nature of the particular case) it is hard to see how any group is denied equal protection. That explains why peremptory challenges coexisted with the Equal Protection Clause for 120 years. This case is a perfect example of how the system as a whole is even-handed. While the only claim before the Court is petitioner's complaint that the prosecutor struck male jurors, for every man struck by the government petitioner's own lawyer struck a woman. To say that men were singled out for discriminatory treatment in this process is preposterous. The situation would be different if both sides systematically struck individuals of one group, so that the strikes evinced group-based animus and served as a proxy for segregated venire lists. The pattern here, however, displays not a systemic sex-based animus but each side's desire to get a jury favorably disposed to its case. That is why the Court's characterization of respondent's argument as "reminiscent of the arguments advanced to justify the total exclusion of women from juries" is patently false. Women were categorically excluded from juries because of doubt that they were competent; women are stricken from juries by peremptory challenge because of doubt that they are well disposed to the striking party's case. * * *

Even if the line of our later cases guaranteed by today's decision limits the theoretically boundless *Batson* principle to race, sex, and perhaps other classifications subject to heightened scrutiny (which presumably would include religious belief [a]), much damage has been done. It has been done, first and foremost, to the peremptory challenge system, which loses its whole character when (in order to defend against "impermissible stereotyping" claims) "reasons" for strikes must be given. * * * And make no mistake about it: there really is no substitute for the peremptory. Voir dire (though it can be expected to expand as a

---

a. In *State v. Davis*, 504 N.W.2d 767 (Minn.1993), defendant objected to the prosecutor's use of a peremptory challenge against a black venireman, but the prosecutor explained she had struck the venireman because he was a Jehovah's Witness and explained that "[i]n my experience Jahovah Witness [sic] are reluctant to exercise authority over their fellow human beings in this Court House." Reading *Batson* as being limited to race-based peremptory challenges, the state supreme court affirmed.

The Supreme Court denied certiorari. *Davis v. Minnesota*, ___ U.S. ___, 114 S.Ct. 2120, 128 L.Ed.2d 679 (1994). Thomas, J., joined by Scalia, J., dissenting, objected that "no principled reason immediately appears for declining to apply *Batson* to any strike based on a classification that is accorded heightened scrutiny under the Equal Protection Clause," and thus concluded "that the Court's decision to deny certiorari stems from an unwillingness to confront forthrightly the ramifications of the decision in *J.E.B.*" Justice Ginsburg, concurring in denial of certiorari, responded that "the dissent's portrayal of the opinion of the Minnesota Supreme Court is incomplete. That court made two key observations: (1) '[R]eligious affiliation (or lack thereof) is not as self-evident as race or gender'; (2) 'Ordinarily ..., inquiry on voir dire into a juror's religious affiliation and beliefs is irrelevant and prejudicial, and to ask such questions is improper.'"

consequence of today's decision) cannot fill the gap. The biases that go along with group characteristics tend to be biases that the juror himself does not perceive, so that it is no use asking about them. It is fruitless to inquire of a male juror whether he harbors any subliminal prejudice in favor of unwed fathers. * * *

8th ed., p. 1433; end of Note 10, add:

11. At Elem's trial, he objected to the prosecutor's use of peremptory challenges to strike two black men from the jury panel, but when the prosecutor explained his strikes the trial court overruled Elem's objection. Elem's conviction was affirmed on appeal, but on habeas corpus the federal court of appeals directed the district court to grant the writ. The court of appeals reasoned that under *Batson* the prosecutor was obligated to "articulate some plausible race-neutral reason," which the prosecutor had not done here in saying that the two prosecutive jurors' "mustaches and ... beards look suspicious to me." But the Supreme Court reversed per curiam in PURKETT v. ELEM, ___ U.S. ___, 115 S.Ct. 1769, 131 L.Ed.2d 834 (1995).

The Court explained that under *Batson,* "once the opponent of a peremptory challenge has made out a prima facie case of racial discrimination (step 1), the burden of production shifts to the proponent of the strike to come forward with a race-neutral explanation (step 2). If a race-neutral explanation is tendered, the trial court must then decide (step 3) whether the opponent of the strike has proved purposeful racial discrimination. * * *

"The Court of Appeals erred by combining *Batson*'s second and third steps into one, requiring that the justification tendered at the second step be not just neutral but also at least minimally persuasive * * *. It is not until the *third* step that the persuasiveness of the justification becomes relevant—the step in which the trial court determines whether the opponent of the strike has carried his burden of proving purposeful discrimination. At that stage, implausible or fantastic justifications may (and probably will) be found to be pretexts for purposeful discrimination. But to say that a trial judge *may choose to disbelieve* a silly or superstitious reason at step 3 is quite different from saying that a trial judge *must terminate* the inquiry at step 2 when the race-neutral reason is silly or superstitious. The latter violates the principle that the ultimate burden of persuasion regarding racial motivation rests with, and never shifts from, the opponent of the strike."

STEVENS and Breyer, JJ., dissenting, objected that "it is unwise for the Court to announce a law-changing decision without first ordering full briefing and argument on the merits of the case," and then concluded: "It is not too much to ask that a prosecutor's explanation for his strikes be race neutral, reasonably specific, *and* trial related. * * * Indeed, in *Hernandez* the Court explained that a trial judge could find pretext based on nothing more than a consistent policy of excluding all Spanish-speaking jurors if that characteristic was entirely unrelated to the case to be tried. Parallel reasoning would justify a finding of pretext based on a policy of excusing jurors with beards if beards have nothing to do with the pending case."

8th ed., p. 1433; end of Note 3, add:

In *Liteky v. United States,* ___ U.S. ___, 114 S.Ct. 1147, 127 L.Ed.2d 474 (1994), the Court held that *both* the federal challenge-for-cause statute, 28 U.S.C. § 144, and the federal recusal statute, 28 U.S.C. § 455, are subject to an "extrajudicial source" limitation, meaning: "First, judicial rulings alone almost never constitute valid basis for a bias or partiality motion. In and of themselves (i.e., apart from surrounding comments or accompanying opinion), they cannot possibly show reliance upon an extrajudicial source; and can only in the rarest circumstances evidence the degree of favoritism or antagonism required (as discussed below) when no extrajudicial source is involved. Almost invariably, they are proper grounds for appeal, not for recusal. Second, opinions formed by the judge on the basis of facts introduced or events occurring in the course of the current proceedings, or of prior proceedings, do not constitute a basis for a bias or partiality motion unless they display a deep-seated favoritism or antagonism that would make fair judgment impossible. Thus, judicial remarks during the course of a trial that are critical or disapproving of, or even hostile to, counsel, the parties, or their cases, ordinarily do not support a bias or partiality challenge. They *may* do so if they reveal an opinion that derives from an extrajudicial source; and they *will* do so if they reveal such a high degree of favoritism or antagonism as to make fair judgment impossible."

Chapter 25
THE CRIMINAL TRIAL

SECTION 3. THE DEFENDANT'S RIGHT TO REMAIN SILENT AND TO TESTIFY

8th ed., p. 1490; end of fn. 3, add:

[Ed. Note—Compare the English position described in the supplement addition at Supp. p. 33.]

SECTION 5. SUBMITTING THE CASE TO THE JURY

8th ed., p. 1511; end of Note 1, add:

Can *Heald* be squared with *United States v. Gaudin,* p. 65 supra?

Chapter 26

REPROSECUTION AND THE BAN AGAINST DOUBLE JEOPARDY

SECTION 3. REPROSECUTION FOLLOWING A CONVICTION

8th ed., p. 1563; add to Note 9:

Consider also *Witte v. United States,* discussed at Supp. p. 54.

SECTION 4. REPROSECUTION BY A DIFFERENT SOVEREIGN

8th ed., p. 1571; add to footnote d:

The federal prosecutions in the "King beating case" also have sparked a reexamination of the *Bartkus* ruling in the scholarly literature, producing a variety of views as to when (if ever) a federal prosecution should be allowed following a state prosecution based on the same events. See Akhil Amar and Jonathan Marcus, *Double Jeopardy Law After Rodney King,* 95 Colum.L.Rev. 1 (1995); Paul Cassell, *The Rodney King Trials and the Double Jeopardy Clause: Some Observations on Original Meaning and the ACLU's Schizophrenic Views of the Dual Sovereign Doctrine,* 41 UCLA L.Rev. 693 (1994); Robert Gorman, *The Second Rodney King Trial: Justice in Jeopardy,* 27 Akron L.Rev. 57 (1993); Susan Herman, *Double Jeopardy All Over Again: Dual Sovereignty, Rodney King, and the ACLU,* 41 UCLA L.Rev. 609 (1994); Susan Herman, *Reconstructing The Bill of Rights: A Reply to Amar and Marcus's Triple Play on Double Jeopardy,* 93 Colum.L.Rev. 1090 (1995); Paul Hoffman, *Double Jeopardy Wars: The Case for a Civil Rights "Exception,"* 41 UCLA L.Rev. 649 (1994); Laurie Levenson, *The Future of State and Federal Civil Rights Prosecutions: the Lessons of the Rodney King Trial,* 41 UCLA L.Rev. 509 (1994).

Consider also Sandra Guerra, *The Myth of Dual Sovereignty, Multijurisdictional Drug Law Enforcement and Double Jeopardy,* 73 N.C.L.Rev. 1159 (1995).

Part Five
APPEALS, POST–CONVICTION REVIEW

Chapter 28
HABEAS CORPUS AND RELATED COLLATERAL REMEDIES

SECTION 2. ISSUES COGNIZABLE

8th ed., p. 1664; following Withrow add:

7. In *Reed v. Farley*, ___ U.S. ___, 114 S.Ct. 2291, 129 L.Ed.2d 277 (1994), also discussed at Supp. p. 57, a state prisoner sought habeas relief on the ground that he was being held in custody in violation of a federal statute, the Interstate Agreement on Detainers, 18 U.S.C. App. § 2, which imposes a 120 day speedy trial requirement as to prisoners transferred under its provisions. The Court of Appeals, relying on *Stone v. Powell*, held that such a claim was not cognizable on habeas review. Three justices (per Ginsburg, J.) rejected reliance on *Stone*, held petitioner's claim to be cognizable, but concluded that petitioner would only be entitled to relief upon a showing that met the "complete miscarriage of justice" standard traditionally applied on § 2255 proceedings to claims by federal prisoners based on violations of federal statutory law. See fn. b, 8th ed. p. 1626. That standard was not met here where the petitioner did not object to the initial setting of the trial date beyond the 120 day period and suffered no prejudice due to the delayed commencement of his trial. Justice Scalia, joined by Justice Thomas, agreed that the traditional § 2255 standard was also applicable to state prisoner claims under federal law, but concluded that a claimed violation of the 120 day time limit therefore was not a cognizable claim. The 120 day requirement, applicable only to prisoners involved in interstate transfer, simply

was too "technical" to fall within that small class of statutory rights whose denial could produce a complete miscarriage of justice. Speaking for four dissenters, Justice Blackmun concluded that the claim not only was cognizable, but that the Court majority erred in assuming without full discussion that the standard applicable to state prisoners presenting claims under federal law was the same as that applied under § 2255 to federal-law claims of federal prisoners, rather than the standard traditionally applied under § 2254 to constitutional claims presented by state prisoners.

SECTION 3. CLAIMS FORECLOSED BY PROCEDURAL DEFAULTS

8th ed., p. 1667; add in lieu of Notes 3 and 4, pp. 1667–70:

SCHLUP v. DELO
___ U.S. ___, 115 S.Ct. 851, 130 L.Ed.2d 808 (1995).

Justice STEVENS delivered the opinion of the Court.

Petitioner Lloyd E. Schlup, Jr., a Missouri prisoner currently under a sentence of death, filed a second federal habeas corpus petition alleging that constitutional error deprived the jury of critical evidence that would have established his innocence. The District Court, without conducting an evidentiary hearing, declined to reach the merits of the petition, holding that petitioner could not satisfy the threshold showing of "actual innocence" required by *Sawyer v. Whitley*, 505 U.S. ___, 112 S.Ct. 2514, 120 L.Ed.2d 269 (1992). Under *Sawyer*, the petitioner must show "by clear and convincing evidence that but for a constitutional error, no reasonable juror would have found the petitioner" guilty. The Court of Appeals affirmed. We granted certiorari to consider whether the *Sawyer* standard provides adequate protection against the kind of miscarriage of justice that would result from the execution of a person who is actually innocent.

On February 3, 1984, on Walk 1 of the high security area of the Missouri State Penitentiary, a black inmate named Arthur Dade was stabbed to death. Three white inmates from Walk 2, including petitioner, were charged in connection with Dade's murder.

At petitioner's trial in December 1985, the State's evidence consisted principally of the testimony of two corrections officers who had witnessed the killing. On the day of the murder, Sergeant Roger Flowers was on duty on Walk 1 and Walk 2, the two walks on the lower floor of the prison's high security area. Flowers testified that he first released the inmates on Walk 2 for their noon meal and relocked their cells. After unlocking the cells to release the inmates on Walk 1, Flowers noticed an inmate named Rodnie Stewart moving against the flow of traffic carrying a container of steaming liquid. Flowers watched as Stewart threw the liquid in Dade's face. According to Flowers,

Schlup then jumped on Dade's back, and Robert O'Neal joined in the attack. Flowers shouted for help, entered the walk, and grabbed Stewart as the two other assailants fled.

Officer John Maylee witnessed the attack from Walk 7, which is three levels and some 40–50 feet above Walks 1 and 2. Maylee first noticed Schlup, Stewart, and O'Neal as they were running from Walk 2 to Walk 1 against the flow of traffic. According to Maylee's testimony, Stewart threw a container of liquid at Dade's face, and then Schlup jumped on Dade's back. O'Neal then stabbed Dade several times in the chest, ran down the walk, and threw the weapon out a window. Maylee did not see what happened to Schlup or Stewart after the stabbing.

The State produced no physical evidence connecting Schlup to the killing, and no witness other than Flowers and Maylee testified to Schlup's involvement in the murder.

Schlup's defense was that the State had the wrong man. He relied heavily on a videotape from a camera in the prisoners' dining room. The tape showed that Schlup was the first inmate to walk into the dining room for the noon meal, and that he went through the line and got his food. Approximately 65 seconds after Schlup's entrance, several guards ran out of the dining room in apparent response to a distress call. Twenty-six seconds later, O'Neal ran into the dining room, dripping blood. Shortly thereafter, Schlup and O'Neal were taken into custody.

Schlup contended that the videotape, when considered in conjunction with testimony that he had walked at a normal pace from his cell to the dining room, demonstrated that he could not have participated in the assault. Because the videotape showed conclusively that Schlup was in the dining room 65 seconds before the guards responded to the distress call, a critical element of Schlup's defense was determining when the distress call went out. Had the distress call sounded shortly after the murder, Schlup would not have had time to get from the prison floor to the dining room, and thus he could not have participated in the murder. Conversely, had there been a delay of several minutes between the murder and the distress call, Schlup might have had sufficient time to participate in the murder and still get to the dining room over a minute before the distress call went out.[6]

The prosecutor adduced evidence tending to establish that such a delay had in fact occurred. First, Flowers testified that none of the officers on the prison floor had radios, thus implying that neither he nor

---

6. A necessary element of Schlup's defense was that Flowers and Maylee were mistaken in their identification of Schlup as one of the participants in the murder. Schlup suggested that Flowers had taken a visitor to Schlup's cell just 30 minutes before the murder. Schlup argued that Flowers therefore had Schlup "on the brain," Trial Tr. 493–494, thus explaining why, in the confusion surrounding the murder, Flowers might have mistakenly believed that he had seen Schlup. Schlup argued that Maylee's identification was suspect because Maylee was three floors away from the murder and did not have an unobstructed view of the murder scene. Schlup further suggested that Maylee's identification of Schlup had been influenced by a postincident conversation between Maylee and another officer who had talked to Flowers.

* * *

any of the other officers on the floor was able to radio for help when the stabbing occurred. Second, Flowers testified that after he shouted for help, it took him "a couple [of] minutes" to subdue Stewart. Flowers then brought Stewart downstairs, encountered Captain James Eberle, and told Eberle that there had been a "disturbance." Eberle testified that he went upstairs to the prison floor, and then radioed for assistance. Eberle estimated that the elapsed time from when he first saw Flowers until he radioed for help was "approximately a minute." The prosecution also offered testimony from a prison investigator who testified that he was able to run from the scene of the crime to the dining room in 33 seconds and to walk the distance at a normal pace in a minute and 37 seconds.

Neither the State nor Schlup was able to present evidence establishing the exact time of Schlup's release from his cell on Walk 2, the exact time of the assault on Walk 1, or the exact time of the radio distress call. Further, there was no evidence suggesting that Schlup had hurried to the dining room.

After deliberating overnight, the jury returned a verdict of guilty. Following the penalty phase, at which the victim of one of Schlup's prior offenses testified extensively about the sordid details of that offense, the jury sentenced Schlup to death. The Missouri Supreme Court affirmed Schlup's conviction and death sentence.

On January 5, 1989, after exhausting his state collateral remedies, Schlup filed a *pro se* petition for a federal writ of habeas corpus, asserting the claim, among others, that his trial counsel was ineffective for failing to interview and to call witnesses who could establish Schlup's innocence. The District Court concluded that Schlup's ineffectiveness claim was procedurally barred, and it denied relief on that claim without conducting an evidentiary hearing. The Court of Appeals affirmed, though it did not rely on the alleged procedural bar. Instead, based on its own examination of the record, the Court found that trial counsel's performance had not been constitutionally ineffective, both because counsel had reviewed statements that Schlup's potential witnesses had given to prison investigators, and because the testimony of those witnesses "would be repetitive of the testimony to be presented at trial."
* * *

On March 11, 1992, represented by new counsel, Schlup filed a second federal habeas corpus petition. That petition raised a number of claims, including that (1) Schlup was actually innocent of Dade's murder, and that his execution would therefore violate the Eighth and Fourteenth Amendments, cf. *Herrera v. Collins* [8th ed., pp. 1516, 1667]; (2) trial counsel was ineffective for failing to interview alibi witnesses; and (3) the State had failed to disclose critical exculpatory evidence. The petition was supported by numerous affidavits from inmates attesting to Schlup's innocence.

The State filed a response arguing that various procedural bars precluded the District Court from reaching the merits of Schlup's claims and that the claims were in any event meritless. Attached to the State's response were transcripts of inmate interviews conducted by prison investigators just five days after the murder. One of the transcripts contained an interview with John Green, an inmate who at the time was the clerk for the housing unit. In his interview, Green stated that he had been in his office at the end of the walks when the murder occurred. Green stated that Flowers had told him to call for help, and that Green had notified base of the disturbance shortly after it began.

Schlup immediately filed a traverse arguing that Green's affidavit provided conclusive proof of Schlup's innocence. Schlup contended that Green's statement demonstrated that a call for help had gone out shortly after the incident. Because the videotape showed that Schlup was in the dining room some 65 seconds before the guards received the distress call, Schlup argued that he could not have been involved in Dade's murder. Schlup emphasized that Green's statement was not likely to have been fabricated, because at the time of Creen's interview, neither he nor anyone else would have realized the significance of Green's call to base. Schlup tried to buttress his claim of innocence with affidavits from inmates who stated that they had witnessed the event and that Schlup had not been present. Two of those affidavits suggested that Randy Jordan—who occupied the cell between O'Neal and Stewart in Walk 2, and who * * * is shown on the videotape arriving at lunch with O'Neal—was the third assailant.

On August 23, 1993, without holding a hearing, the District Court dismissed Schlup's second habeas petition and vacated the stay of execution that was then in effect. The District Court concluded that Schlup's various filings did not provide adequate cause for failing to raise his new claims more promptly. Moreover, the Court concluded that Schlup had failed to meet the *Sawyer v. Whitley* standard for showing that a refusal to entertain those claims would result in a fundamental miscarriage of justice. In its discussion of the evidence, the Court made no separate comment on the significance of Green's statement.

On September 7, 1993, petitioner filed a motion to set aside the order of dismissal, again calling the Court's attention to Green's statement. Two days later, Schlup filed a supplemental motion stating that his counsel had located John Green and had obtained an affidavit from him. That affidavit confirmed Green's postincident statement that he had called base shortly after the assault. Green's affidavit also identified Jordan rather than Schlup as the third assailant. The District Court denied the motion and the supplemental motion without opinion.

Petitioner then sought from the Court of Appeals a stay of execution pending the resolution of his appeal. Relying on Justice Powell's plurality opinion in *Kuhlmann v. Wilson* [8th ed., p. 1683, Note 6], Schlup argued that the District Court should have entertained his second habeas corpus petition, because he had supplemented his constitutional claim "with a colorable showing of factual innocence."

On October 15, 1993, the Court of Appeals denied the stay application. In an opinion that was subsequently vacated, the majority held that petitioner's claim of innocence was governed by the standard announced in *Sawyer v. Whitley,* and it concluded that under that standard, the evidence of Schlup's guilt that had been adduced at trial foreclosed consideration of petitioner's current constitutional claims. Judge Heaney dissented. Relying on Green's affidavit, the videotape, and the affidavits of four other eyewitnesses, Judge Heaney concluded that the petitioner had met both the *Kuhlmann* standard and a proper reading of the *Sawyer* standard. * * *

In the meantime, petitioner's counsel obtained an affidavit from Robert Faherty, the former lieutenant at the prison whom Schlup had passed on the way to lunch on the day of the murder and who had reprimanded Schlup for shouting out the window. Faherty's affidavit stated that Schlup had been in Faherty's presence for at least two and a half minutes; that Schlup was walking at a leisurely pace; and that Schlup "was not perspiring or breathing hard, and he was not nervous."

On November 15, 1993, the Court of Appeals vacated its earlier opinion and substituted a more comprehensive analysis of the law to support its decision to deny Schlup's request for a stay. The majority adhered to its earlier conclusion that *Sawyer* stated the appropriate standard for evaluating Schlup's claim of actual innocence. The opinion also contained an extended discussion of Schlup's new evidence. The Court noted in particular that Green's new affidavit was inconsistent in part with both his prison interview and his testimony at the Stewart trial. The Court viewed Faherty's affidavit as simply "an effort to embellish and expand upon his testimony" and concluded "that a habeas court should not permit retrial on such a basis." * * *

Judge Heaney again dissented, concluding that Schlup had "presented truly persuasive evidence that he is actually innocent," and that the District Court should therefore have addressed the merits of Schlup's constitutional claims. Judge Heaney also argued that Schlup's ineffectiveness claim was substantial. He noted that Schlup's trial counsel failed to conduct individual interviews with Griffin Bey, McCoy, or any of the other inmates who told investigators that they had seen the killing. Moreover, counsel failed to interview Green about his statement that he had called base. In fact, counsel apparently failed to conduct individual interviews with any of the potential witnesses to the crime. Judge Heaney adhered to his conclusion that Schlup's counsel was ineffective, even though counsel allegedly had reviewed 100 interviews conducted by prison investigators. Judge Heaney argued that counsel's review of the interview transcripts—rather than demonstrating counsel's effectiveness—made counsel's failure to conduct his own interviews with Green and the few inmates who admitted seeing the attack even more troubling. * * *

On November 17, 1993, the Court of Appeals denied a suggestion for rehearing en banc. Dissenting from that denial, three judges joined an

opinion describing the question whether the majority should have applied the standard announced in *Sawyer v. Whitley, supra,* rather than the *Kuhlmann* standard as "a question of great importance in habeas corpus jurisprudence." We granted certiorari to consider that question.
* * *

As a preliminary matter, it is important to explain the difference between Schlup's claim of actual innocence and the claim of actual innocence asserted in *Herrera v. Collins* [8th ed., p. 1667, fn. c]. In *Herrera,* the petitioner advanced his claim of innocence to support a novel substantive constitutional claim, namely that the execution of an innocent person would violate the Eighth Amendment. Under petitioner's theory in *Herrera,* even if the proceedings that had resulted in his conviction and sentence were entirely fair and error-free, his innocence would render his execution a "constitutionally intolerable event."

Schlup's claim of innocence, on the other hand, is procedural, rather than substantive. His constitutional claims are based not on his innocence, but rather on his contention that the ineffectiveness of his counsel, see *Strickland v. Washington,* and the withholding of evidence by the prosecution, see *Brady v. Maryland,* denied him the full panoply of protections afforded to criminal defendants by the Constitution. Schlup, however, faces procedural obstacles that he must overcome before a federal court may address the merits of those constitutional claims. Because Schlup has been unable to establish "cause and prejudice" sufficient to excuse his failure to present his evidence in support of his first federal petition, see *McCleskey v. Zant* [8th ed., p. 1660, Note 6], Schlup may obtain review of his constitutional claims only if he falls within the "narrow class of cases ... implicating a fundamental miscarriage of justice." *Id.* Schlup's claim of innocence is offered only to bring him within this "narrow class of cases."

Schlup's claim thus differs in at least two important ways from that presented in *Herrera.* First, Schlup's claim of innocence does not by itself provide a basis for relief. Instead, his claim for relief depends critically on the validity of his *Strickland* and *Brady* claims. Schlup's claim of innocence is thus "not itself a constitutional claim, but instead a gateway through which a habeas petitioner must pass to have his otherwise barred constitutional claim considered on the merits." *Herrera.*

More importantly, a court's assumptions about the validity of the proceedings that resulted in conviction are fundamentally different in Schlup's case than in Herrera's. In *Herrera,* petitioner's claim was evaluated on the assumption that the trial that resulted in his conviction had been error-free. In such a case, when a petitioner has been "tried before a jury of his peers, with the full panoply of protections that our Constitution affords criminal defendants," it is appropriate to apply an " 'extraordinarily high' " standard of review. Id. (O'Connor, J., concurring).

Schlup, in contrast, accompanies his claim of innocence with an assertion of constitutional error at trial. For that reason, Schlup's conviction may not be entitled to the same degree of respect as one, such as Herrera's, that is the product of an error-free trial. Without any new evidence of innocence, even the existence of a concededly meritorious constitutional violation is not in itself sufficient to establish a miscarriage of justice that would allow a habeas court to reach the merits of a barred claim. However, if a petitioner such as Schlup presents evidence of innocence so strong that a court cannot have confidence in the outcome of the trial unless the court is also satisfied that the trial was free of nonharmless constitutional error, the petitioner should be allowed to pass through the gateway and argue the merits of his underlying claims.

Consequently, Schlup's evidence of innocence need carry less of a burden. In *Herrera* (on the assumption that petitioner's claim was, in principle, legally well founded), the evidence of innocence would have had to be strong enough to make his execution "constitutionally intolerable" *even if* his conviction was the product of a fair trial. For Schlup, the evidence must establish sufficient doubt about his guilt to justify the conclusion that his execution would be a miscarriage of justice *unless* his conviction was the product of a fair trial.

Our rather full statement of the facts illustrates the foregoing distinction between a substantive *Herrera* claim and Schlup's procedural claim. Three items of evidence are particularly relevant: the affidavit of black inmates attesting to the innocence of a white defendant in a racially motivated killing; the affidavit of Green describing his prompt call for assistance; and the affidavit of Lieutenant Faherty describing Schlup's unhurried walk to the dining room. If there were no question about the fairness of the criminal trial, a *Herrera*–type claim would have to fail unless the federal habeas court is itself convinced that those new facts unquestionably establish Schlup's innocence. On the other hand, if the habeas court were merely convinced that those new facts raised sufficient doubt about Schlup's guilt to undermine confidence in the result of the trial without the assurance that that trial was untainted by constitutional error, Schlup's threshold showing of innocence would justify a review of the merits of the constitutional claims. * * *

* * * [The] Court [has] held that a habeas court may not ordinarily reach the merits of successive claims, *Kuhlmann v. Wilson,* or abusive claims, *McCleskey,* absent a showing of cause and prejudice, see *Wainwright v. Sykes.* The application of cause and prejudice to successive and abusive claims conformed to this Court's treatment of procedurally defaulted claims. * * * At the same time, the Court has adhered to the principle that habeas corpus is, at its core, an equitable remedy. * * * We firmly established the importance of the equitable inquiry required by the ends of justice in "a trio of 1986 decisions" handed down on the same day. *Sawyer* (referring to *Kuhlmann, Carrier* [8th ed., p. 1667], and *Smith v. Murray* [8th ed., p. 1667]). * * * Thus, while recognizing that successive petitions are generally precluded from review, Justice

Powell's plurality opinion [in *Kuhlmann*] expressly noted that there are "limited circumstances under which the interests of the prisoner in relitigating constitutional claims held meritless on a prior petition may outweigh the countervailing interests served by according finality to the prior judgment." Similarly, writing for the Court in *Carrier,* Justice O'Connor observed that the Court had adopted the cause and prejudice standard in part because of its confidence that that standard would provide adequate protection to " 'victims of a fundamental miscarriage of justice.' " For that reason, " '[i]n appropriate cases,' the principles of comity and finality that inform the concepts of cause and prejudice 'must yield to the imperative of correcting a fundamentally unjust incarceration.' " Id. In subsequent cases, we have consistently reaffirmed the existence and importance of the exception for fundamental miscarriages of justice. See, e.g., *Sawyer*.

To ensure that the fundamental miscarriage of justice exception would remain "rare" and would only be applied in the "extraordinary case," while at the same time ensuring that the exception would extend relief to those who were truly deserving, this Court explicitly tied the miscarriage of justice exception to the petitioner's innocence. In *Kuhlmann,* for example, Justice Powell concluded that a prisoner retains an overriding "interest in obtaining his release from custody if he is innocent of the charge for which he was incarcerated. That interest does not extend, however, to prisoners whose guilt is conceded or plain." Similarly, Justice O'Connor wrote in *Carrier* that "in an extraordinary case, where a constitutional violation has probably resulted in the conviction of one who is actually innocent, a federal habeas court may grant the writ even in the absence of a showing of cause for the procedural default."

The general rule announced in *Kuhlmann, Carrier,* and *Smith,* and confirmed in this Court's more recent decisions, rests in part on the fact that habeas corpus petitions that advance a substantial claim of actual innocence are extremely rare. Judge Friendly's observation a quarter of a century ago [Friendly, 8th ed., p. 1684] that "the one thing almost never suggested on collateral attack is that the prisoner was innocent of the crime" remains largely true today. Explicitly trying the miscarriage of justice exception to innocence thus accommodates both the systemic interests in finality, comity, and conservation of judicial resources, and the overriding individual interest in doing justice in the "extraordinary case," *Carrier.*

In addition to linking miscarriages of justice to innocence, *Carrier,* and *Kuhlmann* also expressed the standard of proof that should govern consideration of those claims. In *Carrier,* for example, the Court stated that the petitioner must show that the constitutional error "probably" resulted in the conviction of one who was actually innocent. The *Kuhlmann* plurality, though using the term "colorable claim of factual innocence," elaborated that the petitioner would be required to establish, by a " 'fair probability,' " that " 'the trier of the facts would have entertained a reasonable doubt of his guilt.' "

In the years following *Kuhlmann* and *Carrier,* we did not expound further on the actual innocence exception. In those few cases that mentioned the standard, the Court continued to rely on the formulations set forth in *Kuhlmann* and *Carrier.* * * * Then, in *Sawyer,* the Court examined the miscarriage of justice exception as applied to a petitioner who claimed he was "actually innocent of the death penalty." In that opinion, the Court struggled to define "actual innocence" in the context of a petitioner's claim that his death sentence was inappropriate. The Court concluded that such actual innocence "must focus on those elements which render a defendant eligible for the death penalty." However, in addition to defining what it means to be "innocent" of the death penalty, the Court departed from *Carrier's* use of "probably" and adopted a more exacting standard of proof to govern these claims: the Court held that a habeas petitioner "must show by *clear and convincing* evidence that but for a constitutional error, no reasonable juror would have found the petitioner eligible for the death penalty." (emphasis added). No attempt was made in *Sawyer* to reconcile this stricter standard with *Carrier's* use of "probably."

In evaluating Schlup's claim of innocence, the Court of Appeals applied Eighth Circuit precedent holding that *Sawyer,* rather than *Carrier,* supplied the proper legal standard. The Court then purported to apply the *Sawyer* standard. Schlup argues that *Sawyer* has no application to a petitioner who claims that he is actually innocent of the crime, and that the Court of Appeals misapplied *Sawyer* in any event. Respondent contends that the Court of Appeals was correct in both its selection and its application of the *Sawyer* standard. Though the Court of Appeals seems to have misapplied *Sawyer,* we do not rest our decision on that ground because we conclude that in a case such as this, the *Sawyer,* standard does not apply.

As we have stated, the fundamental miscarriage of justice exception seeks to balance the societal interests in finality, comity, and conservation of scarce judicial resources with the individual interest in justice that arises in the extraordinary case. We conclude that *Carrier,* rather than *Sawyer,* properly strikes that balance when the claimed injustice is that constitutional error has resulted in the conviction of one who is actually innocent of the crime.

Claims of actual innocence pose less of a threat to scarce judicial resources and to principles of finality and comity than do claims that focus solely on the erroneous imposition of the death penalty. Though challenges to the propriety of imposing a sentence of death are routinely asserted in capital cases, experience has taught us that a substantial claim that constitutional error has caused the conviction of an innocent person is extremely rare. To be credible, such a claim requires petitioner to support his allegations of constitutional error with new reliable evidence—whether it be exculpatory scientific evidence, trustworthy eyewitness accounts, or critical physical evidence—that was not presented at trial. Because such evidence is obviously unavailable in the vast majority of cases, claims of actual innocence are rarely successful. Even under the pre-*Sawyer* regime, "in virtually every case, the allegation of actual innocence has been summarily rejected." Steiker, Innocence and Federal Habeas, 41 UCLA L.Rev. 303 (1993). The threat to judicial resources, finality, and comity posed by claims of actual innocence is thus significantly less than that posed by claims relating only to sentencing.

Of greater importance, the individual interest in avoiding injustice is most compelling in the context of actual innocence. The quintessential miscarriage of justice is the execution of a person who is entirely innocent. Indeed, concern about the injustice that results from the conviction of an innocent person has long been at the core of our criminal justice system. That concern is reflected, for example, in the "fundamental value determination of our society that it is far worse to convict an innocent man than to let a guilty man go free." *In re Winship* [8th ed., p. 850]. * * * The overriding importance of this greater individual interest merits protection by imposing a somewhat less exacting standard of proof on a habeas petitioner alleging a fundamental miscarriage of justice than on one alleging that his sentence is too severe. * * * Though the *Sawyer* standard was fashioned to reflect the relative importance of a claim of an erroneous sentence, application of that standard to petitioners such as Schlup would give insufficient weight to the correspondingly greater injustice that is implicated by a claim of actual innocence. The paramount importance of avoiding the injustice of executing one who is actually innocent thus requires application of the *Carrier* standard.

We recognize, as the State has reminded us, that in *Sawyer* the Court applied its new standard not only to the penalty phase of the case but also to Sawyer's responsibility for arson, one of the elements of the offense of first-degree murder. This fact does not require application of the *Sawyer* standard to a case such as Schlup's. Though formulated as an element of the offense of first-degree murder, the arson functioned essentially as a sentence enhancer. That claim, therefore, is readily distinguishable from a claim, like the one raised by Schlup, that the petitioner is actually innocent. Fealty to the doctrine of *stare decisis* does not, therefore, preclude application of the *Carrier* standard to the facts of this case. * * *

The *Carrier* standard requires the habeas petitioner to show that "a constitutional violation has probably resulted in the conviction of one who is actually innocent." To establish the requisite probability, the petitioner must show that it is more likely than not that no reasonable juror would have convicted him in the light of the new evidence. The petitioner thus is required to make a stronger showing than that needed to establish prejudice. See *Strickland, Bagley*. At the same time, the showing of "more likely than not" imposes a lower burden of proof than the "clear and convincing" standard required under *Sawyer*. The *Carrier* standard thus ensures that petitioner's case is truly "extraordinary," *McCleskey*, while still providing petitioner a meaningful avenue by which to avoid a manifest injustice.

Carrier requires a petitioner to show that he is "actually innocent." As used in *Carrier,* actual innocence is closely related to the definition set forth by this Court in *Sawyer.* To satisfy the *Carrier* gateway standard, a petitioner must show that it is more likely than not that no reasonable juror would have found petitioner guilty beyond a reasonable doubt.

Several observations about this standard are in order. The *Carrier* standard is intended to focus the inquiry on actual innocence. In assessing the adequacy of petitioner's showing, therefore, the district court is not bound by the rules of admissibility that would govern at trial. Instead, the emphasis on "actual innocence" allows the reviewing tribunal also to consider the probative force of relevant evidence that was either excluded or unavailable at trial. Indeed, with respect to this aspect of the *Carrier* standard, we believe that Judge Friendly's description of the inquiry is appropriate: the habeas court must make its determination concerning the petitioner's innocence "in light of all the evidence, including that alleged to have been illegally admitted (but with due regard to any unreliability of it) and evidence tenably claimed to have been wrongly excluded or to have become available only after the trial."

The consideration in federal habeas proceedings of a broader array of evidence does not modify the essential meaning of "innocence." The *Carrier* standard reflects the proposition, firmly established in our legal system, that the line between innocence and guilt is drawn with reference to a reasonable doubt. See *In re Winship.* Indeed, even in *Sawyer,* with its emphasis on eligibility for the death penalty, the Court did not stray from the understanding that the eligibility determination must be made with reference to reasonable doubt. Thus, whether a court is assessing eligibility for the death penalty under *Sawyer,* or is deciding whether a petitioner has made the requisite showing of innocence under *Carrier,* the analysis must incorporate the understanding that proof beyond a reasonable doubt marks the legal boundary between guilt and innocence.

The meaning of actual innocence as formulated by *Sawyer,* and *Carrier* does not merely require a showing that a reasonable doubt exists in the light of the new evidence, but rather that no reasonable juror would have found the defendant guilty. It is not the district court's independent judgment as to whether reasonable doubt exists that the standard addresses; rather the standard requires the district court to make a probabilistic determination about what reasonable, properly instructed jurors would do. Thus, a petitioner does not meet the threshold requirement unless he persuades the district court that, in light of the new evidence, no juror, acting reasonably, would have voted to find him guilty beyond a reasonable doubt.

We note finally that the *Carrier* standard requires a petitioner to show that it is more likely than not that "no reasonable juror" would have convicted him. The word "reasonable" in that formulation is not without meaning. It must be presumed that a reasonable juror would consider fairly all of the evidence presented. It must also be presumed that such a juror would conscientiously obey the instructions of the trial court requiring proof beyond a reasonable doubt.[48]

Though the *Carrier* standard requires a substantial showing, it is by no means equivalent to the standard [of *Jackson v. Virginia,* 443 U.S. 307, 99 S.Ct. 2781, 61 L.Ed.2d 560 (1979)] that governs review of claims of insufficient evidence. The *Jackson* standard, which focuses on whether any rational juror could have convicted, looks to whether there is sufficient evidence which, if credited, could support the conviction. The *Jackson* standard thus differs in at least two important ways from the *Carrier* standard. First, under *Jackson,* the assessment of the credibility of witnesses is generally beyond the scope of review. In contrast, under the gateway standard we describe today, the newly presented evidence may indeed call into question the credibility of the witnesses presented at trial. In such a case, the habeas court may have to make some credibility assessments. Second, and more fundamentally, the focus of the inquiry is different under *Jackson* than under *Carrier.* Under *Jackson,* the use of the word "could" focuses the inquiry on the power of the trier of the fact to reach its conclusion. Under *Carrier,* the use of the word "would" focuses the inquiry on the likely behavior of the trier of fact.

Indeed, our adoption of the phrase "more likely than not" reflects this distinction. Under *Jackson,* the question whether the trier of fact has power to make a finding of guilt requires a binary response: either the trier of fact has power as a matter of law or it does not. Under *Carrier,* in contrast, the habeas court must consider what reasonable triers of fact are likely to do. Under this probabilistic inquiry, it makes sense to have a probabilistic standard such as "more likely than not." Thus, though under *Jackson* the mere existence of sufficient evidence to convict would be determinative of petitioner's claim, that is not true under *Carrier.*

We believe that the Eighth Circuit's erroneous application of the *Sawyer* standard below illustrates this difference. In determining that Schlup had failed to satisfy the *Sawyer* standard, the majority noted that "two prison officials, who were eyewitnesses to the crime, positively identified Mr. Schlup as one of the three perpetrators of the murder. This evidence was clearly admissible and stands unrefuted except to the

---

48. The Chief Justice suggests that the *Carrier* standard is "a classic mixing of apples and oranges." That standard, however, is no more a mixing of apples and oranges than is the standard adopted by the Court in *Sawyer.* Though it is true that " '[m]ore likely than not' " is a "quintessential charge to a finder of fact," that is equally true of the "clear and convincing evidence" component of the *Sawyer* formulation. There is thus no reason to believe that the *Carrier* standard is any more likely than the *Sawyer* standard to be "a source of confusion."

Nor do we accept The Chief Justice's description of the *Carrier* standard as a "hybrid." Finders of fact are often called upon to make predictions about the likely actions of hypothetical "reasonable" actors. Thus, the application of "more likely than not" to the habeas court's assessment of the actions of reasonable jurors is neither illogical nor unusual.

extent that Mr. Schlup now questions its credibility." The majority then continued:

> "[E]ven if we disregard the source of the new evidence, the eleventh-hour nature of the information, and a presentation coming almost six years after the trial; it is simply not possible to say that the appellant has shown by clear and convincing evidence that but for a constitutional error no reasonable jury would have found him guilty."

However, Schlup's evidence includes the sworn statements of several eyewitnesses that Schlup was not involved in the crime. Moreover, Schlup has presented statements from Green and Faherty that cast doubt on whether Schlup could have participated in the murder and still arrived at the dining room 65 seconds before the distress call was received. Those new statements may, of course, be unreliable. But if they are true—as the Court of Appeals assumed for the purpose of applying its understanding of the *Sawyer* standard—it surely cannot be said that a juror, conscientiously following the judge's instructions requiring proof beyond a reasonable doubt, would vote to convict. Under a proper application of either *Sawyer* or *Carrier,* petitioner's showing of innocence is not insufficient solely because the trial record contained sufficient evidence to support the jury's verdict.

In this case, the application of the *Carrier* standard arises in the context of a request for an evidentiary hearing. In applying the *Carrier* standard to such a request, the District Court must assess the probative force of the newly presented evidence in connection with the evidence of guilt adduced at trial. Obviously, the Court is not required to test the new evidence by a standard appropriate for deciding a motion for summary judgment. * * * Instead, the Court may consider how the timing of the submission and the likely credibility of the affiants bear on the probable reliability of that evidence.

Because both the Court of Appeals and the District Court evaluated the record under an improper standard, further proceedings are necessary. The fact-intensive nature of the inquiry, together with the District Court's ability to take testimony from the few key witnesses if it deems that course advisable, convinces us that the most expeditious procedure is to order that the decision of the Court of Appeals be vacated and that the case be remanded to the Court of Appeals with instructions to remand to the District Court for further proceedings consistent with this opinion.

Justice O'CONNOR, concurring.

I write to explain, in light of the dissenting opinions, what I understand the Court to decide and what it does not.

The Court holds that, in order to have an abusive or successive habeas claim heard on the merits, a petitioner who cannot demonstrate cause and prejudice "must show that it is more likely than not that no reasonable juror would have convicted him" in light of newly discovered evidence of innocence. This standard is higher than that required for prejudice, which requires only "a reasonable probability that, absent the errors, the factfinder would have had a reasonable doubt respecting guilt," *Strickland v. Washington.* Instead, a petitioner does not pass through the gateway erected by *Murray v. Carrier* if the district court believes it more likely than not that there is any juror who, acting reasonably, would have found the petitioner guilty beyond a reasonable doubt. And the Court's standard, which focuses the inquiry on the likely behavior of jurors, is substantively different from the rationality standard of *Jackson v. Virginia* * * *. *Jackson,* which emphasizes the authority of the factfinder to make conclusions from the evidence, establishes a standard of review for the sufficiency of record evidence—a standard that would be ill-suited as a burden of proof. * * * The Court today does not sow confusion in the law. Rather, it properly balances the dictates of justice with the need to ensure that the actual innocence exception remains only a " 'safety valve' for the 'extraordinary case.' "

Moreover, the Court does not, and need not, decide whether the fundamental miscarriage of justice exception is a discretionary remedy. It is a paradigmatic abuse of discretion for a court to base its judgment on an erroneous view of the law. Having decided that the district court committed legal error, and thus abused its discretion, by relying on *Sawyer v. Whitley,* instead of *Murray v. Carrier,* the Court need not decide the question—neither argued by the parties nor passed upon by the Court of Appeals—whether abuse of discretion is the proper standard of review. In reversing the judgment of the Court of Appeals, therefore, the Court does not disturb the traditional discretion of district courts in this area, nor does it speak to the standard of appellate review for such judgments. * * * With these observations, I join the Court's opinion.

Chief Justice REHNQUIST, with whom Justice KENNEDY and Justice THOMAS join, dissenting.

* * * In *Sawyer,* we described in some detail the showing of actual innocence required when a habeas petitioner brings an otherwise abusive, successive, or procedurally defaulted claim challenging the imposition of his death sentence, rather than his guilt of the crime. * * * We have never until today had to similarly flesh out the standard of "actual innocence" in the context of a habeas petitioner claiming innocence of the crime. Thus, I agree that the question of what threshold standard should govern is an open one. * * * I disagree with the Court's conclusion that *Carrier,* and not *Sawyer,* provides the proper standard. But far more troubling than the choice of *Carrier* over *Sawyer* is the watered down and confusing version of *Carrier* which is served up by the Court.

* * * The Court informs us that a showing of "actual innocence" requires a habeas petitioner to "show that it is more likely than not that no reasonable juror would have convicted him in the light of the new evidence." But this is a classic mixing of apples and oranges. "More likely than not" is a quintessential charge to a finder of fact, while "no

reasonable juror would have convicted him in the light of the new evidence" is an equally quintessential conclusion of law similar to the standard that courts constantly employ in deciding motions for judgment of acquittal in criminal cases. The hybrid which the Court serves up is bound to be a source of confusion. Because new evidence not presented at trial will almost always be involved in these claims of actual innocence, the legal standard for judgment of acquittal cannot be bodily transposed for the determination of "actual innocence," but the sensible course would be to modify that familiar standard, rather than to create a confusing hybrid.

In the course of elaborating the *Carrier* standard, the Court takes pains to point out that it differs from the standard enunciated in *Jackson v. Virginia,* for review of the sufficiency of the evidence to meet the constitutional standard of proof beyond a reasonable doubt. Under *Jackson,* "the relevant question is whether, after viewing the evidence in the light most favorable to the prosecution, *any* rational trier of fact could have found the essential elements of the crime beyond a reasonable doubt." This standard requires a solely retrospective analysis of the evidence considered by the jury and reflects a healthy respect for the trier of fact's "responsibility ... to resolve conflicts in the testimony, to weigh the evidence, and to draw reasonable inferences from basic facts to the ultimate facts."

The Court fails to acknowledge expressly the similarities between the standard it has adopted and the *Jackson* standard. A habeas court reviewing a claim of actual innocence does not write on a clean slate. * * * Therefore, as the Court acknowledges, a petitioner making a claim of actual innocence under *Carrier* falls short of satisfying his burden if the reviewing court determines that *any* juror reasonably would have found petitioner guilty of the crime. * * * The situation presented by a claim of actual innocence in a federal habeas petition is obviously different from that presented in *Jackson* because the habeas court analyzing an "actual innocence" claim is faced with a body of evidence that has been supplemented since the original trial. The reviewing court must somehow predict the effect that this new evidence would have had on the deliberations of reasonable jurors. It must necessarily weigh this new evidence in some manner, and may need to make credibility determinations as to witnesses who did not appear before the original jury. This new evidence, however, is not a license for the reviewing court to disregard the presumptively proper determination by the original trier of fact.

I think the standard enunciated in *Jackson,* properly modified because of the different body of evidence which must be considered, faithfully reflects the language used in *Carrier.* The habeas judge should initially consider the motion on the basis of the written submissions made by the parties. As the Court suggests, habeas courts will be able to resolve the great majority of "actual innocence" claims routinely without any evidentiary hearing. This fact is important because, as we noted in *Sawyer:* "In the every day context of capital penalty proceedings, a federal district judge typically will be presented with a successive or abusive habeas petition a few days before, or even on the day of, a scheduled execution, and will have only a limited time to determine whether a petitioner has shown that his case falls within the 'actual innocence' exception if such a claim is made."

But in the highly unusual case where the district court believes on the basis of written submissions that the necessary showing of "actual innocence" may be made out, it should conduct a limited evidentiary hearing at which the affiants whose testimony the Court believes to be crucial to the showing of actual innocence are present and may be cross examined as to veracity, reliability, and all of the other elements which affect the weight to be given the testimony of a witness. After such a hearing, the district court would be in as good a position as possible to make the required determination as to the showing of actual innocence.

The present state of our habeas jurisprudence is less than ideal in its complexity, but today's decision needlessly adds to that complexity. I believe that by adopting the *Sawyer* standard both for attacks on the sentence and on the judgment of conviction, we would take a step in the direction of simplifying this jurisprudence. * * * The *Sawyer* standard strikes the proper balance among the State's interest in finality, *McCleskey,* the federal courts' respect for principles of federalism, see, e.g., *Teague v. Lane* [8th ed., p. 1670] and "the ultimate equity on the prisoner's side—a sufficient showing of actual innocence," *Withrow v. Williams* [8th ed., p. 1640] (O'Connor, J., concurring in part and dissenting in part). The Court of Appeals fully analyzed petitioner's new evidence and determined that that petitioner fell way short of " 'show[ing] by clear and convincing evidence [that] no reasonable juror would find him [guilty of murder].' " * * * I agree and therefore would affirm. * * * But if we are to adopt the *Carrier* standard, it should not be the confusing exegesis of that standard contained in the Court's opinion. It should be based on a modified version of *Jackson v. Virginia,* with a clearly defined area in which the district court may exercise its discretion to hold an evidentiary hearing.

Justice SCALIA, with whom Justice THOMAS joins, dissenting.

A federal statute entitled "Finality of Determination"—to be found at § 2244 of Title 28 of the United States Code—specifically addresses the problem of second and subsequent petitions for the writ of habeas corpus. The reader of today's opinion will be unencumbered with knowledge of this law, since it is not there discussed or quoted, and indeed is only cited *en passant.* Rather than asking what the statute says, or even what we have said the statute says, the Court asks only what is the fairest standard to apply, and answers that question by looking to the various semi-consistent standards articulated in our most recent decisions—minutely parsing phrases, and seeking shades of meaning in the interstices of sentences and words, as though a discursive judicial opinion were a statute. * * *

[Under § 2244(b)], a federal district court that receives a second or subsequent petition for the writ of habeas corpus, when a prior petition has been denied on the merits, "need not ... entertai[n]" (i.e. may dismiss) the petition unless it is neither (to use our shorthand terminology) successive nor abusive. * * * Today, however, the Court obliquely but unmistakably pronounces that a successive or abusive petition *must* be entertained and may *not* be dismissed so long as the petitioner makes a sufficiently persuasive showing that a "fundamental miscarriage of justice" has occurred. * * * ("if a petitioner such as Schlup presents [adequate] evidence of innocence ... the petitioner should be allowed to pass through the gateway and argue the merits"), *ante* at [Supp. p. 85, 1st ¶].[1] That conclusion flatly contradicts the statute, and is not required by our precedent.

* * * Three years after *Sanders* [8th ed., p. 1683, Note 6] * * *, Congress amended § 2244 to establish different finality rules for federal prisoner petitions (filed under § 2255) and state prisoner petitions (filed under § 2254). Section 2244(a), which addresses petitions by federal prisoners, retains the "ends of justice" proviso from the old statute; but § 2244(b) omits it, thus restricting the district courts' *obligation* to entertain petitions by state prisoners to cases where the petition is neither successive nor abusive. One might have expected that this not-so-subtle change in the statute would change our interpretation of it, and that we would modify *Sanders* by holding that a district court could exercise its discretion to give controlling weight to the prior denial * * *. Yet when the new version of § 2244(b) was first construed, in *Kuhlmann v. Wilson* [8th ed., p. 1683, Note 6], a plurality of the Court announced that it would "continue to rely on the reference in *Sanders* to the 'ends of justice,'" and concluded that "the 'ends of justice' require federal courts to entertain [successive] petitions only where the prisoner supplements his constitutional claim with a colorable showing of factual innocence." That conclusion contains two complementary propositions. The first is that a habeas court may *not* reach the merits of a barred claim *unless* actual innocence is shown; this was the actual judgment of the opinion (one cannot say the holding, since the opinion was a mere plurality). * * * The second is that a habeas court *must* hear a claim of actual innocence and reach the merits of the petition if the claim is sufficiently persuasive; this was the purest dictum. It is the Court's prerogative to adopt that dictum today, but to adopt it without analysis, as though it were binding precedent, will not do. The *Kuhlmann* plurality opinion lacks formal status as authority, and * * * no holding

---

1. The claim that "the Court does not, and need not, decide whether the fundamental miscarriage of justice exception is a discretionary remedy" (O'Connor, J., concurring), is not in my view an accurate description of what the Court's opinion says. Of course the concurrence's merely making the claim causes it to be an accurate description of what the Court today *holds,* since the narrower ground taken by one of the Justices comprising a five-Justice majority becomes the law.

of this Court binds us to it. A decision to follow it must be justified by reason, not simply asserted by will. * * *

And if reasons are to be given, justification of the *Kuhlmann* opinion will be found difficult indeed. The plurality's central theory is that "the permissive language of § 2244(b) gives federal courts discretion to entertain successive petitions under some circumstances," so that "[u]nless [the] 'rare instances' [in which successive petitions will be entertained] are to be identified by whim or caprice, district judges must be given guidance for determining when to exercise the limited discretion granted them by § 2244(b)." What the plurality then proceeds to do, however, is not to "guide" the discretion, but to eliminate it entirely, dividing the entire universe of successive and abusive petitions into those that *must not* be entertained (where there is no showing of innocence) and those that *must* be entertained (where there is such a showing). This converts a statute redolent of permissiveness ("*need not* entertain") into a rigid command.

The *Kuhlmann* plurality's concern about caprice is met—as it is met for all decisions committed by law to the discretion of lower courts—by applying traditional "abuse of discretion" standards. A judge who dismisses a successive petition because he misconceives some question of law, because he detests the petitioner's religion, or because he would rather play golf, may be reversed. A judge who dismisses a successive petition because it is the petitioner's twenty-second, rather than his second, because its "only purpose is to vex, harass, or delay," *Sanders,* or because the constitutional claims can be seen to be frivolous on the face of the papers—for any of the numerous considerations that have "a *rational* bearing on the propriety of the discharge sought," *Salinger [v. Loisell,* 265 U.S. 224 (1924)] (emphasis added)—may not be commanded to reach the merits because "the ends of justice" require. Here as elsewhere in the law, to say that a district judge may not abuse his discretion is merely to say that the action in question (dismissing a successive petition) may not be done without considering relevant factors and giving a "justifying reason" * * *. It is a failure of logic, and an arrogation of authority, to "guide" that discretion by holding that what Congress authorized the district court to do may not be done at all.

The Court's assumption that the requirement imposed by the *Kuhlmann* plurality should be taken as law can find no support in our subsequent decisions. * * * There is thus no route of escape from the Court's duty to confront the statute today. I would say, as the statute does, that habeas courts need not entertain successive or abusive petitions. The courts whose decisions we review declined to entertain the petition, and I find no abuse of discretion in the record. (I agree with The Chief Justice that they were correct to use *Sawyer v. Whitley,* supra, as the legal standard for determining claims of innocence.) Therefore, "we should sustain [their] action without saying more." *Salinger.*

SECTION 4. THE GOVERNING LEGAL STANDARD

8th ed., p. 1687; at the end of the Note on Brecht, add:

In O'NEAL v. McANINCH, ___ U.S. ___, 115 S.Ct. 992, 130 L.Ed.2d 947 (1995), the Sixth Circuit, relying in part on *Brecht,* held that the habeas petitioner must bear the "burden of establishing" that the alleged constitutional error was prejudicial under the *Brecht–Kotteakos* harmless-error standard—i.e., the habeas petitioner had to establish by a preponderance of the evidence that the error had a " 'substantial and injurious effect or influence in determining the jury's verdict' " (quoting *Brecht,* in turn quoting *Kotteakos*). A divided Supreme Court (6–3), per BREYER, J., held that the Sixth Circuit had erred. The Court concluded: "As a practical matter, this statement [that the petitioner bears the burden of establishing prejudice] apparently means that, if a judge is in grave doubt about the effect on the jury of this kind of error, the petitioner must lose. Thus, O'Neal might have lost in the Court of Appeals, not because the judges concluded that the error *was* harmless, but because the record of the trial left them in grave doubt about the effect of the error. * * * [But] [w]hen a federal judge in a habeas proceeding is in grave doubt about whether a trial error of federal law had 'substantial and injurious effect or influence in determining the jury's verdict,' that error is not harmless. And, the petitioner must win."

In reaching this conclusion, the Court initially noted: "As an initial matter, * * * we deliberately phrase the issue in this case in terms of a judge's grave doubt, instead of in terms of 'burden of proof.' The case before us does not involve a judge who shifts a 'burden' to help control the presentation of evidence at a trial, but rather involves judges who apply a legal standard (harmlessness) to a record that the presentation of evidence is no longer likely to affect. In such a case, we think it conceptually clearer for the judge to ask directly, 'Do I, the judge, think that the error substantially influenced the jury's decision?' than for the judge to try to put the same question in terms of proof burdens (e.g., 'Do I believe the party has borne its burden of showing ...?'). As Chief Justice Traynor said:

> 'Whether or not counsel are helpful, it is still the responsibility of the ... court, once it concludes there was error, to determine whether the error affected the judgment. It must do so without benefit of such aids as presumptions or allocated burdens of proof that expedite fact-finding at the trial.' R. Traynor, The Riddle of Harmless Error 26 (1970).

The case may sometimes arise, however, where the record is so evenly balanced that a conscientious judge is in grave doubt as to the harmlessness of an error. This is the narrow circumstance we address here."

Justice Breyer then turned to "three considerations" that supported "our legal conclusion—that in cases of grave doubt as to harmlessness the petitioner must win." First, that conclusion was supported by precedent. Admittedly, *Brecht* spoke of habeas petitioners not being "entitled to habeas relief based on trial error unless they can establish that it resulted in 'actual prejudice'" (8th ed., p. 1686). But *Brecht* incorporated the *Kotteakos* standard, and the Court there had specifically noted that "*if one is left in grave doubt*, the conviction cannot stand" (emphasis added). So too, as the Court had noted in *Chapman,* " 'the original common-law harmless-error rule put the burden on the beneficiary of the error [here the State] to prove that there was no injury'" (8th ed., p. 1607).

Second, the Court's conclusion was "consistent with the basic purposes underlying the writ of habeas corpus": "[A] legal rule requiring issuance of the writ * * * [where a grave doubt exists] will, at least often avoid a grievous wrong—holding a person 'in custody in violation of the Constitution.' 28 U.S.C. § 2241(c)(3), § 2254(a). * * * [T]he *opposite* rule, denying the writ in cases of grave uncertainty, would virtually guarantee that many, *in fact,* will be held in unlawful custody."

Third, the Court's conclusion would have "certain administrative virtues": "It is consistent with the way that courts have long treated important trial errors. * * * In a highly technical area such as this one, consistency brings with it simplicity, a body of existing case law available for consultation, see *Brecht,* and a consequently diminished risk of further, error-produced, proceedings. Moreover, our rule avoids the need for judges to read lengthy records to determine prejudice in every habeas case. These factors are not determinative, but offer a practical caution against a legal rule that, in respect to precedent and purpose, would run against the judicial grain."

Justice THOMAS' dissent argued that the Court was giving insufficient weight to "the state's interest in finality and the promotion of federal-state comity" in "balancing the costs and benefits associated with disturbing judgments when a court is in grave doubt as to harm." That those interests must be balanced against the potential for ensuring against unlawful imprisonment was acknowledged implicitly by the Court itself in "drawing the line at 'grave doubt' rather than 'significant doubt' or 'any doubt.'" In the habeas context, the dissent argued, these additional interests should produce a harmless error inquiry that shifts to the petitioner a burden that is carried by the state on direct appeal (as in *Kotteakos* and *Chapman*). While the majority viewed the language of the habeas statute as providing no direction as to how an appellate court should apply the harmless error standard, the dissent argued that statute clearly placed the burden of showing prejudice on the petitioner. Unless the petitioner can establish that the constitutional violation "had a 'substantial and injurious effect or influence in determining the jury's verdict,'" he cannot establish that he is being held in custody "in violation of the Constitution"—i.e., that there is a "causal link between the [constitutional] violation and the custody." The dissent concluded by noting that it was "fortunate" that "the rule announced today will affect only a minuscule fraction of cases"—those "in which a judge, after a thorough review of the record remains in equipoise."

Appendix A

SELECTED PROVISIONS OF THE UNITED STATES CONSTITUTION

Article I

Section 9. * * *

[2] The privilege of the Writ of Habeas Corpus shall not be suspended, unless when in Cases of Rebellion or Invasion the public Safety may require it.

[3] No Bill of Attainder or ex post facto Law shall be passed.

Article III

Section 1. The judicial Power of the United States, shall be vested in one supreme Court, and in such inferior Courts as the Congress may from time to time ordain and establish. The Judges, both of the supreme and inferior Courts, shall hold their Offices during good Behaviour, and shall, at stated Times, receive for their Services a Compensation, which shall not be diminished during their Continuance in Office.

Section 2. [1] The judicial Power shall extend to all Cases, in Law and Equity, arising under this Constitution, the Laws of the United States, and Treaties made, or which shall be made, under their Authority;—to all Cases affecting Ambassadors, other public Ministers and Consuls;—to all Cases of admiralty and maritime Jurisdiction;—to Controversies to which the United States shall be a Party;—to Controversies between two or more States;—between a State and Citizens of another State;—between Citizens of different States;—between Citizens of the same State claiming Lands under the Grants of different States, and between a State, or the Citizens thereof, and foreign States, Citizens or Subjects.

[3] The trial of all Crimes, except in Cases of Impeachment, shall be by Jury; and such Trial shall be held in the State where the said Crimes shall have been committed; but when not committed within any State, the Trial shall be at such Place or Places as the Congress may by Law have directed.

Section 3. [1] Treason against the United States, shall consist only in levying War against them, or, in adhering to their Enemies, giving them Aid and Comfort. No Person shall be convicted of Treason unless on the Testimony of two Witnesses to the same overt Act, or on Confession in open Court.

[2] The Congress shall have Power to declare the Punishment of Treason, but no Attainder of Treason shall work Corruption of Blood, or Forfeiture except during the Life of the Person attainted.

Article IV

Section 2. [1] The Citizens of each State shall be entitled to all Privileges and Immunities of Citizens in the several States.

[2] A Person charged in any State with Treason, Felony, or other Crime, who shall flee from Justice, and be found in another State, shall on demand of the executive Authority of the State from which he fled, be delivered up, to be removed to the State having Jurisdiction of the Crime.

Article VI

[2] This Constitution, and the Laws of the United States which shall be made in Pursuance thereof; and all Treaties made, or which shall be made, under the Authority of the United States, shall be the supreme Law.

Amendment I [1791]

Congress shall make no law respecting an establishment of religion, or prohibiting the free exercise thereof; or abridging the freedom of speech, or of the press; or the right of the people peaceably to assemble, and to petition the Government for a redress of grievances.

Amendment II [1791]

A well regulated Militia, being necessary to the security of a free State, the right of the people to keep and bear Arms, shall not be infringed.

Amendment III [1791]

No Soldier shall, in time of peace be quartered in any house, without the consent of the Owner, nor in time of war, but in a manner to be prescribed by law.

Amendment IV [1791]

The right of the people to be secure in their persons, houses, papers, and effects, against unreasonable searches and seizures, shall not be violated, and no Warrants shall issue, but upon probable cause, supported by Oath or affirmation, and particularly describing the place to be searched, and the persons or things to be seized.

Amendment V [1791]

No person shall be held to answer for a capital, or otherwise infamous crime, unless on a presentment or indictment of a Grand Jury, except in cases arising in the land or naval forces, or in the Militia, when in actual service in time of War or public danger; nor shall any person be subject for the same offence to be twice put in jeopardy of life or limb; nor shall be compelled in any criminal case to be a witness against himself, nor be deprived of life, liberty, or property, without due process of law; nor shall private property be taken for public use, without just compensation.

Amendment VI [1791]

In all criminal prosecutions, the accused shall enjoy the right to a speedy and public trial, by an impartial jury of the State and district wherein the crime shall have been committed, which district shall have been previously ascertained by law, and to be informed of the nature and cause of the accusation; to be confronted with the witnesses against him; to have compulsory process for obtaining witnesses in his favor, and to have the Assistance of Counsel for his defence.

Amendment VII [1791]

In Suits at common law, where the value in controversy shall exceed twenty dollars, the right of trial by jury shall be preserved, and no fact tried by jury, shall be otherwise re-examined in any Court of the United States, than according to the rules of the common law.

Amendment VIII [1791]

Excessive bail shall not be required, nor excessive fines imposed, nor cruel and unusual punishments inflicted.

Amendment IX [1791]

The enumeration in the Constitution, of certain rights, shall not be construed to deny or disparage others retained by the people.

Amendment X [1791]

The powers not delegated to the United States by the Constitution, nor prohibited by it to the States, are reserved to the States respectively, or to the people.

Amendment XIII [1865]

Section 1. Neither slavery nor involuntary servitude, except as a punishment for crime whereof the party shall have been duly convicted, shall exist within the United States, or any place subject to their jurisdiction.

Section 2. Congress shall have power to enforce this article by appropriate legislation.

Amendment XIV [1868]

Section 1. All persons born or naturalized in the United States, and subject to the jurisdiction thereof, are citizens of the United States and of the State wherein they reside. No State shall make or enforce any law which shall abridge the privileges or immunities of citizens of the United States; nor shall any State deprive any person of life, liberty, or property, without due process of law; nor deny to any person within its jurisdiction the equal protection of the laws.

Section 5. The Congress shall have power to enforce, by appropriate legislation, the provisions of the article.

Amendment XV [1870]

Section 1. The right of citizens of the United States to vote shall not be denied or abridged by the United States or by any State on account of race, color, or previous condition of servitude.

Section 2. The Congress shall have power to enforce this article by appropriate legislation.

Appendix B

SELECTED FEDERAL STATUTORY PROVISIONS

Analysis

Wire and Electronic Communications Interception and Interception of Oral Communications (18 U.S.C. §§ 2510–2511, 2515–2518, 2520–2521)
Criminal Justice Act (18 U.S.C. § 3006A)
Bail Reform Act of 1984 (18 U.S.C. §§ 3141–3150)
Speedy Trial Act of 1974 (As Amended) (18 U.S.C. §§ 3161–3162, 3164)
Litigation Concerning Sources of Evidence (18 U.S.C. § 3504)
Criminal Appeals Act of 1970 (As Amended) (18 U.S.C. § 3731)
Jury Selection and Service Act of 1968 (As Amended) (28 U.S.C. §§ 1861–1863, 1865–1867)
Habeas Corpus (28 U.S.C. §§ 2241–2244, 2254–2255)
Privacy Protection Act of 1980 (42 U.S.C. §§ 2000aa—2000aa–12)

WIRE AND ELECTRONIC COMMUNICATIONS INTERCEPTION AND INTERCEPTION OF ORAL COMMUNICATIONS

(18 U.S.C. §§ 2510–2511, 2515–2518, 2520–2521).

§ 2510. Definitions

As used in this chapter—

(1) "wire communication" means any aural transfer made in whole or in part through the use of facilities for the transmission of communications by the aid of wire, cable, or other like connection between the point of origin and the point of reception (including the use of such connection in a switching station) furnished or operated by any person engaged in providing or operating such facilities for the transmission of interstate or foreign communications or communications affecting interstate or foreign commerce and such term includes any electronic storage of such communication;

(2) "oral communication" means any oral communication uttered by a person exhibiting an expectation that such communication is not subject to interception under circumstances justifying such expectation, but such term does not include any electronic communication;

(3) "State" means any State of the United States, the District of Columbia, the Commonwealth of Puerto Rico, and any territory or possession of the United States;

(4) "intercept" means the aural or other acquisition of the contents of any wire, electronic, or oral communication through the use of any electronic, mechanical, or other device;

(5) "electronic, mechanical, or other device" means any device or apparatus which can be used to intercept a wire, oral, or electronic communication other than—

   (a) any telephone or telegraph instrument, equipment or facility, or any component thereof, (i) furnished to the subscriber or user by a provider of wire or electronic communication service in the ordinary course of its business and being used by the subscriber or user in the ordinary course of its business or furnished by such subscriber or user for connection to the facilities of such service and used in the ordinary course of its business; or (ii) being used by a provider of wire or electronic communication service in the ordinary course of its business, or by an investigative or law enforcement officer in the ordinary course of his duties;

   (b) a hearing aid or similar device being used to correct subnormal hearing to not better than normal;

(6) "person" means any employee, or agent of the United States or any State or political subdivision thereof, and any individual, partnership, association, joint stock company, trust, or corporation;

(7) "Investigative or law enforcement officer" means any officer of the United States or of a State or political subdivision thereof, who is empowered by law to conduct investigations of or to make arrests for offenses enumerated in this chapter, and any attorney authorized by law to prosecute or participate in the prosecution of such offenses;

(8) "contents", when used with respect to any wire, oral, or electronic communication, includes any information concerning the substance, purport, or meaning of that communication;

(9) "Judge of competent jurisdiction" means—

   (a) a judge of a United States district court or a United States court of appeals; and

   (b) a judge of any court of general criminal jurisdiction of a State who is authorized by a statute of that State to enter orders authorizing interceptions of wire, oral, or electronic communications;

(10) "communication common carrier" shall have the same meaning which is given the term "common carrier" by section 153(h) of title 47 of the United States Code;

(11) "aggrieved person" means a person who was a party to any intercepted wire, oral, or electronic communication or a person against whom the interception was directed;

(12) "electronic communication" means any transfer of signs, signals, writing, images, sounds, data, or intelligence of any nature transmitted in whole or in part by a wire, radio, electromagnetic, photoelectronic or photooptical system that affects interstate or foreign commerce, but does not include—

(A) any wire or oral communication;

(B) any communication made through a tone-only paging device; or

(C) any communication from a tracking device (as defined in section 3117 of this title);

(13) "user" means any person or entity who—

(A) uses an electronic communication service; and

(B) is duly authorized by the provider of such service to engage in such use;

(14) "electronic communications system" means any wire, radio, electromagnetic, photooptical or photoelectronic facilities for the transmission of electronic communications, and any computer facilities or related electronic equipment for the electronic storage of such communications;

(15) "electronic communication service" means any service which provides to users thereof the ability to send or receive wire or electronic communications;

(16) "readily accessible to the general public" means, with respect to a radio communication, that such communication is not—

(A) scrambled or encrypted;

(B) transmitted using modulation techniques whose essential parameters have been withheld from the public with the intention of preserving the privacy of such communication;

(C) carried on a subcarrier or other signal subsidiary to a radio transmission;

(D) transmitted over a communication system provided by a common carrier, unless the communication is a tone only paging system communication;

(E) transmitted on frequencies allocated under part 25, subpart D, E, or F of part 74, or part 94 of the Rules of the Federal Communications Commission, unless, in the case of a communication transmitted on a frequency allocated under part 74 that is not exclusively allocated to broadcast auxiliary services, the communication is a two-way voice communication by radio; or

(F) an electronic communication;

(17) "electronic storage" means—

(A) any temporary, intermediate storage of a wire or electronic communication incidental to the electronic transmission thereof; and

(B) any storage of such communication by an electronic communication service for purposes of backup protection of such communication; and

(18) "aural transfer" means a transfer containing the human voice at any point between and including the point of origin and the point of reception.

§ 2511. Interception and disclosure of wire, oral, or electronic communications prohibited

(1) Except as otherwise specifically provided in this chapter any person who—

(a) intentionally intercepts, endeavors to intercept, or procures any other person to intercept or endeavor to intercept, any wire, oral, or electronic communication;

(b) intentionally uses, endeavors to use, or procures any other person to use or endeavor to use any electronic, mechanical, or other device to intercept any oral communication when—

(i) such device is affixed to, or otherwise transmits a signal through, a wire, cable, or other like connection used in wire communication; or

(ii) such device transmits communications by radio, or interferes with the transmission of such communication; or

(iii) such person knows, or has reason to know, that such device or any component thereof has been sent through the mail or transported in interstate or foreign commerce; or

(iv) such use or endeavor to use (A) takes place on the premises of any business or other commercial establishment the operations of which affect interstate or foreign commerce; or (B) obtains or is for the purpose of obtaining information relating to the operations of any business or other commercial establishment the operations of which affect interstate or foreign commerce; or

(v) such person acts in the District of Columbia, the Commonwealth of Puerto Rico, or any territory or possession of the United States;

(c) intentionally discloses, or endeavors to disclose, to any other person the contents of any wire, oral, or electronic communication, knowing or having reason to know that the information was obtained through the interception of a wire, oral, or electronic communication in violation of this subsection;

(d) intentionally uses, or endeavors to use, the contents of any wire, oral, or electronic communication, knowing or having reason to know that the information was obtained through the interception of a wire, oral, or electronic communication in violation of this subsection; or

(e)(i) intentionally discloses, or endeavors to disclose, to any other person the contents of any wire, oral, or electronic communication, intercepted by means authorized by sections 2511(2)(A)(ii), 2511(b)–(c), 2511(e), 2516, and 2518 of this subchapter, (ii) knowing or having reason to know that the information was obtained through the interception of such a communication in connection with a criminal investigation, (iii) having obtained or received the information in connection with a criminal investigation, and (iv) with intent to improperly obstruct, impede, or interfere with a duly authorized criminal investigation,

shall be punished as provided in subsection (4) or shall be subject to suit as provided in subsection (5).

(2)(a)(i) It shall not be unlawful under this chapter for an operator of a switchboard, or an officer, employee, or agent of a provider of wire or electronic communication service, whose facilities are used in the transmission of a wire or electronic communication, to intercept, disclose, or use that communication in the normal course of his employment while engaged in any activity which is a necessary incident to the rendition of his service or to the protection of the rights or property of the provider of that service, except that a provider of wire communication service to the public shall not utilize service observing or random monitoring except for mechanical or service quality control checks.

(ii) Notwithstanding any other law, providers of wire or electronic communication service, their officers, employees, and agents, landlords, custodians, or other persons, are authorized to provide information, facilities, or technical assistance to persons authorized by law to intercept wire, oral, or electronic communications or to conduct electronic surveillance, as defined in section 101 of the Foreign Intelligence Surveillance Act of 1978, if such provider, its officers, employees, or agents, landlord, custodian, or other specified person, has been provided with—

(A) a court order directing such assistance signed by the authorizing judge, or

(B) a certification in writing by a person specified in section 2518(7) of this title or the Attorney General of the United States that no warrant or court order is required by law, that all statutory requirements have been met, and that the specified assistance is required,

setting forth the period of time during which the provision of the information, facilities, or technical assistance is authorized and specifying the information, facilities, or technical assistance required. No provider of wire or electronic communication service, officer, employee, or agent thereof, or landlord, custodian, or other specified person shall disclose the existence of any interception or surveillance or the device used to accomplish the interception or surveillance with respect to which the person has been furnished a court order or certification under this chapter except as may otherwise be required by legal process and then only after prior notification to the Attorney General or to the principal prosecuting attorney of a State or any political subdivision of a State, as may be appropriate. Any such disclosure, shall render such person liable for the civil damages provided for in section 2520. No cause of action shall lie in any court against any provider of wire or electronic communication service, its officers, employees, or agents, landlord, custodian, or other specified person for providing information, facilities, or assistance in accordance with the terms of an order or certification under this subpar.

(b) It shall not be unlawful under this chapter for an officer, employee, or agent of the Federal Communications Commission, in the normal course of his employment and in discharge of the monitoring responsibilities exercised by the Commission in the enforcement of chapter 5 of title 47 of the United States Code, to intercept a wire or electronic communication, or oral communication transmitted by radio, or to disclose or use the information thereby obtained.

(c) It shall not be unlawful under this chapter for a person acting under color of law to intercept a wire, oral, or electronic communication, where such person is a party to the communication or one of the parties to the communication has given prior consent to such interception.

(d) It shall not be unlawful under this chapter for a person not acting under color of law to intercept a wire, oral, or electronic communication where such person is a party to the communication or where one of the parties to the communication has given prior consent to such interception unless such communication is intercepted for the purpose of committing any criminal or tortious act in violation of the Constitution or laws of the United States or of any State.

(e) Notwithstanding any other provision of this title or section 705 or 706 of the Communications Act of 1934, it shall not be unlawful for an officer, employee, or agent of the United States in the normal course of his official duty to conduct electronic surveillance, as defined in section 101 of the Foreign Intelligence Surveillance Act of 1978, as authorized by that Act.

(f) Nothing contained in this chapter or chapter 121, or section 705 of the Communications Act of 1934, shall be deemed to affect the acquisition by the United States Government of foreign intelligence information from international or foreign communications, or foreign intelligence activities conducted in accordance with otherwise applicable Federal law involving a foreign electronic communications system, utilizing a means other than electronic surveillance as defined in section 101 of the Foreign Intelligence Surveillance Act of 1978, and procedures in this chapter and the Foreign Intelligence Surveillance Act of 1978 shall be the exclusive means by which electronic surveillance, as defined in section 101 of such Act, and the interception of domestic wire and oral communications may be conducted.

(g) It shall not be unlawful under this chapter or chapter 121 of this title for any person—

(i) to intercept or access an electronic communication made through an electronic communication system that is configured so that such electronic communication is readily accessible to the general public;

(ii) to intercept any radio communication which is transmitted—

(I) by any station for the use of the general public, or that relates to ships, aircraft, vehicles, or persons in distress;

(II) by any governmental, law enforcement, civil defense, private land mobile, or public safety communications system, including police and fire, readily accessible to the general public;

(III) by a station operating on an authorized frequency within the bands allocated to the amateur, citizens band, or general mobile radio services; or

(IV) by any marine or aeronautical communications system;

(iii) to engage in any conduct which—

(I) is prohibited by section 633 of the Communications Act of 1934; or

(II) is excepted from the application of section 705(a) of the Communications Act of 1934 by section 705(b) of that Act;

(iv) to intercept any wire or electronic communication the transmission of which is causing harmful interference to any lawfully operating station or consumer electronic equipment, to the extent necessary to identify the source of such interference; or

(v) for other users of the same frequency to intercept any radio communication made through a system that utilizes frequencies monitored by individuals engaged in the provision or the use of such system, if such communication is not scrambled or encrypted.

(h) It shall not be unlawful under this chapter—

(i) to use a pen register or a trap and trace device (as those terms are defined for the purposes of chapter 206 (relating to pen registers and trap and trace devices) of this title); or

(ii) for a provider of electronic communication service to record the fact that a wire or electronic communication was initiated or completed in order to protect such provider, another provider furnishing service toward the completion of the wire or electronic communication, or a user of that service, from fraudulent, unlawful or abusive use of such service.

(3)(a) Except as provided in paragraph (b) of this subsection, a person or entity providing an electronic communication service to the public shall not intentionally divulge the contents of any communication (other than one to such person or entity, or an agent thereof) while in transmission on that service to any person or entity other than an addressee or intended recipient of such communication or an agent of such addressee or intended recipient.

(b) A person or entity providing electronic communication service to the public may divulge the contents of any such communication—

(i) as otherwise authorized in section 2511(2)(a) or 2517 of this title;

(ii) with the lawful consent of the originator or any addressee or intended recipient of such communication;

(iii) to a person employed or authorized, or whose facilities are used, to forward such communication to its destination; or

(iv) which were inadvertently obtained by the service provider and which appear to pertain to the commission of a crime, if such divulgence is made to a law enforcement agency.

(4)(a) Except as provided in paragraph (b) of this subsection or in subsection (5), whoever violates subsection (1) of this section shall be fined under this title or imprisoned not more than five years, or both.

(b) If the offense is a first offense under paragraph (a) of this subsection and is not for a tortious or illegal purpose or for purposes of direct or indirect commercial advantage or private commercial gain, and the wire or electronic communication with respect to which the offense under paragraph

(a) is a radio communication that is not scrambled or encrypted, or transmitted using modulation techniques the essential parameters of which have been withheld from the public with the intention of preserving the privacy of such communication, then—

(i) if the communication is not the radio portion of a cellular telephone communication, a cordless telephone communication that is transmitted between the cordless telephone handset and the base unit, a public land mobile radio service communication or a paging service communication, and the conduct is not that described in subsection (5), the offender shall be fined under this title or imprisoned not more than one year or both; and

(ii) if the communication is the radio portion of a cellular telephone communication, a cordless telephone communication that is transmitted between the cordless telephone handset and the base unit, a public land mobile radio service communication or a paging service communication, the offender shall be fined not more than $500.

(c) Conduct otherwise an offense under this subsection that consists of or relates to the interception of a satellite transmission that is not encrypted or scrambled and that is transmitted—

(i) to a broadcasting station for purposes of retransmission to the general public; or

(ii) as an audio subcarrier intended for redistribution to facilities open to the public, but not including data transmissions or telephone calls,

is not an offense under this subsection unless the conduct is for the purposes of direct or indirect commercial advantage or private financial gain.

(5)(a)(i) If the communication is—

(A) a private satellite video communication that is not scrambled or encrypted and the conduct in violation of this chapter is the private viewing of that communication and is not for a tortious or illegal purpose or for purposes of direct or indirect commercial advantage or private commercial gain; or

(B) a radio communication that is transmitted on frequencies allocated under subpart D of part 74 of the rules of the Federal Communications Commission that is not scrambled or encrypted and the conduct in violation of this chapter is not for a tortious or illegal purpose or for purposes of direct or indirect commercial advantage or private commercial gain,

then the person who engages in such conduct shall be subject to suit by the Federal Government in a court of competent jurisdiction.

(ii) In an action under this subsection—

(A) if the violation of this chapter is a first offense for the person under paragraph (a) of subsection (4) and such person has not been found liable in a civil action under section 2520 of this title, the Federal Government shall be entitled to appropriate injunctive relief; and

(B) if the violation of this chapter is a second or subsequent offense under paragraph (a) of subsection (4) or such person has been found liable in any prior civil action under section 2520, the person shall be subject to a mandatory $500 civil fine.

(b) The court may use any means within its authority to enforce an injunction issued under paragraph (ii)(A), and shall impose a civil fine of not less than $500 for each violation of such an injunction.

§ 2515. Prohibition of use as evidence of intercepted wire or oral communications

Whenever any wire or oral communication has been intercepted, no part of the contents of such communication and no evidence derived therefrom may be received in evidence in any trial, hearing, or other proceeding in or before any court, grand jury, department, officer, agency, regulatory body, legislative committee, or other authority of the United States, a State, or a political subdivision thereof if the disclosure of that information would be in violation of this chapter.

§ 2516. Authorization for interception of wire, oral, or electronic communications

(1) The Attorney General, Deputy Attorney General, Associate Attorney General, any Assistant Attorney General, any acting Assistant Attorney General, or any Deputy Assistant Attorney General or acting Deputy Assistant Attorney General in the Criminal Division specially designated by the Attorney General, may authorize an application to a Federal judge of competent jurisdiction for, and such judge may grant in conformity with section 2518 of this chapter an order authorizing or approving the interception of wire or oral communications by the Federal Bureau of Investigation, or a Federal agency having responsibility for the investigation of the offense as to which the application is made, when such interception may provide or has provided evidence of—

(a) any offense punishable by death or by imprisonment for more than one year under sections 2274 through 2277 of title 42 of the United States Code (relating to the enforcement of the Atomic Energy Act of 1954), section 2284 of title 42 of the United States Code (relating to sabotage of nuclear facilities or fuel), or under the following chapters of this title: chapter 37 (relating to espionage), chapter 105 (relating to sabotage), chapter 115 (relating to treason), chapter 102 (relating to riots); chapter 65 (relating to malicious mischief), chapter 111 (relating to destruction of vessels), or chapter 81 (relating to piracy);

(b) a violation of section 186 or section 501(c) of title 29, United States Code (dealing with restrictions on payments and loans to labor organizations), or any offense which involves murder, kidnapping, robbery, or extortion, and which is punishable under this title;

(c) any offense which is punishable under the following sections of this title: section 201 (bribery of public officials and witnesses), section 224 (bribery in sporting contests), subsection (d), (e), (f), (g), (h), or (i) of section 844 (unlawful use of explosives), section 1084 (transmission of wagering information), section 751 (relating to escape), sections 1503,

1512, and 1513 (influencing or injuring an officer, juror, or witness generally), section 1510 (obstruction of criminal investigations), section 1511 (obstruction of State or local law enforcement), section 1751 (Presidential and Presidential staff assassination, kidnapping, and assault), section 1951 (interference with commerce by threats or violence), section 1952 (interstate and foreign travel or transportation in aid of racketeering enterprises), section 1952A (relating to use of interstate commerce facilities in the commission of murder for hire), section 1952B (relating to violent crimes in aid of racketeering activity), section 1954 (offer, acceptance, or solicitation to influence operations of employee benefit plan), section 1955 (prohibition of business enterprises of gambling), section 1956 (laundering of monetary instruments), section 1957 (relating to engaging in monetary transactions in property derived from specified unlawful activity), section 659 (theft from interstate shipment), section 664 (embezzlement from pension and welfare funds), section 1343 (fraud by wire, radio, or television), sections 2251 and 2252 (sexual exploitation of children), sections 2312, 2313, 2314, and 2315 (interstate transportation of stolen property), the second section 2320 (relating to trafficking in certain motor vehicles or motor vehicle parts), section 1203 (relating to hostage taking), section 1029 (relating to fraud and related activity in connection with access devices), section 3146 (relating to penalty for failure to appear), section 3521(b)(3) (relating to witness relocation and assistance), section 32 (relating to destruction of aircraft or aircraft facilities), section 1963 (violations with respect to racketeer influenced and corrupt organizations), section 115 (relating to threatening or retaliating against a Federal official), the section in chapter 65 (relating to destruction of an energy facility), and section 1341 (relating to mail fraud), section 351 (violations with respect to congressional, Cabinet, or Supreme Court assassinations, kidnapping, and assault), section 831 (relating to prohibited transactions involving nuclear materials), section 33 (relating to destruction of motor vehicles or motor vehicle facilities), section 175 (relating to biological weapons), or section 1992 (relating to wrecking trains);

(d) any offense involving counterfeiting punishable under section 471, 472, or 473 of this title;

(e) any offense involving fraud connected with a case under title 11 or the manufacture, importation, receiving, concealment, buying, selling, or otherwise dealing in narcotic drugs, marihuana, or other dangerous drugs, punishable under any law of the United States;

(f) any offense including extortionate credit transactions under sections 892, 893, or 894 of this title;

(g) a violation of section 5322 of title 31, United States Code (dealing with the reporting of currency transactions);

(h) any felony violation of sections 2511 and 2512 (relating to interception and disclosure of certain communications and to certain intercepting devices) of this title;

(i) any felony violation of chapter 71 (relating to obscenity) of this title;

(j) any violation of section 60123(b) (relating to destruction of a natural gas pipeline) or 46502 (relating to aircraft piracy) of title 49;

(k) any criminal violation of section 2778 of title 22 (relating to the Arms Export Control Act);

(*l*) the location of any fugitive from justice from an offense described in this section; or

(m) any conspiracy to commit any of the foregoing offenses.

(m)[1] any felony violation of sections 922 and 924 of title 18, United States Code (relating to firearms); and

(n) any violation of section 5861 of the Internal Revenue Code of 1986 (relating to firearms).

(2) The principal prosecuting attorney of any State, or the principal prosecuting attorney of any political subdivision thereof, if such attorney is authorized by a statute of that State to make application to a State court judge of competent jurisdiction for an order authorizing or approving the interception of wire, oral, or electronic communications, may apply to such judge for, and such judge may grant in conformity with section 2518 of this chapter and with the applicable State statute an order authorizing, or approving the interception of wire, oral, or electronic communications by investigative or law enforcement officers having responsibility for the investigation of the offense as to which the application is made, when such interception may provide or has provided evidence of the commission of the offense of murder, kidnapping, gambling, robbery, bribery, extortion, or dealing in narcotic drugs, marihuana or other dangerous drugs, or other crime dangerous to life, limb, or property, and punishable by imprisonment for more than one year, designated in any applicable State statute authorizing such interception, or any conspiracy to commit any of the foregoing offenses.

(3) Any attorney for the Government (as such term is defined for the purposes of the Federal Rules of Criminal Procedure) may authorize an application to a Federal judge of competent jurisdiction for, and such judge may grant, in conformity with section 2518 of this title, an order authorizing or approving the interception of electronic communications by an investigative or law enforcement officer having responsibility for the investigation of the offense as to which the application is made, when such interception may provide or has provided evidence of any Federal felony.

§ 2517. Authorization for disclosure and use of intercepted wire, oral, or electronic communications

(1) Any investigative or law enforcement officer who, by any means authorized by this chapter, has obtained knowledge of the contents of any wire, oral, or electronic communication, or evidence derived therefrom, may disclose such contents to another investigative or law enforcement officer to the extent that such disclosure is appropriate to the proper performance of the official duties of the officer making or receiving the disclosure.

---

[1] So in original.

(2) Any investigative or law enforcement officer who, by any means authorized by this chapter, has obtained knowledge of the contents of any wire, oral, or electronic communication or evidence derived therefrom may use such contents to the extent such use is appropriate to the proper performance of his official duties.

(3) Any person who has received, by any means authorized by this chapter, any information concerning a wire, oral, or electronic communication, or evidence derived therefrom intercepted in accordance with the provisions of this chapter may disclose the contents of that communication or such derivative evidence while giving testimony under oath or affirmation in any proceeding held under the authority of the United States or of any State or political subdivision thereof.

(4) No otherwise privileged wire, oral, or electronic communication intercepted in accordance with, or in violation of, the provisions of this chapter shall lose its privileged character.

(5) When an investigative or law enforcement officer, while engaged in intercepting wire, oral, or electronic communications in the manner authorized herein, intercepts wire, oral, or electronic communications relating to offenses other than those specified in the order of authorization or approval, the contents thereof, and evidence derived therefrom, may be disclosed or used as provided in subsections (1) and (2) of this section. Such contents and any evidence derived therefrom may be used under subsection (3) of this section when authorized or approved by a judge of competent jurisdiction where such judge finds on subsequent application that the contents were otherwise intercepted in accordance with the provisions of this chapter. Such application shall be made as soon as practicable.

§ 2518. Procedure for interception of wire, oral, or electronic communications

(1) Each application for an order authorizing or approving the interception of a wire, oral, or electronic communication under this chapter shall be made in writing upon oath or affirmation to a judge of competent jurisdiction and shall state the applicant's authority to make such application. Each application shall include the following information:

 (a) the identity of the investigative or law enforcement officer making the application, and the officer authorizing the application;

 (b) a full and complete statement of the facts and circumstances relied upon by the applicant, to justify his belief that an order should be issued, including (i) details as to the particular offense that has been, is being, is about to be committed, (ii) except as provided in subsection (11), a particular description of the nature and location of the facilities from which or the place where the communication is to be intercepted, (iii) a particular description of the type of communications sought to be intercepted, (iv) the identity of the person, if known, committing the offense and whose communications are to be intercepted;

 (c) a full and complete statement as to whether or not other investigative procedures have been tried and failed or why they reasonably appear to be unlikely to succeed if tried or to be too dangerous;

(d) a statement of the period of time for which the interception is required to be maintained. If the nature of the investigation is such that the authorization for interception should not automatically terminate when the described type of communication has been first obtained, a particular description of facts establishing probable cause to believe that additional communications of the same type will occur thereafter;

(e) a full and complete statement of the facts concerning all previous applications known to the individual authorizing and making the application, made to any judge for authorization to intercept, or for approval of interceptions of, wire, oral, or electronic communications involving any of the same persons, facilities or places specified in the application, and the action taken by the judge on each such application; and

(f) where the application is for the extension of an order, a statement setting forth the results thus far obtained from the interception, or a reasonable explanation of the failure to obtain such results.

(2) The judge may require the applicant to furnish additional testimony or documentary evidence in support of the application.

(3) Upon such application the judge may enter an ex parte order, as requested or as modified, authorizing or approving interception of wire, oral, or electronic communications within the territorial jurisdiction of the court in which the judge is sitting (and outside that jurisdiction but within the United States in the case of a mobile interception device authorized by a Federal court within such jurisdiction), if the judge determines on the basis of the facts submitted by the applicant that—

(a) there is probable cause for belief that an individual is committing, has committed, or is about to commit a particular offense enumerated in section 2516 of this chapter;

(b) there is probable cause for belief that particular communications concerning that offense will be obtained through such interception;

(c) normal investigative procedures have been tried and have failed or reasonably appear to be unlikely to succeed if tried or to be too dangerous;

(d) except as provided in subsection (11), there is probable cause for belief that the facilities from which, or the place where, the wire, oral, or electronic communications are to be intercepted are being used, or are about to be used, in connection with the commission of such offense, or are leased to, listed in the name of, or commonly used by such person.

(4) Each order authorizing or approving the interception of any wire, oral, or electronic communication under this chapter shall specify—

(a) the identity of the person, if known, whose communications are to be intercepted;

(b) the nature and location of the communications facilities as to which, or the place where, authority to intercept is granted;

(c) a particular description of the type of communication sought to be intercepted, and a statement of the particular offense to which it relates;

(d) the identity of the agency authorized to intercept the communications, and of the person authorizing the application; and

(e) the period of time during which such interception is authorized, including a statement as to whether or not the interception shall automatically terminate when the described communication has been first obtained.

An order authorizing the interception of a wire, oral, or electronic communication under this chapter shall, upon request of the applicant, direct that a provider of wire or electronic communication service, landlord, custodian or other person shall furnish the applicant forthwith all information, facilities, and technical assistance necessary to accomplish the interception unobtrusively and with a minimum of interference with the services that such service provider, landlord, custodian, or person is according the person whose communications are to be intercepted. Any provider of wire or electronic communication service, landlord, custodian or other person furnishing such facilities or technical assistance shall be compensated therefor by the applicant for reasonable expenses incurred in providing such facilities or assistance. Pursuant to section 2522 of this chapter, an order may also be issued to enforce the assistance capability requirements under the Communication Assistance for Law Enforcement Act.

(5) No order entered under this section may authorize or approve the interception of any wire, oral, or electronic communication for any period longer than is necessary to achieve the objective of the authorization, nor in any event longer than thirty days. Such thirty-day period begins on the earlier of the day on which the investigative or law enforcement officer first begins to conduct an interception under the order or ten days after the order is entered. Extensions of an order may be granted, but only upon application for an extension made in accordance with subsection (1) of this section and the court making the findings required by subsection (3) of this section. The period of extension shall be no longer than the authorizing judge deems necessary to achieve the purposes for which it was granted and in no event for longer than thirty days. Every order and extension thereof shall contain a provision that the authorization to intercept shall be executed as soon as practicable, shall be conducted in such a way as to minimize the interception of communications not otherwise subject to interception under this chapter, and must terminate upon attainment of the authorized objective, or in any event in thirty days. In the event the intercepted communication is in a code or foreign language, and an expert in that foreign language or code is not reasonably available during the interception period, minimization may be accomplished as soon as practicable after such interception. An interception under this chapter may be conducted in whole or in part by Government personnel, or by an individual operating under a contract with the Government, acting under the supervision of an investigative or law enforcement officer authorized to conduct the interception.

(6) Whenever an order authorizing interception is entered pursuant to this chapter, the order may require reports to be made to the judge who issued the order showing what progress has been made toward achievement of the authorized objective and the need for continued interception. Such reports shall be made at such intervals as the judge may require.

(7) Notwithstanding any other provision of this chapter, any investigative or law enforcement officer, specially designated by the Attorney General, the Deputy Attorney General, the Associate Attorney General or by the principal prosecuting attorney of any State or subdivision thereof acting pursuant to a statute of that State, who reasonably determines that—

    (a) an emergency situation exists that involves—

        (i) immediate danger of death or serious physical injury to any person,

        (ii) conspiratorial activities threatening the national security interest, or

        (iii) conspiratorial activities characteristic of organized crime,

that requires a wire, oral, or electronic communication to be intercepted before an order authorizing such interception can, with due diligence, be obtained, and

    (b) there are grounds upon which an order could be entered under this chapter to authorize such interception,

may intercept such wire, oral, or electronic communication if an application for an order approving the interception is made in accordance with this section within forty-eight hours after the interception has occurred, or begins to occur. In the absence of an order, such interception shall immediately terminate when the communication sought is obtained or when the application for the order is denied, whichever is earlier. In the event such application for approval is denied, or in any other case where the interception is terminated without an order having been issued, the contents of any wire, oral, or electronic communication intercepted shall be treated as having been obtained in violation of this chapter, and an inventory shall be served as provided for in subsection (d) of this section on the person named in the application.

(8)(a) The contents of any wire, oral, or electronic communication intercepted by any means authorized by this chapter shall, if possible, be recorded on tape or wire or other comparable device. The recording of the contents of any wire, oral or electronic communication under this subsection shall be done in such way as will protect the recording from editing or other alterations. Immediately upon the expiration of the period of the order, or extensions thereof, such recordings shall be made available to the judge issuing such order and sealed under his directions. Custody of the recordings shall be wherever the judge orders. They shall not be destroyed except upon an order of the issuing or denying judge and in any event shall be kept for ten years. Duplicate recordings may be made for use or disclosure pursuant to the provisions of subsections (1) and (2) of section 2517 of this chapter for investigations. The presence of the seal provided for by this subsection, or a satisfactory explanation for the absence thereof, shall be a prerequisite for the use or disclosure of the contents of any wire, oral, or electronic communication or evidence derived therefrom under subsection (3) of section 2517.

(b) Applications made and orders granted under this chapter shall be sealed by the judge. Custody of the applications and orders shall be wherever the judge directs. Such applications and orders shall be disclosed only upon a showing of good cause before a judge of competent jurisdiction and shall not be destroyed except on order of the issuing or denying judge, and in any event shall be kept for ten years.

(c) Any violation of the provisions of this subsection may be punished as contempt of the issuing or denying judge.

(d) Within a reasonable time but not later than ninety days after the filing of an application for an order of approval under section 2518(7)(b) which is denied or the termination of the period of an order or extensions thereof, the issuing or denying judge shall cause to be served, on the persons named in the order or the application, and such other parties to intercepted communications as the judge may determine in his discretion that is in the interest of justice, an inventory which shall include notice of—

(1) the fact of the entry of the order or the application;

(2) the date of the entry and the period of authorized, approved or disapproved interception, or the denial of the application; and

(3) the fact that during the period wire, oral or electronic communications were or were not intercepted.

The judge, upon the filing of a motion, may in his discretion make available to such person or his counsel for inspection such portions of the intercepted communications, applications and orders as the judge determines to be in the interest of justice. On an ex parte showing of good cause to a judge of competent jurisdiction the serving of the inventory required by this subsection may be postponed.

(9) The contents of any wire, oral, or electronic communication intercepted pursuant to this chapter or evidence derived therefrom shall not be received in evidence or otherwise disclosed in any trial, hearing, or other proceeding in a Federal or State court unless each party, not less than ten days before the trial, hearing, or proceeding, has been furnished with a copy of the court order, and accompanying application, under which the interception was authorized or approved. This ten-day period may be waived by the judge if he finds that it was not possible to furnish the party with the above information ten days before the trial, hearing, or proceeding and that the party will not be prejudiced by the delay in receiving such information.

(10)(a) Any aggrieved person in any trial, hearing, or proceeding in or before any court, department, officer, agency, regulatory body, or other authority of the United States, a State, or a political subdivision thereof, may move to suppress the contents of any wire or oral communication intercepted pursuant to this chapter, or evidence derived therefrom, on the grounds that—

(i) the communication was unlawfully intercepted;

(ii) the order of authorization or approval under which it was intercepted is insufficient on its face; or

(iii) the interception was not made in conformity with the order of authorization or approval.

Such motion shall be made before the trial, hearing, or proceeding unless there was no opportunity to make such motion or the person was not aware of the grounds of the motion. If the motion is granted, the contents of the intercepted wire or oral communication, or evidence derived therefrom, shall be treated as having been obtained in violation of this chapter. The judge, upon the filing of such motion by the aggrieved person, may in his discretion make available to the aggrieved person or his counsel for inspection such portions of the intercepted communication or evidence derived therefrom as the judge determines to be in the interests of justice.

(b) In addition to any other right to appeal, the United States shall have the right to appeal from an order granting a motion to suppress made under paragraph (a) of this subsection, or the denial of an application for an order of approval, if the United States attorney shall certify to the judge or other official granting such motion or denying such application that the appeal is not taken for purposes of delay. Such appeal shall be taken within thirty days after the date the order was entered and shall be diligently prosecuted.

(c) The remedies and sanctions described in this chapter with respect to the interception of electronic communications are the only judicial remedies and sanctions for nonconstitutional violations of this chapter involving such communications.

(11) The requirements of subsections (1)(b)(ii) and (3)(d) of this section relating to the specification of the facilities from which, or the place where, the communication is to be intercepted do not apply if—

(a) in the case of an application with respect to the interception of an oral communication—

(i) the application is by a Federal investigative or law enforcement officer and is approved by the Attorney General, the Deputy Attorney General, the Associate Attorney General, an Assistant Attorney General, or an acting Assistant Attorney General;

(ii) the application contains a full and complete statement as to why such specification is not practical and identifies the person committing the offense and whose communications are to be intercepted; and

(iii) the judge finds that such specification is not practical; and

(b) in the case of an application with respect to a wire or electronic communication—

(i) the application is by a Federal investigative or law enforcement officer and is approved by the Attorney General, the Deputy Attorney General, the Associate Attorney General, an Assistant Attorney General, or an acting Assistant Attorney General;

(ii) the application identifies the person believed to be committing the offense and whose communications are to be intercepted and the applicant makes a showing of a purpose, on the part of that person, to thwart interception by changing facilities; and

(iii) the judge finds that such purpose has been adequately shown.

(12) An interception of a communication under an order with respect to which the requirements of subsections (1)(b)(ii) and (3)(d) of this section do not apply by reason of subsection (11) shall not begin until the facilities from which, or the place where, the communication is to be intercepted is

ascertained by the person implementing the interception order. A provider of wire or electronic communications service that has received an order as provided for in subsection (11)(b) may move the court to modify or quash the order on the ground that its assistance with respect to the interception cannot be performed in a timely or reasonable fashion. The court, upon notice to the government, shall decide such a motion expeditiously.

§ 2520. Recovery of civil damages authorized

(a) In general.—Except as provided in section 2511(2)(a)(ii), any person whose wire, oral, or electronic communication is intercepted, disclosed, or intentionally used in violation of this chapter may in a civil action recover from the person or entity which engaged in that violation such relief as may be appropriate.

(b) Relief.—In an action under this section, appropriate relief includes—

(1) such preliminary and other equitable or declaratory relief as may be appropriate;

(2) damages under subsection (c) and punitive damages in appropriate cases; and

(3) a reasonable attorney's fee and other litigation costs reasonably incurred.

(c) Computation of damages.—(1) In an action under this section, if the conduct in violation of this chapter is the private viewing of a private satellite video communication that is not scrambled or encrypted or if the communication is a radio communication that is transmitted on frequencies allocated under subpart D of part 74 of the rules of the Federal Communications Commission that is not scrambled or encrypted and the conduct is not for a tortious or illegal purpose or for purposes of direct or indirect commercial advantage or private commercial gain, then the court shall assess damages as follows:

(A) If the person who engaged in that conduct has not previously been enjoined under section 2511(5) and has not been found liable in a prior civil action under this section, the court shall assess the greater of the sum of actual damages suffered by the plaintiff, or statutory damages of not less than $50 and not more than $500.

(B) If, on one prior occasion, the person who engaged in that conduct has been enjoined under section 2511(5) or has been found liable in a civil action under this section, the court shall assess the greater of the sum of actual damages suffered by the plaintiff, or statutory damages of not less than $100 and not more than $1000.

(2) In any other action under this section, the court may assess as damages whichever is the greater of—

(A) the sum of the actual damages suffered by the plaintiff and any profits made by the violator as a result of the violation; or

(B) statutory damages of whichever is the greater of $100 a day for each day of violation or $10,000.

(d) Defense.—A good faith reliance on—

(1) a court warrant or order, a grand jury subpoena, a legislative authorization, or a statutory authorization;

(2) a request of an investigative or law enforcement officer under section 2518(7) of this title; or

(3) a good faith determination that section 2511(3) of this title permitted the conduct complained of;

is a complete defense against any civil or criminal action brought under this chapter or any other law.

(e) Limitation.—A civil action under this section may not be commenced later than two years after the date upon which the claimant first has a reasonable opportunity to discover the violation.

§ 2521. Injunction against illegal interception

Whenever it shall appear that any person is engaged or is about to engage in any act which constitutes or will constitute a felony violation of this chapter, the Attorney General may initiate a civil action in a district court of the United States to enjoin such violation. The court shall proceed as soon as practicable to the hearing and determination of such an action, and may, at any time before final determination, enter such a restraining order or prohibition, or take such other action, as is warranted to prevent a continuing and substantial injury to the United States or to any person or class of persons for whose protection the action is brought. A proceeding under this section is governed by the Federal Rules of Civil Procedure, except that, if an indictment has been returned against the respondent, discovery is governed by the Federal Rules of Criminal Procedure.

CRIMINAL JUSTICE ACT

(18 U.S.C. § 3006A).

§ 3006A. Adequate representation of defendants

(a) Choice of plan.—Each United States district court, with the approval of the judicial council of the circuit, shall place in operation throughout the district a plan for furnishing representation for any person financially unable to obtain adequate representation in accordance with this section. Representation under each plan shall include counsel and investigative, expert, and other services necessary for adequate representation. Each plan shall provide the following:

(1) Representation shall be provided for any financially eligible person who—

(A) is charged with a felony or a Class A misdemeanor;

(B) is a juvenile alleged to have committed an act of juvenile delinquency as defined in section 5031 of this title;

(C) is charged with a violation of probation;

(D) is under arrest, when such representation is required by law;

(E) is charged with a violation of supervised release or faces modification, reduction, or enlargement of a condition, or extension or revocation of a term of supervised release;

(F) is subject to a mental condition hearing under chapter 313 of this title;

(G) is in custody as a material witness;

(H) is entitled to appointment of counsel under the sixth amendment to the Constitution; or

(I) faces loss of liberty in a case, and Federal law requires the appointment of counsel; or

(J) is entitled to the appointment of counsel under section 4019 of this title.

(2) Whenever the United States magistrate or the court determines that the interests of justice so require, representation may be provided for any financially eligible person who—

(A) is charged with a Class B or C misdemeanor, or an infraction for which a sentence to confinement is authorized; or

(B) is seeking relief under section 2241, 2254, or 2255 of title 28.

(3) Private attorneys shall be appointed in a substantial proportion of the cases. Each plan may include, in addition to the provisions for private attorneys, either of the following or both:

(A) Attorneys furnished by a bar association or a legal aid agency.

(B) Attorneys furnished by a defender organization established in accordance with the provisions of subsection (g).

Prior to approving the plan for a district, the judicial council of the circuit shall supplement the plan with provisions for representation on appeal. The district court may modify the plan at any time with the approval of the judicial council of the circuit. It shall modify the plan when directed by the judicial council of the circuit. The district court shall notify the Administrative Office of the United States Courts of any modification of its plan.

(b) Appointment of counsel.—Counsel furnishing representation under the plan shall be selected from a panel of attorneys designated or approved by the court, or from a bar association, legal aid agency, or defender organization furnishing representation pursuant to the plan. In every case in which a person entitled to representation under a plan approved under subsection (a) appears without counsel, the United States magistrate or the court shall advise the person that he has the right to be represented by counsel and that counsel will be appointed to represent him if he is financially unable to obtain counsel. Unless the person waives representation by counsel, the United States magistrate or the court, if satisfied after appropriate inquiry that the person is financially unable to obtain counsel, shall appoint counsel to represent him. Such appointment may be made retroactive to include any representation furnished pursuant to the plan prior to appointment. The United States magistrate or the court shall appoint separate counsel for persons having interests that cannot properly be represented by the same counsel, or when other good cause is shown.

(c) **Duration and substitution of appointments.**—A person for whom counsel is appointed shall be represented at every stage of the proceedings from his initial appearance before the United States magistrate or the court through appeal, including ancillary matters appropriate to the proceedings. If at any time after the appointment of counsel the United States magistrate or the court finds that the person is financially able to obtain counsel or to make partial payment for the representation, it may terminate the appointment of counsel or authorize payment as provided in subsection (f), as the interests of justice may dictate. If at any stage of the proceedings, including an appeal, the United States magistrate or the court finds that the person is financially unable to pay counsel whom he had retained, it may appoint counsel as provided in subsection (b) and authorize payment as provided in subsection (d), as the interests of justice may dictate. The United States magistrate or the court may, in the interests of justice, substitute one appointed counsel for another at any stage of the proceedings.

(d) **Payment for representation.**—

(1) **Hourly rate.**—Any attorney appointed pursuant to this section or a bar association or legal aid agency or community defender organization which has provided the appointed attorney shall, at the conclusion of the representation or any segment thereof, be compensated at a rate not exceeding $60 per hour for time expended in court or before a United States magistrate and $40 per hour for time reasonably expended out of court, unless the Judicial Conference determines that a higher rate of not in excess of $75 per hour is justified for a circuit or for particular districts within a circuit, for time expended in court or before a United States magistrate and for time expended out of court. The Judicial Conference shall develop guidelines for determining the maximum hourly rates for each circuit in accordance with the preceding sentence, with variations by district, where appropriate, taking into account such factors as the minimum range of the prevailing hourly rates for qualified attorneys in the district in which the representation is provided and the recommendations of the judicial councils of the circuits. Not less than 3 years after the effective date of the Criminal Justice Act Revision of 1986, the Judicial Conference is authorized to raise the maximum hourly rates specified in this paragraph up to the aggregate of the overall average percentages of the adjustments in the rates of pay under the General Schedule made pursuant to section 5305 of title 5 on or after such effective date. After the rates are raised under the preceding sentence, such maximum hourly rates may be raised at intervals of not less than 1 year each, up to the aggregate of the overall average percentages of such adjustments made since the last raise was made under this paragraph. Attorneys shall be reimbursed for expenses reasonably incurred, including the costs of transcripts authorized by the United States magistrate or the court.

(2) **Maximum amounts.**—For representation of a defendant before the United States magistrate or the district court, or both, the compensation to be paid to an attorney or to a bar association or legal aid agency or community defender organization shall not exceed $3,500 for each attorney

in a case in which one or more felonies are charged, and $1,000 for each attorney in a case in which only misdemeanors are charged. For representation of a defendant in an appellate court, the compensation to be paid to an attorney or to a bar association or legal aid agency or community defender organization shall not exceed $2,500 for each attorney in each court. For representation of an offender before the United States Parole Commission in a proceeding under section 4106A of this title, the compensation shall not exceed $750 for each attorney in each proceeding; for representation of an offender in an appeal from a determination of such Commission under such section, the compensation shall not exceed 2,500 for each attorney in each court. For any other representation required or authorized by this section, the compensation shall not exceed $750 for each attorney in each proceeding.

(3) **Waiving maximum amounts.**—Payment in excess of any maximum amount provided in paragraph (2) of this subsection may be made for extended or complex representation whenever the court in which the representation was rendered, or the United States magistrate if the representation was furnished exclusively before him, certifies that the amount of the excess payment is necessary to provide fair compensation and the payment is approved by the chief judge of the circuit. The chief judge of the circuit may delegate such approval authority to an active circuit judge.

(4) **Filing claims.**—A separate claim for compensation and reimbursement shall be made to the district court for representation before the United States magistrate and the court, and to each appellate court before which the attorney provided representation to the person involved. Each claim shall be supported by a sworn written statement specifying the time expended, services rendered, and expenses incurred while the case was pending before the United States magistrate and the court, and the compensation and reimbursement applied for or received in the same case from any other source. The court shall fix the compensation and reimbursement to be paid to the attorney or to the bar association or legal aid agency or community defender organization which provided the appointed attorney. In cases where representation is furnished exclusively before a United States magistrate, the claim shall be submitted to him and he shall fix the compensation and reimbursement to be paid. In cases where representation is furnished other than before the United States magistrate, the district court, or an appellate court, claims shall be submitted to the district court which shall fix the compensation and reimbursement to be paid.

(5) **New trials.**—For purposes of compensation and other payments authorized by this section, an order by a court granting a new trial shall be deemed to initiate a new case.

(6) **Proceedings before appellate courts.**—If a person for whom counsel is appointed under this section appeals to an appellate court or petitions for a writ of certiorari, he may do so without prepayment of fees and costs or security therefor and without filing the affidavit required by section 1915(a) of title 28.

(e) **Services other than counsel.—**

(1) **Upon request.**—Counsel for a person who is financially unable to obtain investigative, expert, or other services necessary for an adequate representation may request them in an ex parte application. Upon finding,

after appropriate inquiry in an ex parte proceeding, that the services are necessary and that the person is financially unable to obtain them, the court, or the United States magistrate if the services are required in connection with a matter over which he has jurisdiction, shall authorize counsel to obtain the services.

(2) **Without prior request.**—(A) Counsel appointed under this section may obtain, subject to later review, investigative, expert, and other services without prior authorization if necessary for adequate representation. Except as provided in subparagraph (B) of this paragraph, the total cost of services obtained without prior authorization may not exceed $300 and expenses reasonably incurred.

(B) The court, or the United States magistrate (if the services were rendered in a case disposed of entirely before the United States magistrate), may, in the interest of justice, and upon the finding that timely procurement of necessary services could not await prior authorization, approve payment for such services after they have been obtained, even if the cost of such services exceeds $300.

(3) **Maximum amounts.**—Compensation to be paid to a person for services rendered by him to a person under this subsection, or to be paid to an organization for services rendered by an employee thereof, shall not exceed $1,000, exclusive of reimbursement for expenses reasonably incurred, unless payment in excess of that limit is certified by the court, or by the United States magistrate if the services were rendered in connection with a case disposed of entirely before him, as necessary to provide fair compensation for services of an unusual character or duration, and the amount of the excess payment is approved by the chief judge of the circuit. The chief judge of the circuit may delegate such approval authority to an active circuit judge.

(f) **Receipt of other payments.**—Whenever the United States magistrate or the court finds that funds are available for payment from or on behalf of a person furnished representation, it may authorize or direct that such funds be paid to the appointed attorney, to the bar association or legal aid agency or community defender organization which provided the appointed attorney, to any person or organization authorized pursuant to subsection (e) to render investigative, expert, or other services, or to the court for deposit in the Treasury as a reimbursement to the appropriation, current at the time of payment, to carry out the provisions of this section. Except as so authorized or directed, no such person or organization may request or accept any payment or promise of payment for representing a defendant.

(g) **Defender organization.**—

(1) **Qualifications.**—A district or a part of a district in which at least two hundred persons annually require the appointment of counsel may establish a defender organization as provided for either under subparagraphs (A) or (B) of paragraph (2) of this subsection or both. Two adjacent districts or parts of districts may aggregate the number of persons required to be represented to establish eligibility for a defender organization to serve both areas. In the event that adjacent districts or parts of districts are located in different circuits, the plan for furnishing representation shall be approved by the judicial council of each circuit.

(2) Types of defender organizations.—

(A) Federal Public Defender Organization.—A Federal Public Defender Organization shall consist of one or more full-time salaried attorneys. An organization for a district or part of a district or two adjacent districts or parts of districts shall be supervised by a Federal Public Defender appointed by the court of appeals of the circuit, without regard to the provisions of title 5 governing appointments in the competitive service, after considering recommendations from the district court or courts to be served. Nothing contained herein shall be deemed to authorize more than one Federal Public Defender within a single judicial district. The Federal Public Defender shall be appointed for a term of four years, unless sooner removed by the court of appeals of the circuit for incompetency, misconduct in office, or neglect of duty. Upon the expiration of his term, a Federal Public Defender may, by a majority vote of the judges of the court of appeals, continue to perform the duties of his office until his successor is appointed, or until one year after the expiration of such Defender's term, whichever is earlier. The compensation of the Federal Public Defender shall be fixed by the court of appeals of the circuit at a rate not to exceed the compensation received by the United States attorney for the district where representation is furnished or, if two districts or parts of districts are involved, the compensation of the higher paid United States attorney of the districts. The Federal Public Defender may appoint, without regard to the provisions of title 5 governing appointments in the competitive service, full-time attorneys in such number as may be approved by the court of appeals of the circuit and other personnel in such number as may be approved by the Director of the Administrative Office of the United States Courts. Compensation paid to such attorneys and other personnel of the organization shall be fixed by the Federal Public Defender at a rate not to exceed that paid to attorneys and other personnel of similar qualifications and experience in the Office of the United States attorney in the district where representation is furnished or, if two districts or parts of districts are involved, the higher compensation paid to persons of similar qualifications and experience in the districts. Neither the Federal Public Defender nor any attorney so appointed by him may engage in the private practice of law. Each organization shall submit to the Director of the Administrative Office of the United States Courts, at the time and in the form prescribed by him, reports of its activities and financial position and its proposed budget. The Director of the Administrative Office shall submit, in accordance with section 605 of title 28, a budget for each organization for each fiscal year and shall out of the appropriations therefor make payments to and on behalf of each organization. Payments under this subparagraph to an organization shall be in lieu of payments under subsection (d) or (e).

(B) Community Defender Organization.—A Community Defender Organization shall be a nonprofit defense counsel service established and administered by any group authorized by the plan to provide representation. The organization shall be eligible to furnish attorneys and receive payments under this section if its bylaws are set forth in the plan of the district or districts in which it will serve. Each organization shall submit to the Judicial Conference of the United States an annual report setting forth its activities and financial position and the anticipated caseload and expenses for the next fiscal year. Upon application an organization may, to the extent approved by the Judicial Conference of the United States:

(i) receive an initial grant for expenses necessary to establish the organization; and

(ii) in lieu of payments under subsection (d) or (e), receive periodic sustaining grants to provide representation and other expenses pursuant to this section. * * *

BAIL REFORM ACT OF 1984

(18 U.S.C. §§ 3141–3150).

§ 3141. Release and detention authority generally

(a) Pending Trial.—A judicial officer authorized to order the arrest of a person under section 3041 of this title before whom an arrested person is brought shall order that such person be released or detained, pending judicial proceedings, under this chapter.

(b) Pending sentence or appeal.—A judicial officer of a court of original jurisdiction over an offense, or a judicial officer of a Federal appellate court, shall order that, pending imposition or execution of sentence, or pending appeal of conviction or sentence, a person be released or detained under this chapter.

§ 3142. Release or detention of a defendant pending trial

(a) In general.—Upon the appearance before a judicial officer of a person charged with an offense, the judicial officer shall issue an order that, pending trial, the person be—

(1) released on his personal recognizance or upon execution of an unsecured appearance bond, under subsection (b) of this section;

(2) released on a condition or combination of conditions under subsection (c) of this section;

(3) temporarily detained to permit revocation of conditional release, deportation, or exclusion under subsection (d) of this section; or

(4) detained under subsection (e) of this section.

(b) Release on personal recognizance or unsecured appearance bond.—The judicial officer shall order the pretrial release of the person on personal recognizance, or upon execution of an unsecured appearance bond in an amount specified by the court, subject to the condition that the person not commit a Federal, State, or local crime during the period of release, unless the judicial officer determines that such release will not reasonably assure the appearance of the person as required or will endanger the safety of any other person or the community.

(c) Release on conditions.—(1) If the judicial officer determines that the release described in subsection (b) of this section will not reasonably assure the appearance of the person as required or will endanger the safety of any other person or the community, such judicial officer shall order the pretrial release of the person—

(A) subject to the condition that the person not commit a Federal, State, or local crime during the period of release; and

(B) subject to the least restrictive further condition, or combination of conditions, that such judicial officer determines will reasonably assure the appearance of the person as required and the safety of any other person and the community, which may include the condition that the person—

(i) remain in the custody of a designated person, who agrees to assume supervision and to report any violation of a release condition to the court, if the designated person is able reasonably to assure the judicial officer that the person will appear as required and will not pose a danger to the safety of any other person or the community;

(ii) maintain employment, or, if unemployed, actively seek employment;

(iii) maintain or commence an educational program;

(iv) abide by specified restrictions on personal associations, place of abode, or travel;

(v) avoid all contact with an alleged victim of the crime and with a potential witness who may testify concerning the offense;

(vi) report on a regular basis to a designated law enforcement agency, pretrial services agency, or other agency;

(vii) comply with a specified curfew;

(viii) refrain from possessing a firearm, destructive device, or other dangerous weapon;

(ix) refrain from excessive use of alcohol, or any use of a narcotic drug or other controlled substance, as defined in section 102 of the Controlled Substances Act (21 U.S.C. 802), without a prescription by a licensed medical practitioner;

(x) undergo available medical or psychiatric treatment, including treatment for drug or alcohol dependency, and remain in a specified institution if required for that purpose;

(xi) execute an agreement to forfeit upon failing to appear as required, such designated property, including money, as is reasonably necessary to assure the appearance of the person as required, and post with the court such indicia of ownership of the property or such percentage of the money as the judicial officer may specify;

(xii) execute a bail bond with solvent sureties in such amount as is reasonably necessary to assure the appearance of the person as required;

(xiii) return to custody for specified hours following release for employment, schooling, or other limited purposes; and

(xiv) satisfy any other condition that is reasonably necessary to assure the appearance of the person as required and to assure the safety of any other person and the community.

(2) The judicial officer may not impose a financial condition that results in the pretrial detention of the person.

(3) The judicial officer may at any time amend the order to impose additional or different conditions of release.

(d) Temporary detention to permit revocation of conditional release, deportation, or exclusion.—If the judicial officer determines that—

(1) the person—

(A) is, and was at the time the offense was committed, on—

(i) release pending trial for a felony under Federal, State, or local law;

(ii) release pending imposition or execution of sentence, appeal of sentence or conviction, or completion of sentence, for any offense under Federal, State, or local law; or

(iii) probation or parole for any offense under Federal, State, or local law; or

(B) is not a citizen of the United States or lawfully admitted for permanent residence, as defined in section 101(a)(20) of the Immigration and Nationality Act (8 U.S.C. 1101(a)(20)); and

(2) the person may flee or pose a danger to any other person or the community;

such judicial officer shall order the detention of the person, for a period of not more than ten days, excluding Saturdays, Sundays, and holidays, and direct the attorney for the Government to notify the appropriate court, probation or parole official, or State or local law enforcement official, or the appropriate official of the Immigration and Naturalization Service. If the official fails or declines to take the person into custody during that period, the person shall be treated in accordance with the other provisions of this section, notwithstanding the applicability of other provisions of law governing release pending trial or deportation or exclusion proceedings. If temporary detention is sought under paragraph (1)(B) of this subsection, the person has the burden of proving to the court such person's United States citizenship or lawful admission for permanent residence.

(e) Detention.—If, after a hearing pursuant to the provisions of subsection (f) of this section, the judicial officer finds that no condition or combination of conditions will reasonably assure the appearance of the person as required and the safety of any other person and the community, such judicial officer shall order the detention of the person before trial. In a case described in (f)(1) of this section, a rebuttable presumption arises that no condition or combination of conditions will reasonably assure the safety of any other person and the community if such judicial officer finds that—

(1) the person has been convicted of a Federal offense that is described in subsection (f)(1) of this section, or of a State or local offense that would have been an offense described in subsection (f)(1) of this section if a circumstance giving rise to Federal jurisdiction had existed;

(2) the offense described in paragraph (1) of this subsection was committed while the person was on release pending trial for a Federal, State, or local offense; and

(3) a period of not more than five years has elapsed since the date of conviction, or the release of the person from imprisonment, for the offense described in paragraph (1) of this subsection, whichever is later.

Subject to rebuttal by the person, it shall be presumed that no condition or combination of conditions will reasonably assure the appearance of the person as required and the safety of the community if the judicial officer finds that there is probable cause to believe that the person committed an offense for which a maximum term of imprisonment of ten years or more is prescribed in the Controlled Substances Act (21 U.S.C. 801 et seq.), the Controlled Substances Import and Export Act (21 U.S.C. 951 et seq.), section 1 of the Act of September 15, 1980 (21 U.S.C. 955a), or an offense under section 924(c) of title 18 of the United States Code.

(f) Detention hearing.—The judicial officer shall hold a hearing to determine whether any condition or combination of conditions set forth in subsection (c) of this section will reasonably assure the appearance of the person as required and the safety of any other person and the community in a case—

(1) upon motion of the attorney for the Government, that involves—

(A) a crime of violence;*

(B) an offense for which the maximum sentence is life imprisonment or death;

(C) an offense for which a maximum term of imprisonment of ten years or more is prescribed in the Controlled Substances Act (21 U.S.C. 801 et seq.), the Controlled Substances Import and Export Act (21 U.S.C. 951 et seq.), or section 1 of the Act of September 15, 1980 (21 U.S.C. 955a); or

(D) any felony if the person had been convicted of two or more prior offenses described in subparagraphs (A) through (C) of this paragraph, or two or more State or local offenses that would have been offenses described in subparagraphs (A) through (C) of this paragraph if a circumstance giving rise to Federal jurisdiction had existed or a combination of such offenses; or

(2) upon motion of the attorney for the Government or upon the judicial officer's own motion in a case, that involves—

(A) a serious risk that such person will flee;

---

* The phrase "crime of violence" is defined in 18 U.S.C. § 3156(a)(4) as meaning: "(A) an offense that has an element of the offense the use, attempted use, or threatened use of physical force against the person or property of another, or (B) any other offense that is a felony and that, by its nature, involves a substantial risk that physical force against the person or property of another may be used in the course of committing the offense."

(B) a serious risk that the person will obstruct or attempt to obstruct justice, or threaten, injure, or intimidate, or attempt to threaten, injure, or intimidate, a prospective witness or juror.

The hearing shall be held immediately upon the person's first appearance before the judicial officer unless that person, or the attorney for the Government, seeks a continuance. Except for good cause, a continuance on motion of the person may not exceed five days, and a continuance on motion of the attorney for the Government may not exceed three days. During a continuance, the person shall be detained, and the judicial officer, on motion of the attorney for the Government or sua sponte, may order that, while in custody, a person who appears to be a narcotics addict receive a medical examination to determine whether such person is an addict. At the hearing, the person has the right to be represented by counsel, and, if financially unable to obtain adequate representation, to have counsel appointed. The person shall be afforded an opportunity to testify, to present witnesses, to cross-examine witnesses who appear at the hearing, and to present information by proffer or otherwise. The rules concerning admissibility of evidence in criminal trials do not apply to the presentation and consideration of information at the hearing. The facts the judicial officer uses to support a finding pursuant to subsection (e) that no condition or combination of conditions will reasonably assure the safety of any other person and the community shall be supported by clear and convincing evidence. The person may be detained pending completion of the hearing. The hearing may be reopened before or after a determination by the judicial officer, at any time before trial if the judicial officer finds that information exists that was not known to the movant at the time of the hearing and that has a material bearing on the issue of whether there are conditions of release that will reasonably assure the appearance of the person as required and the safety of any other person and the community.

(g) Factors to be considered.—The judicial officer shall, in determining whether there are conditions of release that will reasonably assure the appearance of the person as required and the safety of any other person and the community, take into account the available information concerning—

(1) the nature and circumstances of the offense charged, including whether the offense is a crime of violence or involves a narcotic drug;

(2) the weight of the evidence against the person;

(3) the history and characteristics of the person, including—

(A) the person's character, physical and mental condition, family ties, employment, financial resources, length of residence in the community, community ties, past conduct, history relating to drug or alcohol abuse, criminal history, and record concerning appearance at court proceedings; and

(B) whether, at the time of the current offense or arrest, the person was on probation, on parole, or on other release pending trial, sentencing, appeal, or completion of sentence for an offense under Federal, State, or local law; and

(4) the nature and seriousness of the danger to any person or the community that would be posed by the person's release. In considering

the conditions of release described in subsection (c)(2)(K) or (c)(2)(L) [eds. note: intended references are to what is now subsection (c)(1)(B)(xi) or (c)(1)(B)(xii)], the judicial officer may upon his own motion, or shall upon the motion of the Government, conduct an inquiry into the source of the property to be designated for potential forfeiture or offered as collateral to secure a bond, and shall decline to accept the designation, or the use as collateral, of property that, because of its source, will not reasonably assure the appearance of the person as required.

(h) Contents of release order.—In a release order issued under subsection (b) or (c) of this section, the judicial officer shall—

(1) include a written statement that sets forth all the conditions to which the release is subject, in a manner sufficiently clear and specific to serve as a guide for the person's conduct; and

(2) advise the person of—

(A) the penalties for violating a condition of release, including the penalties for committing an offense while on pretrial release;

(B) the consequences of violating a condition of release, including the immediate issuance of a warrant for the person's arrest; and

(C) the provisions of sections 1503 of this title (relating to intimidation of witnesses, jurors, and officers of the court), 1510 (relating to obstruction of criminal investigations), 1512 (tampering with a witness, victim, or an informant), and 1513 (retaliating against a witness, victim, or an informant).

(i) Contents of detention order.—In a detention order issued under subsection (e) of this section, the judicial officer shall—

(1) include written findings of fact and a written statement of the reasons for the detention;

(2) direct that the person be committed to the custody of the Attorney General for confinement in a corrections facility separate, to the extent practicable, from persons awaiting or serving sentences or being held in custody pending appeal;

(3) direct that the person be afforded reasonable opportunity for private consultation with counsel; and

(4) direct that, on order of a court of the United States or on request of an attorney for the Government, the person in charge of the corrections facility in which the person is confined deliver the person to a United States marshal for the purpose of an appearance in connection with a court proceeding.

The judicial officer may, by subsequent order, permit the temporary release of the person, in the custody of a United States marshal or another appropriate person, to the extent that the judicial officer determines such release to be necessary for preparation of the person's defense or for another compelling reason.

(j) Presumption of innocence.—Nothing in this section shall be construed as modifying or limiting the presumption of innocence.

§ 3143. Release or detention of a defendant pending sentence or appeal

(a) Release or detention pending sentence.—(1) Except as provided in paragraph (2), the judicial officer shall order that a person who has been found guilty of an offense and who is awaiting imposition or execution of sentence, other than a person for whom the applicable guideline promulgated pursuant to 28 U.S.C. 994 does not recommend a term of imprisonment, be detained, unless the judicial officer finds by clear and convincing evidence that the person is not likely to flee or pose a danger to the safety of any other person or the community if released under section 3142(b) or (c). If the judicial officer makes such a finding, such judicial officer shall order the release of the person in accordance with section 3142(b) or (c).

(2) The judicial officer shall order that a person who has been found guilty of an offense in a case described in subparagraph (A), (B), or (C) of subsection (f)(1) of section 3142 and is awaiting imposition or execution of sentence be detained unless—

(A)(i) the judicial officer finds there is a substantial likelihood that a motion for acquittal or new trial will be granted; or

(ii) an attorney for the Government has recommended that no sentence of imprisonment be imposed on the person; and

(B) the judicial officer finds by clear and convincing evidence that the person is not likely to flee or pose a danger to any other person or the community.

(b) Release or detention pending appeal by the defendant.—(1) Except as provided in subparagraph (B)(iv) of this paragraph, the judicial officer shall order that a person who has been found guilty of an offense and sentenced to a term of imprisonment, and who has filed an appeal or a petition for a writ of certiorari, be detained, unless the judicial officer finds—

(A) by clear and convincing evidence that the person is not likely to flee or pose a danger to the safety of any other person or the community if released under section 3142(b) or (c) of this title; and

(B) that the appeal is not for the purpose of delay and raises a substantial question of law or fact likely to result in—

(i) reversal,

(ii) an order for a new trial,

(iii) a sentence that does not include a term of imprisonment, or

(iv) a reduced sentence to a term of imprisonment less than the total of the time already served plus the expected duration of the appeal process.

If the judicial officer makes such findings, such judicial officer shall order the release of the person in accordance with section 3142(b) or (c) of this title, except that in the circumstance described in subparagraph (B)(iv) of this paragraph, the judicial officer shall order the detention terminated at the expiration of the likely reduced sentence.

(2) The judicial officer shall order that a person who has been found guilty of an offense in a case described in subparagraph (A), (B), or (C) of subsection (f)(1) of section 3142 and sentenced to a term of imprisonment, and who has filed an appeal or a petition for a writ of certiorari, be detained.

(c) Release or detention pending appeal by the government.— The judicial officer shall treat a defendant in a case in which an appeal has been taken by the United States under section 3731 of this title, in accordance with section 3142 of this title, unless the defendant is otherwise subject to a release or detention order.

Except as provided in subsection (b) of this section, the judicial officer, in a case in which an appeal has been taken by the United States under section 3742, shall—

(1) if the person has been sentenced to a term of imprisonment, order that person detained; and

(2) in any other circumstance, release or detain the person under section 3142.

§ 3144. Release or detention of a material witness

If it appears from an affidavit filed by a party that the testimony of a person is material in a criminal proceeding, and if it is shown that it may become impracticable to secure the presence of the person by subpena, a judicial officer may order the arrest of the person and treat the person in accordance with the provisions of section 3142 of this title. No material witness may be detained because of inability to comply with any condition of release if the testimony of such witness can adequately be secured by deposition, and if further detention is not necessary to prevent a failure of justice. Release of a material witness may be delayed for a reasonable period of time until the deposition of the witness can be taken pursuant to the Federal Rules of Criminal Procedure.

§ 3145. Review and appeal of a release or detention order

(a) Review of a release order.—If a person is ordered released by a magistrate, or by a person other than a judge of a court having original jurisdiction over the offense and other than a Federal appellate court—

(1) the attorney for the Government may file, with the court having original jurisdiction over the offense, a motion for revocation of the order or amendment of the conditions of release; and

(2) the person may file, with the court having original jurisdiction over the offense, a motion for amendment of the conditions of release.

The motion shall be determined promptly.

(b) Review of a detention order.—If a person is ordered detained by a magistrate, or by a person other than a judge of a court having original jurisdiction over the offense and other than a Federal appellate court, the person may file, with the court having original jurisdiction over the offense, a motion for revocation or amendment of the order. The motion shall be determined promptly.

(c) Appeal from a release or detention order.—An appeal from a release or detention order, or from a decision denying revocation or amendment of such an order, is governed by the provisions of section 1291 of title 28 and section 3731 of this title. The appeal shall be determined promptly. A person subject to detention pursuant to section 3143(a)(2) or (b)(2), and who meets the conditions of release set forth in section 3143(a)(1) or (b)(1), may be ordered released, under appropriate conditions, by the judicial officer, if it is clearly shown that there are exceptional reasons why such person's detention would not be appropriate.

§ 3146. Penalty for failure to appear

(a) Offense.—Whoever, having been released under this chapter knowingly—

(1) fails to appear before a court as required by the conditions of his release; or

(2) fails to surrender for service of sentence pursuant to a court order; shall be punished as provided in subsection (b) of this section.

(b) Punishment.—(1) The punishment for an offense under this section is—

(A) if the person was released in connection with a charge of, or while awaiting sentence, surrender for service of sentence, or appeal or certiorari after conviction, for—

(i) an offense punishable by death, life imprisonment, or imprisonment for a term of 15 years or more, a fine under this title or imprisonment for not more than ten years, or both;

(ii) an offense punishable by imprisonment for a term of five years or more, a fine under this title or imprisonment for not more than five years, or both;

(iii) any other felony, a fine under this title or imprisonment for not more than two years, or both; or

(iv) a misdemeanor, a fine under this title or imprisonment for not more than one year, or both; and

(B) if the person was released for appearance as a material witness, a fine under this chapter or imprisonment for not more than one year, or both.

(2) A term of imprisonment imposed under this section shall be consecutive to the sentence of imprisonment for any other offense.

(c) Affirmative defense.—It is an affirmative defense to a prosecution under this section that uncontrollable circumstances prevented the person from appearing or surrendering, and that the person did not contribute to the creation of such circumstances in reckless disregard of the requirement that he appear or surrender, and that the person appeared or surrendered as soon as such circumstances ceased to exist.

(d) Declaration of forfeiture.—If a person fails to appear before a court as required, and the person executed an appearance bond pursuant to section 3142(b) of this title or is subject to the release condition set forth in clause (xi) or (xii) of section 3142(c)(1)(B) of this title, the judicial officer may, regardless of whether the person has been charged with an offense under this section, declare any property designated pursuant to that section to be forfeited to the United States.

§ 3147. Penalty for an offense committed while on release

A person convicted of an offense committed while released under this chapter shall be sentenced, in addition to the sentence prescribed for the offense to—

(1) a term of imprisonment of not less than two years and not more than ten years if the offense is a felony; or

(2) a term of imprisonment of not less than ninety days and not more than one year if the offense is a misdemeanor.

A term of imprisonment imposed under this section shall be consecutive to any other sentence of imprisonment.

§ 3148. Sanctions for violation of a release condition

(a) Available sanctions.—A person who has been released under section 3142 of this title, and who has violated a condition of his release, is subject to a revocation of release, an order of detention, and a prosecution for contempt of court.

(b) Revocation of release.—The attorney for the Government may initiate a proceeding for revocation of an order of release by filing a motion with the district court. A judicial officer may issue a warrant for the arrest of a person charged with violating a condition of release, and the person shall be brought before a judicial officer in the district in which such person's arrest was ordered for a proceeding in accordance with this section. To the extent practicable, a person charged with violating the condition of release that such person not commit a Federal, State, or local crime during the period of release shall be brought before the judicial officer who ordered the release and whose order is alleged to have been violated. The judicial officer shall enter an order of revocation and detention if, after a hearing, the judicial officer—

(1) finds that there is—

(A) probable cause to believe that the person has committed a Federal, State, or local crime while on release; or

(B) clear and convincing evidence that the person has violated any other condition of his release; and

(2) finds that—

(A) based on the factors set forth in section 3142(g) of this title, there is no condition or combination of conditions of release that will assure that the person will not flee or pose a danger to the safety of any other person or the community; or

(B) the person is unlikely to abide by any condition or combination of conditions of release.

If there is probable cause to believe that, while on release, the person committed a Federal, State, or local felony, a rebuttable presumption arises that no condition or combination of conditions will assure that the person will not pose a danger to the safety of any other person or the community. If the judicial officer finds that there are conditions of release that will assure that the person will not flee or pose a danger to the safety of any other person or the community, and that the person will abide by such conditions, the judicial officer shall treat the person in accordance with the provisions of section 3142 of this title and may amend the conditions of release accordingly.

(c) Prosecution for contempt.—The judge may commence a prosecution for contempt, pursuant to the provisions of section 401 of this title, if the person has violated a condition of release.

§ 3149. Surrender of an offender by a surety

A person charged with an offense, who is released upon the execution of an appearance bond with a surety, may be arrested by the surety, and if so arrested, shall be delivered promptly to a United States marshal and brought before a judicial officer. The judicial officer shall determine in accordance with the provisions of section 3148(b) whether to revoke the release of the person, and may absolve the surety of responsibility to pay all or part of the bond in accordance with the provisions of Rule 46 of the Federal Rules of Criminal Procedure. The person so committed shall be held in official detention until released pursuant to this chapter or another provision of law.

§ 3150. Applicability to a case removed from a State court

The provisions of this chapter apply to a criminal case removed to a Federal court from a State court.

SPEEDY TRIAL ACT OF 1974 (AS AMENDED)

(18 U.S.C. §§ 3161–3162, 3164).

§ 3161. Time limits and exclusions

(a) In any case involving a defendant charged with an offense, the appropriate judicial officer, at the earliest practicable time, shall, after consultation with the counsel for the defendant and the attorney for the Government, set the case for trial on a day certain, or list it for trial on a weekly or other short-term trial calendar at a place within the judicial district, so as to assure a speedy trial.

(b) Any information or indictment charging an individual with the commission of an offense shall be filed within thirty days from the date on which such individual was arrested or served with a summons in connection with such charges. If an individual has been charged with a felony in a district in which no grand jury has been in session during such thirty-day period, the period of time for filing of the indictment shall be extended an additional thirty days.

(c) (1) In any case in which a plea of not guilty is entered, the trial of a defendant charged in an information or indictment with the commission of an offense shall commence within seventy days from the filing date (and making public) of the information or indictment, or from the date the defendant has appeared before a judicial officer of the court in which such charge is pending, whichever date last occurs. If a defendant consents in writing to be tried before a magistrate on a complaint, the trial shall commence within seventy days from the date of such consent.

(2) Unless the defendant consents in writing to the contrary, the trial shall not commence less than thirty days from the date on which the defendant first appears through counsel or expressly waives counsel and elects to proceed pro se.

(d) (1) If any indictment or information is dismissed upon motion of the defendant, or any charge contained in a complaint filed against an individual is dismissed or otherwise dropped, and thereafter a complaint is filed against such defendant or individual charging him with the same offense or an offense based on the same conduct or arising from the same criminal episode, or an information or indictment is filed charging such defendant with the same offense or an offense based on the same conduct or arising from the same criminal episode, the provisions of subsections (b) and (c) of this section shall be applicable with respect to such subsequent complaint, indictment, or information, as the case may be.

(2) If the defendant is to be tried upon an indictment or information dismissed by a trial court and reinstated following an appeal, the trial shall commence within seventy days from the date the action occasioning the trial becomes final, except that the court retrying the case may extend the period for trial not to exceed one hundred and eighty days from the date the action occasioning the trial becomes final if the unavailability of witnesses or other factors resulting from the passage of time shall make trial within seventy days impractical. The periods of delay enumerated in section 3161(h) are excluded in computing the time limitations specified in this section. The sanctions of section 3162 apply to this subsection.

(e) If the defendant is to be tried again following a declaration by the trial judge of a mistrial or following an order of such judge for a new trial, the trial shall commence within seventy days from the date the action occasioning the retrial becomes final. If the defendant is to be tried again following an appeal or a collateral attack, the trial shall commence within seventy days from the date the action occasioning the retrial becomes final, except that the court retrying the case may extend the period for retrial not to exceed one hundred and eighty days from the date the action occasioning the retrial becomes final if unavailability of witnesses or other factors resulting from passage of time shall make trial within seventy days impractical. The periods of delay enumerated in section 3161(h) are excluded in computing the time limitations specified in this section. The sanctions of section 3162 apply to this subsection. * * *

(h) The following periods of delay shall be excluded in computing the time within which an information or an indictment must be filed, or in computing the time within which the trial of any such offense must commence:

(1) Any period of delay resulting from other proceedings concerning the defendant, including but not limited to—

(A) delay resulting from any proceeding, including any examinations, to determine the mental competency or physical capacity of the defendant;

(B) delay resulting from any proceeding, including any examination of the defendant, pursuant to section 2902 of title 28, United States Code;

(C) delay resulting from deferral of prosecution pursuant to section 2902 of title 28, United States Code;

(D) delay resulting from trial with respect to other charges against the defendant;

(E) delay resulting from any interlocutory appeal;

(F) delay resulting from any pretrial motion, from the filing of the motion through the conclusion of the hearing on, or other prompt disposition of, such motion;

(G) delay resulting from any proceeding relating to the transfer of a case or the removal of any defendant from another district under the Federal Rules of Criminal Procedure;

(H) delay resulting from transportation of any defendant from another district, or to and from places of examination or hospitalization, except that any time consumed in excess of ten days from the date an order of removal or an order directing such transportation, and the defendant's arrival at the destination shall be presumed to be unreasonable;

(I) delay resulting from consideration by the court of a proposed plea agreement to be entered into by the defendant and the attorney for the Government; and

(J) delay reasonably attributable to any period, not to exceed thirty days, during which any proceeding concerning the defendant is actually under advisement by the court.

(2) Any period of delay during which prosecution is deferred by the attorney for the Government pursuant to written agreement with the defendant, with the approval of the court, for the purpose of allowing the defendant to demonstrate his good conduct.

(3) (A) Any period of delay resulting from the absence or unavailability of the defendant or an essential witness.

(B) For purposes of subparagraph (A) of this paragraph, a defendant or an essential witness shall be considered absent when his whereabouts are unknown and, in addition, he is attempting to avoid apprehension or prosecution or his whereabouts cannot be determined by due diligence. For purposes of such subparagraph, a defendant or an essential witness shall be considered unavailable whenever his whereabouts are known but his presence for trial cannot be obtained by due diligence or he resists appearing at or being returned for trial.

(4) Any period of delay resulting from the fact that the defendant is mentally incompetent or physically unable to stand trial.

(5) Any period of delay resulting from the treatment of the defendant pursuant to section 2902 of title 28, United States Code.

(6) If the information or indictment is dismissed upon motion of the attorney for the Government and thereafter a charge is filed against the defendant for the same offense, or any offense required to be joined with that offense, any period of delay from the date the charge was dismissed to the date the time limitation would commence to run as to the subsequent charge had there been no previous charge.

(7) A reasonable period of delay when the defendant is joined for trial with a codefendant as to whom the time for trial has not run and no motion for severance has been granted.

(8) (A) Any period of delay resulting from a continuance granted by any judge on his own motion or at the request of the defendant or his counsel or at the request of the attorney for the Government, if the judge granted such continuance on the basis of his findings that the ends of justice served by taking such action outweigh the best interest of the public and the defendant in a speedy trial. No such period of delay resulting from a continuance granted by the court in accordance with this paragraph shall be excludable under this subsection unless the court sets forth, in the record of the case, either orally or in writing, its reasons for finding that the ends of justice served by the granting of such continuance outweigh the best interests of the public and the defendant in a speedy trial.

(B) The factors, among others, which a judge shall consider in determining whether to grant a continuance under subparagraph (A) of this paragraph in any case are as follows:

(i) Whether the failure to grant such a continuance in the proceeding would be likely to make a continuation of such proceeding impossible, or result in a miscarriage of justice.

(ii) Whether the case is so unusual or so complex, due to the number of defendants, the nature of the prosecution, or the existence of novel questions of fact or law, that it is unreasonable to expect adequate preparation for pretrial proceedings or for the trial itself within the time limits established by this section.

(iii) Whether, in a case in which arrest precedes indictment, delay in the filing of the indictment is caused because the arrest occurs at a time such that it is unreasonable to expect return and filing of the indictment within the period specified in section 3161(b), or because the facts upon which the grand jury must base its determination are unusual or complex.

(iv) Whether the failure to grant such a continuance in a case which, taken as a whole, is not so unusual or so complex as to fall within clause (ii), would deny the defendant reasonable time to obtain counsel, would unreasonably deny the defendant or the Government continuity of counsel, or would deny counsel for the defendant or the attorney for the Government the reasonable time necessary for effective preparation, taking into account the exercise of due diligence.

(C) No continuance under subparagraph (A) of this paragraph shall be granted because of general congestion of the court's calendar, or lack of diligent preparation or failure to obtain available witnesses on the part of the attorney for the Government.

(9) Any period of delay, not to exceed one year, ordered by a district court upon an application of a party and a finding by a preponderance of the evidence that an official request, as defined in section 3292 of this title, has been made for evidence of any such offense and that it reasonably appears, or reasonably appeared at the time the request was made, that such evidence is, or was, in such foreign country.

(i) If trial did not commence within the time limitation specified in section 3161 because the defendant had entered a plea of guilty or nolo contendere subsequently withdrawn to any or all charges in an indictment or information, the defendant shall be deemed indicted with respect to all charges therein contained within the meaning of section 3161, on the day the order permitting withdrawal of the plea becomes final.

(j) (1) If the attorney for the Government knows that a person charged with an offense is serving a term of imprisonment in any penal institution, he shall promptly—

(A) undertake to obtain the presence of the prisoner for trial; or

(B) cause a detainer to be filed with the person having custody of the prisoner and request him to so advise the prisoner and to advise the prisoner of his right to demand trial.

(2) If the person having custody of such prisoner receives a detainer, he shall promptly advise the prisoner of the charge and of the prisoner's right to demand trial. If at any time thereafter the prisoner informs the person having custody that he does demand trial, such person shall cause notice to that effect to be sent promptly to the attorney for the Government who caused the detainer to be filed.

(3) Upon receipt of such notice, the attorney for the Government shall promptly seek to obtain the presence of the prisoner for trial.

(4) When the person having custody of the prisoner receives from the attorney for the Government a properly supported request for temporary custody of such prisoner for trial, the prisoner shall be made available to that attorney for the Government (subject, in cases of interjurisdictional transfer, to any right of the prisoner to contest the legality of his delivery).

(k) (1) If the defendant is absent (as defined by subsection (h)(3)) on the day set for trial, and the defendant's subsequent appearance before the court on a bench warrant or other process or surrender to the court occurs more than 21 days after the day set for trial, the defendant shall be deemed to have first appeared before a judicial officer of the court in which the information or indictment is pending within the meaning of subsection (c) on the date of the defendant's subsequent appearance before the court.

(2) If the defendant is absent (as defined by subsection (h)(3)) on the day set for trial, and the defendant's subsequent appearance before the court

on a bench warrant or other process or surrender to the court occurs not more than 21 days after the day set for trial, the time limit required by subsection (c), as extended by subsection (h), shall be further extended by 21 days.

§ 3162. Sanctions

(a) (1) If, in the case of any individual against whom a complaint is filed charging such individual with an offense, no indictment or information is filed within the time limit required by section 3161(b) as extended by section 3161(h) of this chapter, such charge against that individual contained in such complaint shall be dismissed or otherwise dropped. In determining whether to dismiss the case with or without prejudice, the court shall consider, among others, each of the following factors: the seriousness of the offense; the facts and circumstances of the case which led to the dismissal; and the impact of a reprosecution on the administration of this chapter and on the administration of justice.

(2) If a defendant is not brought to trial within the time limit required by section 3161(c) as extended by section 3161(h), the information or indictment shall be dismissed on motion of the defendant. The defendant shall have the burden of proof of supporting such motion but the Government shall have the burden of going forward with the evidence in connection with any exclusion of time under subparagraph 3161(h)(3). In determining whether to dismiss the case with or without prejudice, the court shall consider, among others, each of the following factors: the seriousness of the offense; the facts and circumstances of the case which led to the dismissal; and the impact of a reprosecution on the administration of this chapter and on the administration of justice. Failure of the defendant to move for dismissal prior to trial or entry of a plea of guilty or nolo contendere shall constitute a waiver of the right to dismissal under this section.

(b) In any case in which counsel for the defendant or the attorney for the Government (1) knowingly allows the case to be set for trial without disclosing the fact that a necessary witness would be unavailable for trial; (2) files a motion solely for the purpose of delay which he knows is totally frivolous and without merit; (3) makes a statement for the purpose of obtaining a continuance which he knows to be false and which is material to the granting of a continuance; or (4) otherwise willfully fails to proceed to trial without justification consistent with section 3161 of this chapter, the court may punish any such counsel or attorney, as follows:

(A) in the case of an appointed defense counsel, by reducing the amount of compensation that otherwise would have been paid to such counsel pursuant to section 3006A of this title in an amount not to exceed 25 per centum thereof;

(B) in the case of a counsel retained in connection with the defense of a defendant, by imposing on such counsel a fine of not to exceed 25 per centum of the compensation to which he is entitled in connection with his defense of such defendant;

(C) by imposing on any attorney for the Government a fine of not to exceed $250;

(D) by denying any such counsel or attorney for the Government the right to practice before the court considering such case for a period of not to exceed ninety days; or

(E) by filing a report with an appropriate disciplinary committee.

The authority to punish provided for by this subsection shall be in addition to any other authority or power available to such court.

(c) The court shall follow procedures established in the Federal Rules of Criminal Procedure in punishing any counsel or attorney for the Government pursuant to this section.

§ 3164. Persons detained or designated as being of high risk

(a) The trial or other disposition of cases involving—

(1) a detained person who is being held in detention solely because he is awaiting trial, and

(2) a released person who is awaiting trial and has been designated by the attorney for the Government as being of high risk,

shall be accorded priority.

(b) The trial of any person described in subsection (a)(1) or (a)(2) of this section shall commence not later than ninety days following the beginning of such continuous detention or designation of high risk by the attorney for the Government. The periods of delay enumerated in section 3161(h) are excluded in computing the time limitation specified in this section.

(c) Failure to commence trial of a detainee as specified in subsection (b), through no fault of the accused or his counsel, or failure to commence trial of a designated releasee as specified in subsection (b), through no fault of the attorney for the Government, shall result in the automatic review by the court of the conditions of release. No detainee, as defined in subsection (a), shall be held in custody pending trial after the expiration of such ninety-day period required for the commencement of his trial. A designated releasee, as defined in subsection (a), who is found by the court to have intentionally delayed the trial of his case shall be subject to an order of the court modifying his nonfinancial conditions of release under this title to insure that he shall appear at trial as required.

LITIGATION CONCERNING SOURCES OF EVIDENCE

(18 U.S.C. § 3504).

§ 3504. Litigation concerning sources of evidence

(a) In any trial, hearing, or other proceeding in or before any court, grand jury, department, officer, agency, regulatory body, or other authority of the United States—

(1) upon a claim by a party aggrieved that evidence is inadmissible because it is the primary product of an unlawful act or because it was obtained by the exploitation of an unlawful act, the opponent of the claim shall affirm or deny the occurrence of the alleged unlawful act;

(2) disclosure of information for a determination if evidence is inadmissible because it is the primary product of an unlawful act occurring prior to June 19, 1968, or because it was obtained by the exploitation of an unlawful act occurring prior to June 19, 1968, shall not be required unless such information may be relevant to a pending claim of such inadmissibility; and

(3) no claim shall be considered that evidence of an event is inadmissible on the ground that such evidence was obtained by the exploitation of an unlawful act occurring prior to June 19, 1968, if such event occurred more than five years after such allegedly unlawful act.

(b) As used in this section "unlawful act" means any act the use of any electronic, mechanical, or other device (as defined in section 2510(5) of this title) in violation of the Constitution or laws of the United States or any regulation or standard promulgated pursuant thereto.

CRIMINAL APPEALS ACT OF 1970 (AS AMENDED)

(18 U.S.C. § 3731).

§ 3731. Appeal by United States

In a criminal case an appeal by the United States shall lie to a court of appeals from a decision, judgment, or order of a district court dismissing an indictment or information or granting a new trial after verdict or judgment, as to any one or more counts, except that no appeal shall lie where the double jeopardy clause of the United States Constitution prohibits further prosecution.

An appeal by the United States shall lie to a court of appeals from a decision or order of a district court suppressing or excluding evidence or requiring the return of seized property in a criminal proceeding, not made after the defendant has been put in jeopardy and before the verdict or finding on an indictment or information, if the United States attorney certifies to the district court that the appeal is not taken for purpose of delay and that the evidence is a substantial proof of a fact material in the proceeding.

An appeal by the United States shall lie to a court of appeals from a decision or order, entered by a district court of the United States, granting the release of a person charged with or convicted of an offense, or denying a motion for revocation of, or modification of the conditions of, a decision or order granting release.

The appeal in all such cases shall be taken within thirty days after the decision, judgment or order has been rendered and shall be diligently prosecuted.

The provisions of this section shall be liberally construed to effectuate its purposes.

JURY SELECTION AND SERVICE ACT OF 1968 (AS AMENDED)

(28 U.S.C. §§ 1861–1863, 1865–1867).

§ 1861. Declaration of policy

It is the policy of the United States that all litigants in Federal courts entitled to trial by jury shall have the right to grand and petit juries selected at random from a fair cross section of the community in the district or division wherein the court convenes. It is further the policy of the United States that all citizens shall have the opportunity to be considered for service on grand and petit juries in the district courts of the United States, and shall have an obligation to serve as jurors when summoned for that purpose.

§ 1862. Discrimination prohibited

No citizen shall be excluded from service as a grand or petit juror in the district courts of the United States or in the Court of International Trade on account of race, color, religion, sex, national origin, or economic status.

§ 1863. Plan for random jury selection

(a) Each United States district court shall devise and place into operation a written plan for random selection of grand and petit jurors that shall be designed to achieve the objectives of sections 1861 and 1862 of this title, and that shall otherwise comply with the provisions of this title. The plan shall be placed into operation after approval by a reviewing panel consisting of the members of the judicial council of the circuit and either the chief judge of the district whose plan is being reviewed or such other active district judge of that district as the chief judge of the district may designate. The panel shall examine the plan to ascertain that it complies with the provisions of this title. * * * The district court may modify a plan at any time and it shall modify the plan when so directed by the reviewing panel. * * *

(b) Among other things, such plan shall—

(1) either establish a jury commission, or authorize the clerk of the court, to manage the jury selection process. If the plan establishes a jury commission, the district court shall appoint one citizen to serve with the clerk of the court as the jury commission. * * * The citizen jury commissioner shall not belong to the same political party as the clerk serving with him. The clerk or the jury commission, as the case may be, shall act under the supervision and control of the chief judge of the district court or such other judge of the district court as the plan may provide. * * *

(2) specify whether the names of prospective jurors shall be selected from the voter registration lists or the lists of actual voters of the political subdivisions within the district or division. The plan shall prescribe some other source or sources of names in addition to voter lists where necessary to foster the policy and protect the rights secured by sections 1861 and 1862 of this title. * * *

(3) specify detailed procedures to be followed by the jury commission or clerk in selecting names from the sources specified in paragraph (2) of this subsection. These procedures shall be designed to ensure the random selection of a fair cross section of the persons residing in the community in the district or division wherein the court convenes. They shall ensure that names of persons residing in each of the counties, parishes, or similar political subdivisions within the judicial district or division are placed in a master jury wheel; and shall ensure that each county, parish, or similar political subdivision within the district or division is substantially proportionally represented in the master jury wheel for that judicial district, division, or combination of divisions. For the purposes of determining proportional representation in the master jury wheel, either the number of actual voters at the last general election in each county, parish, or similar political subdivision, or the number of registered voters if registration of voters is uniformly required throughout the district or division, may be used.

(4) provide for a master jury wheel (or a device similar in purpose and function) into which the names of those randomly selected shall be placed. The plan shall fix a minimum number of names to be placed initially in the master jury wheel, which shall be at least one-half of 1 per centum of the total number of persons on the lists used as a source of names for the district or division; but if this number of names is believed to be cumbersome and unnecessary, the plan may fix a smaller number of names to be placed in the master wheel, but in no event less than one thousand. The chief judge of the district court, or such other district court judge as the plan may provide, may order additional names to be placed in the master jury wheel from time to time as necessary. The plan shall provide for periodic emptying and refilling of the master jury wheel at specified times, the interval for which shall not exceed four years.

(5) (A) except as provided in subparagraph (B), specify those groups of persons or occupational classes whose members shall, on individual request therefor, be excused from jury service. Such groups or classes shall be excused only if the district court finds, and the plan states, that jury service by such class or group would entail undue hardship or extreme inconvenience to the members thereof, and excuse of members thereof would not be inconsistent with sections 1861 and 1862 of this title.

(B) specify that volunteer safety personnel, upon individual request, shall be excused from jury service. For purposes of this subparagraph, the term "volunteer safety personnel" means individuals serving a public agency (as defined in section 1203(6) of title I of the Omnibus Crime Control and Safe Streets Act of 1968) in an official capacity, without compensation, as firefighters or members of a rescue squad or ambulance crew.

(6) specify that the following persons are barred from jury service on the ground that they are exempt: (A) members in active service in the Armed Forces of the United States; (B) members of the fire or police departments of any State, the District of Columbia, any territory

or possession of the United States, or any subdivision of a State, the District of Columbia, or such territory or possession; (C) public officers in the executive, legislative, or judicial branches of the Government of the United States, or of any State, the District of Columbia, any territory or possession of the United States, or any subdivision of a State, the District of Columbia, or such territory or possession, who are actively engaged in the performance of official duties.

(7) fix the time when the names drawn from the qualified jury wheel shall be disclosed to parties and to the public. If the plan permits these names to be made public, it may nevertheless permit the chief judge of the district court, or such other district court judge as the plan may provide, to keep these names confidential in any case where the interests of justice so require.

(8) specify the procedures to be followed by the clerk or jury commission in assigning persons whose names have been drawn from the qualified jury wheel to grand and petit jury panels. * * *

§ 1865. Qualifications for jury service

(a) The chief judge of the district court, or such other district court judge as the plan may provide, on his initiative or upon recommendation of the clerk or jury commission, shall determine solely on the basis of information provided on the juror qualification form and other competent evidence whether a person is unqualified for, or exempt, or to be excused from jury service. The clerk shall enter such determination in the space provided on the juror qualification form and the alphabetical list of names drawn from the master jury wheel. If a person did not appear in response to a summons, such fact shall be noted on said list.

(b) In making such determination the chief judge of the district court, or such other district court judge as the plan may provide, shall deem any person qualified to serve on grand and petit juries in the district court unless he—

(1) is not a citizen of the United States eighteen years old who has resided for a period of one year within the judicial district;

(2) is unable to read, write, and understand the English language with a degree of proficiency sufficient to fill out satisfactorily the juror qualification form;

(3) is unable to speak the English language;

(4) is incapable, by reason of mental or physical infirmity, to render satisfactory jury service; or

(5) has a charge pending against him for the commission of, or has been convicted in a State or Federal court of record of, a crime punishable by imprisonment for more than one year and his civil rights have not been restored.

§ 1866. Selection and summoning of jury panels
* * *

(c) Except as provided in section 1865 of this title or in any jury selection plan provision adopted pursuant to paragraph (5) or (6) of section

1863(b) of this title, no person or class of persons shall be disqualified, excluded, excused, or exempt from service as jurors: *Provided*, That any person summoned for jury service may be (1) excused by the court, or by the clerk under supervision of the court if the court's jury selection plan so authorizes, upon a showing of undue hardship or extreme inconvenience, for such period as the court deems necessary, at the conclusion of which such person either shall be summoned again for jury service under subsections (b) and (c) of this section or, if the court's jury selection plan so provides, the name of such person shall be reinserted into the qualified jury wheel for selection pursuant to subsection (a) of this section, or (2) excluded by the court on the ground that such person may be unable to render impartial jury service or that his service as a juror would be likely to disrupt the proceedings, or (3) excluded upon peremptory challenge as provided by law, or (4) excluded pursuant to the procedure specified by law upon a challenge by any party for good cause shown, or (5) excluded upon determination by the court that his service as a juror would be likely to threaten the secrecy of the proceedings, or otherwise adversely affect the integrity of jury deliberations. No person shall be excluded under clause (5) of this subsection unless the judge, in open court, determines that such is warranted and that exclusion of the person will not be inconsistent with sections 1861 and 1862 of this title. The number of persons excluded under clause (5) of this subsection shall not exceed one per centum of the number of persons who return executed jury qualification forms during the period, specified in the plan, between two consecutive fillings of the master jury wheel. The names of persons excluded under clause (5) of this subsection, together with detailed explanations for the exclusions, shall be forwarded immediately to the judicial council of the circuit, which shall have the power to make any appropriate order, prospective or retroactive, to redress any misapplication of clause (5) of this subsection, but otherwise exclusions effectuated under such clause shall not be subject to challenge under the provisions of this title. Any person excluded from a particular jury under clause (2), (3), or (4) of this subsection shall be eligible to sit on another jury if the basis for his initial exclusion would not be relevant to his ability to serve on such other jury. * * *

§ 1867. Challenging compliance with selection procedures

(a) In criminal cases, before the voir dire examination begins, or within seven days after the defendant discovered or could have discovered, by the exercise of diligence, the grounds therefor, whichever is earlier, the defendant may move to dismiss the indictment or stay the proceedings against him on the ground of substantial failure to comply with the provisions of this title in selecting the grand or petit jury.

(b) In criminal cases, before the voir dire examination begins, or within seven days after the Attorney General of the United States discovered or could have discovered, by the exercise of diligence, the grounds therefor, whichever is earlier, the Attorney General may move to dismiss the indictment or stay the proceedings on the ground of substantial failure to comply with the provisions of this title in selecting the grand or petit jury. * * *

(d) Upon motion filed under subsection (a), (b), or (c) of this section, containing a sworn statement of facts which, if true, would constitute a substantial failure to comply with the provisions of this title, the moving party shall be entitled to present in support of such motion the testimony of the jury commission or clerk, if available, any relevant records and papers not public or otherwise available used by the jury commissioner or clerk, and any other relevant evidence. If the court determines that there has been a substantial failure to comply with the provisions of this title in selecting a grand jury, the court shall stay the proceedings pending the selection of a grand jury in conformity with this title or dismiss the indictment, whichever is appropriate. If the court determines that there has been a substantial failure to comply with the provisions of this title in selecting the petit jury, the court shall stay the proceedings pending the selection of a petit jury in conformity with this title.

(e) The procedures prescribed by this section shall be the exclusive means by which a person accused of a Federal crime, the Attorney General of the United States or a party in a civil case may challenge any jury on the ground that such jury was not selected in conformity with the provisions of this title. Nothing in this section shall preclude any person or the United States from pursuing any other remedy, civil or criminal, which may be available for the vindication or enforcement of any law prohibiting discrimination on account of race, color, religion, sex, national origin or economic status in the selection of persons for service on grand or petit juries. * * *

HABEAS CORPUS

(28 U.S.C. §§ 2241–2244, 2254–2255).

§ 2241. Power to grant writ

(a) Writs of habeas corpus may be granted by the Supreme Court, any justice thereof, the district courts and any circuit judge within their respective jurisdictions. The order of a circuit judge shall be entered in the records of the district court of the district wherein the restraint complained of is had.

(b) The Supreme Court, any justice thereof, and any circuit judge may decline to entertain an application for a writ of habeas corpus and may transfer the application for hearing and determination to the district court having jurisdiction to entertain it.

(c) The writ of habeas corpus shall not extend to a prisoner unless—

(1) He is in custody under or by color of the authority of the United States or is committed for trial before some court there of; or

(2) He is in custody for an act done or omitted in pursuance of an Act of Congress, or an order, process, judgment or decree of a court or judge of the United States; or

(3) He is in custody in violation of the Constitution or laws or treaties of the United States; or

(4) He, being a citizen of a foreign state and domiciled therein is in custody for an act done or omitted under any alleged right, title, authority, privilege, protection, or exemption claimed under the commission, order or sanction of any foreign state, or under color thereof, the validity and effect of which depend upon the law of nations; or

(5) It is necessary to bring him into court to testify or for trial.

(d) Where an application for a writ of habeas corpus is made by a person in custody under the judgment and sentence of a State court of a State which contains two or more Federal judicial districts, the application may be filed in the district court for the district wherein such person is in custody or in the district court for the district within which the State court was held which convicted and sentenced him and each of such district courts shall have concurrent jurisdiction to entertain the application. The district court for the district wherein such an application is filed in the exercise of its discretion and in furtherance of justice may transfer the application to the other district court for hearing and determination.

§ 2242. Application

Application for a writ of habeas corpus shall be in writing signed and verified by the person for whose relief it is intended or by someone acting in his behalf.

It shall allege the facts concerning the applicant's commitment or detention, the name of the person who has custody over him and by virtue of what claim or authority, if known.

It may be amended or supplemented as provided in the rules of procedure applicable to civil actions.

If addressed to the Supreme Court, a justice thereof or a circuit judge it shall state the reasons for not making application to the district court of the district in which the applicant is held.

§ 2243. Issuance of writ; return; hearing; decision

A court, justice or judge entertaining an application for a writ of habeas corpus shall forthwith award the writ or issue an order directing the respondent to show cause why the writ should not be granted, unless it appears from the application that the applicant or person detained is not entitled thereto.

The writ, or order to show cause shall be directed to the person having custody of the person detained. It shall be returned within three days unless for good cause additional time, not exceeding twenty days, is allowed.

The person to whom the writ or order is directed shall make a return certifying the true cause of the detention.

When the writ or order is returned a day shall be set for hearing, not more than five days after the return unless for good cause additional time is allowed.

Unless the application for the writ and the return present only issues of law the person to whom the writ is directed shall be required to produce at the hearing the body of the person detained.

The applicant or the person detained may, under oath, deny any of the facts set forth in the return or allege any other material facts.

The return and all suggestions made against it may be amended, by leave of court, before or after being filed.

The court shall summarily hear and determine the facts, and dispose of the matter as law and justice require.

§ 2244. Finality of determination

(a) No circuit or district judge shall be required to entertain an application for a writ of habeas corpus to inquire into the detention of a person pursuant to a judgment of a court of the United States if it appears that the legality of such detention has been determined by a judge or court of the United States on a prior application for a writ of habeas corpus and the petition presents no new ground not theretofore presented and determined, and the judge of court is satisfied that the ends of justice will not be served by such inquiry.

(b) When after an evidentiary hearing on the merits of a material factual issue, or after a hearing on the merits of an issue of law, a person in custody pursuant to the judgment of a State court has been denied by a court of the United States or a justice or judge of the United States release from custody or other remedy on an application for a writ of habeas corpus, a subsequent application for a writ of habeas corpus in behalf of such person need not be entertained by a court of the United States or a justice or judge of the United States unless the application alleges and is predicated on a factual or other ground not adjudicated on the hearing of the earlier application for the writ, and unless the court, justice, or judge is satisfied that the applicant has not on the earlier application deliberately withheld the newly asserted ground or otherwise abused the writ.

(c) In a habeas corpus proceeding brought in behalf of a person in custody pursuant to the judgment of a State court, a prior judgment of the Supreme Court of the United States on an appeal or review by a writ of certiorari at the instance of the prisoner of the decision of such State court, shall be conclusive as to all issues of fact or law with respect to an asserted denial of a Federal right which constitutes ground for discharge in a habeas corpus proceeding, actually adjudicated by the Supreme Court therein, unless the applicant for the writ of habeas corpus shall plead and the court shall find the existence of a material and controlling fact which did not appear in the record of the proceeding in the Supreme Court and the court shall further find that the applicant for the writ of habeas corpus could not have caused such fact to appear in such record by the exercise of reasonable diligence.

§ 2254. State custody; remedies in State courts

(a) The Supreme Court, a Justice thereof, a circuit judge, or a district court shall entertain an application for a writ of habeas corpus in behalf of a person in custody pursuant to the judgment of a State court only on the ground that he is in custody in violation of the Constitution or laws or treaties of the United States.

(b) An application for a writ of habeas corpus in behalf of a person in custody pursuant to the judgment of a State court shall not be granted unless it appears that the applicant has exhausted the remedies available in the courts of the State, or that there is either an absence of available State corrective process or the existence of circumstances rendering such process ineffective to protect the rights of the prisoner.

(c) An applicant shall not be deemed to have exhausted the remedies available in the courts of the State, within the meaning of this section, if he has the right under the law of the State to raise, by any available procedure, the question presented.

(d) In any proceeding instituted in a Federal court by an application for a writ of habeas corpus by a person in custody pursuant to the judgment of a State court, a determination after a hearing on the merits of a factual issue, made by a State court of competent jurisdiction in a proceeding to which the applicant for the writ and the State or an officer or agent thereof were parties, evidenced by a written finding, written opinion, or other reliable and adequate written indicia, shall be presumed to be correct, unless the applicant shall establish or it shall otherwise appear, or the respondent shall admit—

(1) that the merits of the factual dispute were not resolved in the State court hearing;

(2) that the factfinding procedure employed by the State court was not adequate to afford a full and fair hearing;

(3) that the material facts were not adequately developed at the State court hearing;

(4) that the State court lacked jurisdiction of the subject matter or over the person of the applicant in the State court proceeding;

(5) that the applicant was an indigent and the State court, in deprivation of his constitutional right, failed to appoint counsel to represent him in the State court proceeding;

(6) that the applicant did not receive a full, fair, and adequate hearing in the State court proceeding; or

(7) that the applicant was otherwise denied due process of law in the State court proceeding;

(8) or unless that part of the record of the State court proceeding in which the determination of such factual issue was made, pertinent to a determination of the sufficiency of the evidence to support such factual determination, is produced as provided for hereinafter, and the Federal court on a consideration of such part of the record as a whole concludes that such factual determination is not fairly supported by the record:

And in an evidentiary hearing in the proceeding in the Federal court, when due proof of such factual determination has been made, unless the existence of one or more of the circumstances respectively set forth in paragraphs numbered (1) to (7), inclusive, is shown by the applicant, otherwise appears, or is admitted by the respondent, or unless the court concludes pursuant to the provisions of paragraph numbered (8) that the record in the State court proceeding, considered as a whole, does not fairly support such factual determination, the burden shall rest upon the applicant to establish by convincing evidence that the factual determination by the State court was erroneous.

(e) If the applicant challenges the sufficiency of the evidence adduced in such State court proceeding to support the State court's determination of a factual issue made therein, the applicant, if able, shall produce that part of the record pertinent to a determination of the sufficiency of the evidence to support such determination. If the applicant, because of indigency or other reason is unable to produce such part of the record, then the State shall produce such part of the record and the Federal court shall direct the State to do so by order directed to an appropriate State official. If the State cannot provide such pertinent part of the record, then the court shall determine under the existing facts and circumstances what weight shall be given to the State court's factual determination.

(f) A copy of the official records of the State court, duly certified by the clerk of such court to be a true and correct copy of a finding, judicial opinion, or other reliable written indicia showing such a factual determination by the State court shall be admissible in the Federal court proceeding.

§ 2255. Federal custody; remedies on motion attacking sentence

A prisoner in custody under sentence of a court established by Act of Congress claiming the right to be released upon the ground that the sentence was imposed in violation of the Constitution or laws of the United States, or that the court was without jurisdiction to impose such sentence, or that the sentence was in excess of the maximum authorized by law, or is otherwise subject to collateral attack, may move the court which imposed the sentence to vacate, set aside or correct the sentence.

A motion for such relief may be made at any time.

Unless the motion and the files and records of the case conclusively show that the prisoner is entitled to no relief, the court shall cause notice thereof to be served upon the United States attorney, grant a prompt hearing thereon, determine the issues and make findings of fact and conclusions of law with respect thereto. If the court finds that the judgment was rendered without jurisdiction, or that the sentence imposed was not authorized by law or otherwise open to collateral attack, or that there has been such a denial or infringement of the constitutional rights of the prisoner as to render the judgment vulnerable to collateral attack, the court shall vacate and set the judgment aside and shall discharge the prisoner or resentence him or grant a new trial or correct the sentence as may appear appropriate.

A court may entertain and determine such motion without requiring the production of the prisoner at the hearing.

The sentencing court shall not be required to entertain a second or successive motion for similar relief on behalf of the same prisoner.

An appeal may be taken to the court of appeals from the order entered on the motion as from a final judgment on application for a writ of habeas corpus.

An application for a writ of habeas corpus in behalf of a prisoner who is authorized to apply for relief by motion pursuant to this section, shall not be entertained if it appears that the applicant has failed to apply for relief, by motion, to the court which sentenced him, or that such court has denied him relief, unless it also appears that the remedy by motion is inadequate or ineffective to test the legality of his detention.

PRIVACY PROTECTION ACT OF 1980

(42 U.S.C. §§ 2000aa–2000aa–12).

§ 2000aa. Searches and seizures by government officers and employees in connection with investigation or prosecution of criminal offenses

(a) Notwithstanding any other law, it shall be unlawful for a government officer or employee, in connection with the investigation or prosecution of a criminal offense, to search for or seize any work product materials possessed by a person reasonably believed to have a purpose to disseminate to the public a newspaper, book, broadcast, or other similar form of public communication, in or affecting interstate or foreign commerce; but this provision shall not impair or affect the ability of any government officer or employee, pursuant to otherwise applicable law, to search for or seize such materials, if—

(1) there is probable cause to believe that the person possessing such materials has committed or is committing the criminal offense to which the materials relate: *Provided, however*, That a government officer or employee may not search for or seize such materials under the provisions of this paragraph if the offense to which the materials relate consists of the receipt, possession, communication, or withholding of such materials or the information contained therein (but such a search or seizure may be conducted under the provisions of this paragraph if the offense consists of the receipt, possession, or communication of information relating to the national defense, classified information, or restricted data under the provisions of section 793, 794, 797, or 798 of Title 18, or section 2274, 2275 or 2277 of this title, or section 783 of Title 50); or

(2) there is reason to believe that the immediate seizure of such materials is necessary to prevent the death of, or serious bodily injury to, a human being.

(b) Notwithstanding any other law, it shall be unlawful for a government officer or employee, in connection with the investigation or prosecution of a criminal offense, to search for or seize documentary materials, other than work product materials, possessed by a person in connection with a purpose to disseminate to the public a newspaper, book, broadcast, or other similar form of public communication, in or affecting interstate or foreign commerce; but this provision shall not impair or affect the ability of any government officer or employee, pursuant to otherwise applicable law, to search for or seize such materials, if—

(1) there is probable cause to believe that the person possessing such materials has committed or is committing the criminal offense to which the materials relate: *Provided, however*, That a government officer or employee may not search for or seize such materials under the provisions of this paragraph if the offense to which the materials relate

consists of the receipt, possession, communication, or withholding of such materials or the information contained therein (but such a search or seizure may be conducted under the provisions of this paragraph if the offense consists of the receipt, possession, or communication of information relating to the national defense, classified information, or restricted data under the provisions of section 793, 794, 797, or 798 of Title 18, or section 2274, 2275 or 2277 of this title, or section 783 of Title 50);

(2) there is reason to believe that the immediate seizure of such materials is necessary to prevent the death of, or serious bodily injury to, a human being;

(3) there is reason to believe that the giving of notice pursuant to a subpena duces tecum would result in the destruction, alteration, or concealment of such materials; or

(4) such materials have not been produced in response to a court order directing compliance with a subpena duces tecum, and—

(A) all appellate remedies have been exhausted; or

(B) there is reason to believe that the delay in an investigation or trial occasioned by further proceedings relating to the subpena would threaten the interests of justice.

(c) In the event a search warrant is sought pursuant to paragraph (4)(B) of subsection (b) of this section, the person possessing the materials shall be afforded adequate opportunity to submit an affidavit setting forth the basis for any contention that the materials sought are not subject to seizure.

§ 2000aa–5. Border and customs searches

This chapter shall not impair or affect the ability of a government officer or employee, pursuant to otherwise applicable law, to conduct searches and seizures at the borders of, or at international points of, entry into the United States in order to enforce the customs laws of the United States.

§ 2000aa–6. Civil actions by aggrieved persons

(a) A person aggrieved by a search for or seizure of materials in violation of this chapter shall have a civil cause of action for damages for such search or seizure—

(1) against the United States, against a State which has waived its sovereign immunity under the Constitution to a claim for damages resulting from a violation of this chapter, or against any other governmental unit, all of which shall be liable for violations of this chapter by their officers or employees while acting within the scope or under color of their office or employment; and

(2) against an officer or employee of a State who has violated this chapter while acting within the scope or under color of his office or employment, if such State has not waived its sovereign immunity as provided in paragraph (1).

(b) It shall be a complete defense to a civil action brought under paragraph (2) of subsection (a) of this section that the officer or employee had a reasonable good faith belief in the lawfulness of his conduct.

(c) The United States, a State, or any other governmental unit liable for violations of this chapter under subsection (a)(1) of this section, may not assert as a defense to a claim arising under this chapter the immunity of the officer or employee whose violation is complained of or his reasonable good faith belief in the lawfulness of his conduct, except that such a defense may be asserted if the violation complained of is that of a judicial officer.

(d) The remedy provided by subsection (a)(1) of this section against the United States, a State, or any other governmental unit is exclusive of any other civil action or proceeding for conduct constituting a violation of this chapter, against the officer or employee whose violation gave rise to the claim, or against the estate of such officer or employee.

(e) Evidence otherwise admissible in a proceeding shall not be excluded on the basis of a violation of this chapter.

(f) A person having a cause of action under this section shall be entitled to recover actual damages but not less than liquidated damages of $1,000, and such reasonable attorneys' fees and other litigation costs reasonably incurred as the court, in its discretion, may award: *Provided, however*, That the United States, a State, or any other governmental unit shall not be liable for interest prior to judgment.

(g) The Attorney General may settle a claim for damages brought against the United States under this section, and shall promulgate regulations to provide for the commencement of an administrative inquiry following a determination of a violation of this chapter by an officer or employee of the United States and for the imposition of administrative sanctions against such officer or employee, if warranted.

(h) The district courts shall have original jurisdiction of all civil actions arising under this section.

§ 2000aa-7. Definitions

(a) "Documentary materials", as used in this chapter, means materials upon which information is recorded, and includes, but is not limited to, written or printed materials, photographs, motion picture films, negatives, video tapes, audio tapes, and other mechanically, magnetically or electronically recorded cards, tapes, or discs, but does not include contraband or the fruits of a crime or things otherwise criminally possessed, or property designed or intended for use, or which is or has been used as, the means of committing a criminal offense.

(b) "Work product materials", as used in this chapter, means materials, other than contraband or the fruits of a crime or things otherwise criminally possessed, or property designed or intended for use, or which is or has been used, as the means of committing a criminal offense, and—

(1) in anticipation of communicating such materials to the public, are prepared, produced, authored, or created, whether by the person in possession of the materials or by any other person;

(2) are possessed for the purposes of communicating such materials to the public; and

(3) include mental impressions, conclusions, opinions, or theories of the person who prepared, produced, authored, or created such material.

(c) "Any other governmental unit", as used in this chapter, includes the District of Columbia, the Commonwealth of Puerto Rico, any territory or possession of the United States, and any local government, unit of local government, or any unit of State government.

§ 2000aa–11. Guidelines for federal officers and employees

(a) The Attorney General shall * * * issue guidelines for the procedures to be employed by any Federal officer or employee, in connection with the investigation or prosecution of an offense, to obtain documentary materials in the private possession of a person when the person is not reasonably believed to be a suspect in such offense or related by blood or marriage to such a suspect, and when the materials sought are not contraband or the fruits or instrumentalities of an offense. * * *

§ 2000aa–12. Binding nature of guidelines; disciplinary actions for violations; legal proceedings for non-compliance prohibited

Guidelines issued by the Attorney General under this subchapter shall have the full force and effect of Department of Justice regulations and any violation of these guidelines shall make the employee or officer involved subject to appropriate administrative disciplinary action. However, an issue relating to the compliance, or the failure to comply, with guidelines issued pursuant to this subchapter may not be litigated, and a court may not entertain such an issue as the basis for the suppression or exclusion of evidence.

[EDITOR'S NOTE: These guidelines appear in 28 C.F.R. Pt. 59. The procedural provisions are set out below.]

§ 59.4 Procedures

(a) *Provisions governing the use of search warrants generally.*

(1) A search warrant should not be used to obtain documentary materials believed to be in the private possession of a disinterested third party unless it appears that the use of a subpoena, summons, request, or other less intrusive alternative means of obtaining the materials would substantially jeopardize the availability or usefulness of the materials sought, and the application for the warrant has been authorized as provided in paragraph (a)(2) of this section.

(2) No federal officer or employee shall apply for a warrant to search for and seize documentary materials believed to be in the private possession of a disinterested third party unless the application for the warrant has been authorized by an attorney for the government. Provided, however, that in an emergency situation in which the immediacy of the need to seize the materials does not permit an opportunity to secure the authorization of an attorney for the government, the application may be authorized by a

supervisory law enforcement officer in the applicant's department or agency, if the appropriate United States Attorney (or where the case is not being handled by a United States Attorney's Office, the appropriate supervisory official of the Department of Justice) is notified of the authorization and the basis for justifying such authorization under this part within 24 hours of the authorization.

(b) *Provisions governing the use of search warrants which may intrude upon professional, confidential relationships.*

(1) A search warrant should not be used to obtain documentary materials believed to be in the private possession of a disinterested third party physician, lawyer, or clergyman, under circumstances in which the materials sought, or other materials likely to be reviewed during the execution of the warrant, contain confidential information on patients, clients, or parishioners which was furnished or developed for the purposes of professional counseling or treatment, unless—

   (i) It appears that the use of a subpoena, summons, request or other less intrusive alternative means of obtaining the materials would substantially jeopardize the availability or usefulness of the materials sought;

   (ii) Access to the documentary materials appears to be of substantial importance to the investigation or prosecution for which they are sought; and

   (iii) The application for the warrant has been approved as provided in paragraph (b)(2) of this section.

(2) No federal officer or employee shall apply for a warrant to search for and seize documentary materials believed to be in the private possession of a disinterested third party physician, lawyer, or clergyman under the circumstances described in paragraph (b)(1) of this section, unless, upon the recommendation of the United States Attorney (or where a case is not being handled by a United States Attorney's Office, upon the recommendation of the appropriate supervisory official of the Department of Justice), an appropriate Deputy Assistant Attorney General has authorized the application for the warrant. Provided, however, that in an emergency situation in which the immediacy of the need to seize the materials does not permit an opportunity to secure the authorization of a Deputy Assistant Attorney General, the application may be authorized by the United States Attorney (or where the case is not being handled by a United States Attorney's Office, by the appropriate supervisory official of the Department of Justice) if an appropriate Deputy Assistant Attorney General is notified of the authorization and the basis for justifying such authorization under this part within 72 hours of the authorization.

(3) Whenever possible, a request for authorization by an appropriate Deputy Assistant Attorney General of a search warrant application pursuant to paragraph (b)(2) of this section shall be made in writing and shall include:

   (i) The application for the warrant; and

   (ii) A brief description of the facts and circumstances advanced as the basis for recommending authorization of the application under this part.

If a request for authorization of the application is made orally or if, in an emergency situation, the application is authorized by the United States Attorney or a supervisory official of the Department of Justice as provided in paragraph (b)(2) of this section, a written record of the request including the materials specified in paragraphs (b)(3)(i) and (ii) of this section shall be transmitted to an appropriate Deputy Assistant Attorney General within 7 days. The Deputy Assistant Attorneys General shall keep a record of the disposition of all requests for authorizations of search warrant applications made under paragraph (b) of this section.

(4) A search warrant authorized under paragraph (b)(2) of this section shall be executed in such a manner as to minimize, to the greatest extent practicable, scrutiny of confidential materials.

(5) Although it is impossible to define the full range of additional doctor-like therapeutic relationships which involve the furnishing or development of private information, the United States Attorney (or where a case is not being handled by a United States Attorney's Office, the appropriate supervisory official of the Department of Justice) should determine whether a search for documentary materials held by other disinterested third party professionals involved in such relationships (e.g. psychologists or psychiatric social workers or nurses) would implicate the special privacy concerns which are addressed in paragraph (b) of this section. If the United States Attorney (or other supervisory official of the Department of Justice) determines that such a search would require review of extremely confidential information furnished or developed for the purposes of professional counseling or treatment, the provisions of this subsection should be applied. Otherwise, at a minimum, the requirements of paragraph (a) of this section must be met.

(c) *Considerations bearing on choice of methods.*

In determining whether, as an alternative to the use of a search warrant, the use of a subpoena or other less intrusive means of obtaining documentary materials would substantially jeopardize the availability or usefulness of the materials sought, the following factors, among others, should be considered:

(1) Whether it appears that the use of a subpoena or other alternative which gives advance notice of the government's interest in obtaining the materials would be likely to result in the destruction, alteration, concealment, or transfer of the materials sought; considerations, among others, bearing on this issue may include:

(i) Whether a suspect has access to the materials sought;

(ii) Whether there is a close relationship of friendship, loyalty, or sympathy between the possessor of the materials and a suspect;

(iii) Whether the possessor of the materials is under the domination or control of a suspect;

(iv) Whether the possessor of the materials has an interest in preventing the disclosure of the materials to the government;

(v) Whether the possessor's willingness to comply with a subpoena or request by the government would be likely to subject him to intimidation or threats of reprisal;

(vi) Whether the possessor of the materials has previously acted to obstruct a criminal investigation or judicial proceeding or refused to comply with or acted in defiance of court orders; or

(vii) Whether the possessor has expressed an intent to destroy, conceal, alter, or transfer the materials;

(2) The immediacy of the government's need to obtain the materials; considerations, among others, bearing on this issue may include:

(i) Whether the immediate seizure of the materials is necessary to prevent injury to persons or property;

(ii) Whether the prompt seizure of the materials is necessary to preserve their evidentiary value;

(iii) Whether delay in obtaining the materials would significantly jeopardize an ongoing investigation or prosecution; or

(iv) Whether a legally enforceable form of process, other than a search warrant, is reasonably available as a means of obtaining the materials.

The fact that the disinterested third party possessing the materials may have grounds to challenge a subpoena or other legal process is not in itself a legitimate basis for the use of a search warrant.

Appendix C

FEDERAL RULES OF CRIMINAL PROCEDURE FOR THE UNITED STATES DISTRICT COURTS

I. SCOPE, PURPOSE, AND CONSTRUCTION

Rule 1. Scope

These rules govern the procedure in all criminal proceedings in the courts of the United States, as provided in Rule 54(a); and, whenever specifically provided in one of the rules, to preliminary, supplementary, and special proceedings before United States magistrate judges and at proceedings before state and local judicial officers.

Rule 2. Purpose and Construction

These rules are intended to provide for the just determination of every criminal proceeding. They shall be construed to secure simplicity in procedure, fairness in administration and the elimination of unjustifiable expense and delay.

II. PRELIMINARY PROCEEDINGS

Rule 3. The Complaint

The complaint is a written statement of the essential facts constituting the offense charged. It shall be made upon oath before a magistrate judge.

Rule 4. Arrest Warrant or Summons upon Complaint

(a) Issuance. If it appears from the complaint, or from an affidavit or affidavits filed with the complaint, that there is probable cause to believe that an offense has been committed and that the defendant has committed it, a warrant for the arrest of the defendant shall issue to any officer authorized by law to execute it. Upon the request of the attorney for the government a summons instead of a warrant shall issue. More than one warrant or summons may issue on the same complaint. If a defendant fails to appear in response to the summons, a warrant shall issue.

(b) Probable Cause. The finding of probable cause may be based upon hearsay evidence in whole or in part.

(c) Form.

(1) Warrant. The warrant shall be signed by the magistrate judge and shall contain the name of the defendant or, if the defendant's name is unknown, any name or description by which the defendant can be identified with reasonable certainty. It shall describe the offense charged in the complaint. It shall command that the defendant be arrested and brought before the nearest available magistrate judge.

(2) Summons. The summons shall be in the same form as the warrant except that it shall summon the defendant to appear before a magistrate at a stated time and place.

(d) Execution or Service; and Return.

(1) By Whom. The warrant shall be executed by a marshal or by some other officer authorized by law. The summons may be served by any person authorized to serve a summons in a civil action.

(2) Territorial Limits. The warrant may be executed or the summons may be served at any place within the jurisdiction of the United States.

(3) Manner. The warrant shall be executed by the arrest of the defendant. The officer need not have the warrant at the time of the arrest but upon request shall show the warrant to the defendant as soon as possible. If the officer does not have the warrant at the time of the arrest, the officer shall then inform the defendant of the offense charged and of the fact that a warrant has been issued. The summons shall be served upon a defendant by delivering a copy to the defendant personally, or by leaving it at the defendant's dwelling house or usual place of abode with some person of suitable age and discretion then residing therein and by mailing a copy of the summons to the defendant's last known address.

(4) Return. The officer executing a warrant shall make return thereof to the magistrate judge or other officer before whom the defendant is brought pursuant to Rule 5. At the request of the attorney for the government any unexecuted warrant shall be returned to and canceled by the magistrate judge by whom it was issued. On or before the return day the person to whom a summons was delivered for service shall make return thereof to the magistrate judge before whom the summons is returnable. At the request of the attorney for the government made at any time while the complaint is pending, a warrant returned unexecuted and not canceled or a summons returned unserved or a duplicate thereof may be delivered by the magistrate judge to the marshal or other authorized person for execution or service.

Rule 5. Initial Appearance Before the Magistrate Judge

(a) In General. An officer making an arrest under a warrant issued upon a complaint or any person making an arrest without a warrant shall take the arrested person without unnecessary delay before the nearest available federal magistrate judge or, in the event that a federal magistrate judge is not reasonably available, before a state or local judicial officer authorized by 18 U.S.C. § 3041. If a person arrested without a warrant is brought before a magistrate judge, a complaint shall be filed forthwith which shall comply with the requirements of Rule 4(a) with respect to the showing of probable cause. When a person, arrested with or without a warrant or given a summons, appears initially before the magistrate judge, the magistrate judge shall proceed in accordance with the applicable subdivisions of this rule.

(b) Misdemeanors and Other Petty Offenses. If the charge against the defendant is a misdemeanor or other petty offense triable by a United States magistrate judge under 18 U.S.C. § 3401, the United States magistrate judge shall proceed in accordance with Rule 58.

(c) Offenses Not Triable by the United States Magistrate Judge. If the charge against the defendant is not triable by the United States magistrate judge, the defendant shall not be called upon to plead. The magistrate judge shall inform the defendant of the complaint against the defendant and of any affidavit filed therewith, of the defendant's right to retain counsel or to request the assignment of counsel if the defendant is unable to obtain counsel, and of the general circumstances under which the defendant may secure pretrial release. The magistrate judge shall inform the defendant that the defendant is not required to make a statement and that any statement made by the defendant may be used against the defendant. The magistrate judge shall also inform the defendant of the right to a preliminary examination. The magistrate judge shall allow the defendant reasonable time and opportunity to consult counsel and shall detain or conditionally release the defendant as provided by statute or in these rules.

A defendant is entitled to a preliminary examination, unless waived, when charged with any offense, other than a petty offense, which is to be tried by a judge of the district court. If the defendant waives preliminary examination, the magistrate judge shall forthwith hold the defendant to answer in the district court. If the defendant does not waive the preliminary examination, the magistrate judge shall schedule a preliminary examination. Such examination shall be held within a reasonable time but in any event not later than 10 days following the initial appearance if the defendant is in custody and no later than 20 days if the defendant is not in custody, provided, however, that the preliminary examination shall not be held if the defendant is indicted or if an information against the defendant is filed in district court before the date set for the preliminary examination. With the consent of the defendant and upon a showing of good cause, taking into account the public interest in the prompt disposition of criminal cases, time limits specified in this subdivision may be extended one or more times by a federal magistrate judge. In the absence of such consent by the defendant, time limits may be extended by a judge of the United States only upon a showing that extraordinary circumstances exist and that delay is indispensable to the interests of justice.

Rule 5.1. Preliminary Examination

(a) Probable Cause Finding. If from the evidence it appears that there is probable cause to believe that an offense has been committed and that the defendant committed it, the federal magistrate judge shall forthwith hold the defendant to answer in district court. The finding of probable cause may be based upon hearsay evidence in whole or in part. The defendant may cross-examine adverse witnesses and may introduce evidence. Objections to evidence on the ground that it was acquired by unlawful means are not properly made at the preliminary examination. Motions to suppress must be made to the trial court as provided in Rule 12.

(b) Discharge of Defendant. If from the evidence it appears that there is no probable cause to believe that an offense has been committed or that the defendant committed it, the federal magistrate judge shall dismiss the complaint and discharge the defendant. The discharge of the defendant shall not preclude the government from instituting a subsequent prosecution for the same offense.

(c) Records. After concluding the proceeding the federal magistrate judge shall transmit forthwith to the clerk of the district court all papers in the proceeding. The magistrate judge shall promptly make or cause to be made a record or summary of such proceeding.

(1) On timely application to a federal magistrate judge, the attorney for a defendant in a criminal case may be given the opportunity to have the recording of the hearing on preliminary examination made available to that attorney in connection with any further hearing or preparation for trial. The court may, by local rule, appoint the place for and define the conditions under which such opportunity may be afforded counsel.

(2) On application of a defendant addressed to the court or any judge thereof, an order may issue that the federal magistrate judge make available a copy of the transcript, or of a portion thereof, to defense counsel. Such order shall provide for prepayment of costs of such transcript by the defendant unless the defendant makes a sufficient affidavit that the defendant is unable to pay or to give security therefor, in which case the expense shall be paid by the Director of the Administrative Office of the United States Courts from available appropriated funds. Counsel for the government may move also that a copy of the transcript, in whole or in part, be made available to it, for good cause shown, and an order may be entered granting such motion in whole or in part, on appropriate terms, except that the government need not prepay costs nor furnish security therefor.

III. INDICTMENT AND INFORMATION
Rule 6. The Grand Jury

(a) Summoning Grand Juries.

(1) Generally. The court shall order one or more grand juries to be summoned at such time as the public interest requires. The grand jury shall consist of not less than 16 nor more than 23 members. The court shall direct that a sufficient number of legally qualified persons be summoned to meet this requirement.

(2) Alternate Jurors. The court may direct that alternate jurors may be designated at the time a grand jury is selected. Alternate jurors in the order in which they were designated may thereafter be impanelled as provided in subdivision (g) of this rule. Alternate jurors shall be drawn in the same manner and shall have the same qualifications as the regular jurors, and if impanelled shall be subject to the same challenges, shall take the same oath and shall have the same functions, powers, facilities and privileges as the regular jurors.

(b) Objections to Grand Jury and to Grand Jurors.

(1) Challenges. The attorney for the government or a defendant who has been held to answer in the district court may challenge the array of jurors on the ground that the grand jury was not selected, drawn or summoned in accordance with law, and may challenge an individual juror on the ground that the juror is not legally qualified. Challenges shall be made before the administration of the oath to the jurors and shall be tried by the court.

(2) Motion to Dismiss. A motion to dismiss the indictment may be based on objections to the array or on the lack of legal qualification of an individual juror, if not previously determined upon challenge. It shall be made in the manner prescribed in 28 U.S.C. § 1867(e) and shall be granted under the conditions prescribed in that statute. An indictment shall not be dismissed on the ground that one or more members of the grand jury were not legally qualified if it appears from the record kept pursuant to subdivision (c) of this rule that 12 or more jurors, after deducting the number not legally qualified, concurred in finding the indictment.

(c) Foreperson and Deputy Foreperson. The court shall appoint one of the jurors to be foreperson and another to be deputy foreperson. The foreperson shall have power to administer oaths and affirmations and shall sign all indictments. The foreperson or another juror designated by the foreperson shall keep record of the number of jurors concurring in the finding of every indictment and shall file the record with the clerk of the court, but the record shall not be made public except on order of the court. During the absence of the foreperson, the deputy foreperson shall act as foreperson.

(d) Who May Be Present. Attorneys for the government, the witness under examination, interpreters when needed and, for the purpose of taking the evidence, a stenographer or operator of a recording device may be present while the grand jury is in session, but no person other than the jurors may be present while the grand jury is deliberating or voting.

(e) Recording and Disclosure of Proceedings.

(1) Recording of Proceedings. All proceedings, except when the grand jury is deliberating or voting, shall be recorded stenographically or by an electronic recording device. An unintentional failure of any recording to reproduce all or any portion of a proceeding shall not affect the validity of the prosecution. The recording or reporter's notes or any transcript prepared therefrom shall remain in the custody or control of the attorney for the government unless otherwise ordered by the court in a particular case.

(2) General Rule of Secrecy. A grand juror, an interpreter, a stenographer, an operator of a recording device, a typist who transcribes recorded testimony, an attorney for the government, or any person to whom disclosure is made under paragraph (3)(A)(ii) of this subdivision shall not disclose matters occurring before the grand jury, except as otherwise provided for in these rules. No obligation of secrecy may be imposed on any person except in accordance with this rule. A knowing violation of Rule 6 may be punished as a contempt of court.

(3) Exceptions.

(A) Disclosure otherwise prohibited by this rule of matters occurring before the grand jury, other than its deliberations and the vote of any grand juror, may be made to—

 (i) an attorney for the government for use in the performance of such attorney's duty; and

 (ii) such government personnel (including personnel of a state or subdivision of a state) as are deemed necessary by an attorney for the government to assist an attorney for the government in the performance of such attorney's duty to enforce federal criminal law.

(B) Any person to whom matters are disclosed under subparagraph (A)(ii) of this paragraph shall not utilize that grand jury material for any purpose other than assisting the attorney for the government in the performance of such attorney's duty to enforce federal criminal law. An attorney for the government shall promptly provide the district court, before which was impaneled the grand jury whose material has been so disclosed, with the names of the persons to whom such disclosure has been made, and shall certify that the attorney has advised such persons of their obligation of secrecy under this rule.

(C) Disclosure otherwise prohibited by this rule of matters occurring before the grand jury may also be made—

 (i) when so directed by a court preliminarily to or in connection with a judicial proceeding;

 (ii) when permitted by a court at the request of the defendant, upon a showing that grounds may exist for a motion to dismiss the indictment because of matters occurring before the grand jury;

 (iii) when the disclosure is made by an attorney for the government to another federal grand jury; or

 (iv) when permitted by a court at the request of an attorney for the government, upon a showing that such matters may disclose a violation of state criminal law, to an appropriate official of a state or subdivision of a state for the purpose of enforcing such law.

If the court orders disclosure of matters occurring before the grand jury, the disclosure shall be made in such manner, at such time, and under such conditions as the court may direct.

(D) A petition for disclosure pursuant to subdivision (e)(3)(C)(i) shall be filed in the district where the grand jury convened. Unless the hearing is ex parte, which it may be when the petitioner is the government, the petitioner shall serve written notice of the petition upon (i) the attorney for the government, (ii) the parties to the judicial proceeding if disclosure is sought in connection with such a proceeding, and (iii) such other persons as the court may direct. The court shall afford those persons a reasonable opportunity to appear and be heard.

(E) If the judicial proceeding giving rise to the petition is in a federal district court in another district, the court shall transfer the matter to that court unless it can reasonably obtain sufficient knowledge of the proceeding to determine whether disclosure is proper. The court shall order transmitted to the court to which the matter is transferred the material sought to be disclosed, if feasible, and a written evaluation of the need for continued grand jury secrecy. The court to which the matter is transferred shall afford the aforementioned persons a reasonable opportunity to appear and be heard.

(4) Sealed Indictments. The federal magistrate judge to whom an indictment is returned may direct that the indictment be kept secret until the defendant is in custody or has been released pending trial. Thereupon the clerk shall seal the indictment and no person shall disclose the return of the indictment except when necessary for the issuance and execution of a warrant or summons.

(5) Closed Hearing. Subject to any right to an open hearing in contempt proceedings, the court shall order a hearing on matters affecting a grand jury proceeding to be closed to the extent necessary to prevent disclosure of matters occurring before a grand jury.

(6) Sealed Records. Records, orders and subpoenas relating to grand jury proceedings shall be kept under seal to the extent and for such time as is necessary to prevent disclosure of matters occurring before a grand jury.

(f) Finding and Return of Indictment. An indictment may be found only upon the concurrence of 12 or more jurors. The indictment shall be returned by the grand jury to a federal magistrate judge in open court. If a complaint or information is pending against the defendant and 12 jurors do not concur in finding an indictment, the foreperson shall so report to a federal magistrate judge in writing forthwith.

(g) Discharge and Excuse. A grand jury shall serve until discharged by the court, but no grand jury may serve more than 18 months unless the court extends the service of the grand jury for a period of six months or less upon a determination that such extension is in the public interest. At any time for cause shown the court may excuse a juror either temporarily or permanently, and in the latter event the court may impanel another person in place of the juror excused.

Rule 7. The Indictment and the Information

(a) Use of Indictment or Information. An offense which may be punished by death shall be prosecuted by indictment. An offense which may be punished by imprisonment for a term exceeding one year or at hard labor shall be prosecuted by indictment or, if indictment is waived, it may be prosecuted by information. Any other offense may be prosecuted by indictment or by information. An information may be filed without leave of court.

(b) Waiver of Indictment. An offense which may be punished by imprisonment for a term exceeding one year or at hard labor may be prosecuted by information if the defendant, after having been advised of the nature of the charge and of the rights of the defendant, waives in open court prosecution by indictment.

(c) Nature and Contents.

(1) In General. The indictment or the information shall be a plain, concise and definite written statement of the essential facts constituting the offense charged. It shall be signed by the attorney for the government. It need not contain a formal commencement, a formal conclusion or any other matter not necessary to such statement. Allegations made in one count may be incorporated by reference in another count. It may be alleged in a single count that the means by which the defendant committed the offense are unknown or that the defendant committed it by one or more specified means. The indictment or information shall state for each count the official or customary citation of the statute, rule, regulation or other provision of law which the defendant is alleged therein to have violated.

(2) Criminal Forfeiture. No judgment of forfeiture may be entered in a criminal proceeding unless the indictment or the information shall allege the extent of the interest or property subject to forfeiture.

(3) Harmless Error. Error in the citation or its omission shall not be ground for dismissal of the indictment or information or for reversal of a conviction if the error or omission did not mislead the defendant to the defendant's prejudice.

(d) Surplusage. The court on motion of the defendant may strike surplusage from the indictment or information.

(e) Amendment of Information. The court may permit an information to be amended at any time before verdict or finding if no additional or different offense is charged and if substantial rights of the defendant are not prejudiced.

(f) Bill of Particulars. The court may direct the filing of a bill of particulars. A motion for a bill of particulars may be made before arraignment or within ten days after arraignment or at such later time as the court may permit. A bill of particulars may be amended at any time subject to such conditions as justice requires.

Rule 8. Joinder of Offenses and of Defendants

(a) Joinder of Offenses. Two or more offenses may be charged in the same indictment or information in a separate count for each offense if the offenses charged, whether felonies or misdemeanors or both, are of the same or similar character or are based on the same act or transaction or on two or more acts or transactions connected together or constituting parts of a common scheme or plan.

(b) Joinder of Defendants. Two or more defendants may be charged in the same indictment or information if they are alleged to have participated in the same act or transaction or in the same series of acts or transactions constituting an offense or offenses. Such defendants may be charged in one or more counts together or separately and all of the defendants need not be charged in each count.

Rule 9. Warrant or Summons Upon Indictment or Information

(a) Issuance. Upon the request of the attorney for the government the court shall issue a warrant for each defendant named in an information supported by a showing of probable cause under oath as is required by Rule 4(a), or in an indictment. Upon the request of the attorney for the government a summons instead of a warrant shall issue. If no request is made, the court may issue either a warrant or a summons in its discretion. More than one warrant or summons may issue for the same defendant. The clerk shall deliver the warrant or summons to the marshal or other person authorized by law to execute or serve it. If a defendant fails to appear in response to the summons, a warrant shall issue. When a defendant arrested with a warrant or given a summons appears initially before a magistrate judge, the magistrate judge shall proceed in accordance with the applicable subdivisions of Rule 5.

(b) Form.

(1) Warrant. The form of the warrant shall be as provided in Rule 4(c)(1) except that it shall be signed by the clerk, it shall describe the offense charged in the indictment or information and it shall command that the defendant be arrested and brought before the nearest available magistrate judge. The amount of bail may be fixed by the court and endorsed on the warrant.

(2) Summons. The summons shall be in the same form as the warrant except that it shall summon the defendant to appear before a magistrate judge at a stated time and place.

(c) Execution or Service; and Return.

(1) Execution or Service. The warrant shall be executed or the summons served as provided in Rule 4(d)(1), (2) and (3). A summons to a corporation shall be served by delivering a copy to an officer or to a managing or general agent or to any other agent authorized by appointment or by law to receive service of process and, if the agent is one authorized by statute to receive service and the statute so requires, by also mailing a copy to the corporation's last known address within the district or at its principal place of business elsewhere in the United States. The officer executing the warrant shall bring the arrested person without unnecessary delay before the nearest available federal magistrate judge or, in the event that a federal magistrate judge is not reasonably available, before a state or local judicial officer authorized by 18 U.S.C. § 3041.

(2) Return. The officer executing a warrant shall make return thereof to the magistrate judge or other officer before whom the defendant is brought. At the request of the attorney for the government any unexecuted warrant shall be returned and cancelled. On or before the return day the person to whom a summons was delivered for service shall make return thereof. At the request of the attorney for the government made at any time while the indictment or information is pending, a warrant returned unexecuted and not cancelled or a summons returned unserved or a duplicate thereof may be delivered by the clerk to the marshal or other authorized person for execution or service.

[(d) Remand to United States Magistrate for Trial of Minor Offenses] (Abrogated Apr. 28, 1982, eff. Aug. 1, 1982).

IV. ARRAIGNMENT AND PREPARATION FOR TRIAL

Rule 10. Arraignment

Arraignment shall be conducted in open court and shall consist of reading the indictment or information to the defendant or stating to the defendant the substance of the charge and calling on the defendant to plead thereto. The defendant shall be given a copy of the indictment or information before being called upon to plead.

Rule 11. Pleas

(a) Alternatives.

(1) In General. A defendant may plead not guilty, guilty, or nolo contendere. If a defendant refuses to plead or if a defendant corporation fails to appear, the court shall enter a plea of not guilty.

(2) Conditional Pleas. With the approval of the court and the consent of the government, a defendant may enter a conditional plea of guilty or nolo contendere, reserving in writing the right, on appeal from the judgment, to review of the adverse determination of any specified pretrial motion. A defendant who prevails on appeal shall be allowed to withdraw the plea.

(b) Nolo Contendere. A defendant may plead nolo contendere only with the consent of the court. Such a plea shall be accepted by the court only after due consideration of the views of the parties and the interest of the public in the effective administration of justice.

(c) Advice to Defendant. Before accepting a plea of guilty or nolo contendere, the court must address the defendant personally in open court and inform the defendant of, and determine that the defendant understands, the following:

(1) the nature of the charge to which the plea is offered, the mandatory minimum penalty provided by law, if any, and the maximum possible penalty provided by law, including the effect of any special parole or supervised release term, the fact that the court is required to consider any applicable sentencing guidelines but many depart from those guidelines under some circumstances, and, when applicable, that the court may also order the defendant to make restitution to any victim of the offense; and

(2) if the defendant is not represented by an attorney, that the defendant has the right to be represented by an attorney at every stage of the proceeding and, if necessary, one will be appointed to represent the defendant; and

(3) that the defendant has the right to plead not guilty or to persist in that plea if it has already been made, the right to be tried by a jury and at that trial the right to the assistance of counsel, the right to confront and cross-examine adverse witnesses, and the right against compelled self-incrimination; and

(4) that if a plea of guilty or nolo contendere is accepted by the court there will not be a further trial of any kind, so that by pleading guilty or nolo contendere the defendant waives the right to a trial; and

(5) if the court intends to question the defendant under oath, on the record, and in the presence of counsel about the offense to which the defendant has pleaded, that the defendant's answers may later be used against the defendant in a prosecution for perjury or false statement.

(d) Insuring That the Plea is Voluntary. The court shall not accept a plea of guilty or nolo contendere without first, by addressing the defendant personally in open court, determining that the plea is voluntary and not the result of force or threats or of promises apart from a plea agreement. The court shall also inquire as to whether the defendant's willingness to plead guilty or nolo contendere results from prior discussions between the attorney for the government and the defendant or the defendant's attorney.

(e) Plea Agreement Procedure.

(1) In General. The attorney for the government and the attorney for the defendant or the defendant when acting pro se may engage in discussions with a view toward reaching an agreement that, upon the entering of a plea of guilty or nolo contendere to a charged offense or to a lesser or related offense, the attorney for the government will do any of the following:

(A) move for dismissal of other charges; or

(B) make a recommendation, or agree not to oppose the defendant's request, for a particular sentence, with the understanding that such recommendation or request shall not be binding upon the court; or

(C) agree that a specific sentence is the appropriate disposition of the case.

The court shall not participate in any such discussions.

(2) Notice of Such Agreement. If a plea agreement has been reached by the parties, the court shall, on the record, require the disclosure of the agreement in open court or, on a showing of good cause, in camera, at the time the plea is offered. If the agreement is of the type specified in subdivision (e)(1)(A) or (C), the court may accept or reject the agreement, or may defer its decision as to the acceptance or rejection until there has been an opportunity to consider the presentence report. If the agreement is of the type specified in subdivision (e)(1)(B), the court shall advise the defendant that if the court does not accept the recommendation or request the defendant nevertheless has no right to withdraw the plea.

(3) Acceptance of a Plea Agreement. If the court accepts the plea agreement, the court shall inform the defendant that it will embody in the judgment and sentence the disposition provided for in the plea agreement.

(4) Rejection of a Plea Agreement. If the court rejects the plea agreement, the court shall, on the record, inform the parties of this fact, advise the defendant personally in open court or, on a showing of good cause, in camera, that the court is not bound by the plea agreement, afford the defendant the opportunity to then withdraw the plea, and advise the defendant that if the defendant persists in a guilty plea or plea of nolo contendere the disposition of the case may be less favorable to the defendant than that contemplated by the plea agreement.

(5) Time of Plea Agreement Procedure. Except for good cause shown, notification to the court of the existence of a plea agreement shall be given at the arraignment or at such other time, prior to trial, as may be fixed by the court.

(6) Inadmissibility of Pleas, Plea Discussions, and Related Statements. Except as otherwise provided in this paragraph, evidence of the following is not, in any civil or criminal proceeding, admissible against the defendant who made the plea or was a participant in the plea discussions:

> (A) a plea of guilty which was later withdrawn;
>
> (B) a plea of nolo contendere;
>
> (C) any statement made in the course of any proceedings under this rule regarding either of the foregoing pleas; or
>
> (D) any statement made in the course of plea discussions with an attorney for the government which do not result in a plea of guilty or which result in a plea of guilty later withdrawn.

However, such a statement is admissible (i) in any proceeding wherein another statement made in the course of the same plea or plea discussions has been introduced and the statement ought in fairness be considered contemporaneously with it, or (ii) in a criminal proceeding for perjury or false statement if the statement was made by the defendant under oath, on the record, and in the presence of counsel.

(f) Determining Accuracy of Plea. Notwithstanding the acceptance of a plea of guilty, the court should not enter a judgment upon such plea without making such inquiry as shall satisfy it that there is a factual basis for the plea.

(g) Record of Proceedings. A verbatim record of the proceedings at which the defendant enters a plea shall be made and, if there is a plea of guilty or nolo contendere, the record shall include, without limitation, the court's advice to the defendant, the inquiry into the voluntariness of the plea including any plea agreement, and the inquiry into the accuracy of a guilty plea.

(h) Harmless Error. Any variance from the procedures required by this rule which does not affect substantial rights shall be disregarded.

Rule 12. Pleadings and Motions Before Trial; Defenses and Objections

(a) Pleadings and Motions. Pleadings in criminal proceedings shall be the indictment and the information, and the pleas of not guilty, guilty and nolo contendere. All other pleas, and demurrers and motions to quash are abolished, and defenses and objections raised before trial which heretofore could have been raised by one or more of them shall be raised only by motion to dismiss or to grant appropriate relief, as provided in these rules.

(b) Pretrial Motions. Any defense, objection, or request which is capable of determination without the trial of the general issue may be raised before trial by motion. Motions may be written or oral at the discretion of the judge. The following must be raised prior to trial:

(1) Defenses and objections based on defects in the institution of the prosecution; or

(2) Defenses and objections based on defects in the indictment or information (other than that it fails to show jurisdiction in the court or to charge an offense which objections shall be noticed by the court at any time during the pendency of the proceedings); or

(3) Motions to suppress evidence; or

(4) Requests for discovery under Rule 16; or

(5) Requests for a severance of charges or defendants under Rule 14.

(c) Motion Date. Unless otherwise provided by local rule, the court may, at the time of the arraignment or as soon thereafter as practicable, set a time for the making of pretrial motions or requests and, if required, a later date of hearing.

(d) Notice by the Government of the Intention to Use Evidence.

(1) At the Discretion of the Government. At the arraignment or as soon thereafter as is practicable, the government may give notice to the defendant of its intention to use specified evidence at trial in order to afford the defendant an opportunity to raise objections to such evidence prior to trial under subdivision (b)(3) of this rule.

(2) At the Request of the Defendant. At the arraignment or as soon thereafter as is practicable the defendant may, in order to afford an opportunity to move to suppress evidence under subdivision (b)(3) of this rule, request notice of the government's intention to use (in its evidence in chief at trial) any evidence which the defendant may be entitled to discover under Rule 16 subject to any relevant limitations prescribed in Rule 16.

(e) Ruling on Motion. A motion made before trial shall be determined before trial unless the court, for good cause, orders that it be deferred for determination at the trial of the general issue or until after verdict, but no such determination shall be deferred if a party's right to appeal is adversely affected. Where factual issues are involved in determining a motion, the court shall state its essential findings on the record.

(f) Effect of Failure To Raise Defenses or Objections. Failure by a party to raise defenses or objections or to make requests which must be made prior to trial, at the time set by the court pursuant to subdivision (c), or prior to any extension thereof made by the court, shall constitute waiver thereof, but the court for cause shown may grant relief from the waiver.

(g) Records. A verbatim record shall be made of all proceedings at the hearing, including such findings of fact and conclusions of law as are made orally.

(h) Effect of Determination. If the court grants a motion based on a defect in the institution of the prosecution or in the indictment or information, it may also order that the defendant be continued in custody or that bail be continued for a specified time pending the filing of a new indictment or information. Nothing in this rule shall be deemed to affect the provisions of any Act of Congress relating to periods of limitations.

(i) Production of Statements at Suppression Hearing. Rule 26.2 applies at a hearing on a motion to suppress evidence under subdivision (b)(3) of this rule. For purposes of this subdivision, a law enforcement officer is deemed a government witness.

Rule 12.1. Notice of Alibi

(a) Notice by Defendant. Upon written demand of the attorney for the government stating the time, date, and place at which the alleged offense was committed, the defendant shall serve within ten days, or at such different time as the court may direct, upon the attorney for the government a written notice of the defendant's intention to offer a defense of alibi. Such notice by the defendant shall state the specific place or places at which the defendant claims to have been at the time of the alleged offense and the names and addresses of the witnesses upon whom the defendant intends to rely to establish such alibi.

(b) Disclosure of Information and Witness. Within ten days thereafter, but in no event less than ten days before trial, unless the court otherwise directs, the attorney for the government shall serve upon the defendant or the defendant's attorney a written notice stating the names and addresses of the witnesses upon whom the government intends to rely to establish the defendant's presence at the scene of the alleged offense and any other witnesses to be relied on to rebut testimony of any of the defendant's alibi witnesses.

(c) Continuing Duty to Disclose. If prior to or during trial, a party learns of an additional witness whose identity, if known, should have been included in the information furnished under subdivision (a) or (b), the party shall promptly notify the other party or the other party's attorney of the existence and identity of such additional witness.

(d) Failure to Comply. Upon the failure of either party to comply with the requirements of this rule, the court may exclude the testimony of any undisclosed witness offered by such party as to the defendant's absence from or presence at, the scene of the alleged offense. This rule shall not limit the right of the defendant to testify.

(e) Exceptions. For good cause shown, the court may grant an exception to any of the requirements of subdivisions (a) through (d) of this rule.

(f) Inadmissibility of Withdrawn Alibi. Evidence of an intention to rely upon an alibi defense, later withdrawn, or of statements made in connection with such intention, is not, in any civil or criminal proceeding, admissible against the person who gave notice of the intention.

Rule 12.2. Notice of Insanity Defense or Expert Testimony of Defendant's Mental Condition

(a) Defense of Insanity. If a defendant intends to rely upon the defense of insanity at the time of the alleged offense, the defendant shall, within the time provided for the filing of pretrial motions or at such later time as the court may direct, notify the attorney for the government in writing of such intention and file a copy of such notice with the clerk. If there is a failure to comply with the requirements of this subdivision, insanity may not be raised as a defense. The court may for cause shown allow late filing of the notice or grant additional time to the parties to prepare for trial or make such other order as may be appropriate.

(b) Expert Testimony of Defendant's Mental Condition. If a defendant intends to introduce expert testimony relating to a mental disease or defect or any other mental condition of the defendant bearing upon the issue of guilt, the defendant shall, within the time provided for the filing of pretrial motions or at such later time as the court may direct, notify the attorney for the government in writing of such intention and file a copy of such notice with the clerk. The court may for cause shown allow late filing of the notice or grant additional time to the parties to prepare for trial or make such other order as may be appropriate.

(c) Mental Examination of Defendant. In an appropriate case the court may, upon motion of the attorney for the government, order the defendant to submit to an examination pursuant to 18 U.S.C. 4241 or 4242. No statement made by the defendant in the course of any examination provided for by this rule, whether the examination be with or without the consent of the defendant, no testimony by the expert based upon such statement, and no other fruits of the statement shall be admitted in evidence against the defendant in any criminal proceeding except on an issue respecting mental condition on which the defendant has introduced testimony.

(d) Failure To Comply. If there is a failure to give notice when required by subdivision (b) of this rule or to submit to an examination when ordered under subdivision (c) of this rule, the court may exclude the testimony of any expert witness offered by the defendant on the issue of the defendant's guilt.

(e) Inadmissibility of Withdrawn Intention. Evidence of an intention as to which notice was given under subdivision (a) or (b), later withdrawn, is not, in any civil or criminal proceeding, admissible against the person who gave notice of the intention.

Rule 12.3. Notice of Defense Based Upon Public Authority

(a) Notice by Defendant; Government Response; Disclosure of Witnesses.

(1) Defendant's Notice and Government's Response. A defendant intending to claim a defense of actual or believed exercise of public authority on behalf of a law enforcement or Federal intelligence agency at the time of the alleged offense shall, within the time provided for the filing of pretrial motions or at such later time as the court may direct, serve upon the attorney for the Government a written notice of such intention and file a copy of such notice with the clerk. Such notice shall identify the law enforcement or Federal intelligence agency and any member of such agency on behalf of which and the period of time in which the defendant claims the actual or believed exercise of public authority occurred. If the notice identifies a Federal intelligence agency, the copy filed with the clerk shall be under seal. Within ten days after receiving the defendant's notice, but in no event less than twenty days before the trial, the attorney for the Government shall serve upon the defendant or the defendant's attorney a written response which shall admit or deny that the defendant exercised the public authority identified in the defendant's notice.

(2) Disclosure of Witnesses. At the time that the Government serves its response to the notice or thereafter, but in no event less than twenty days before the trial, the attorney for the Government may serve upon the defendant or the defendant's attorney a written demand for the names and addresses of the witnesses, if any, upon whom the defendant intends to rely in establishing the defense identified in the notice. Within seven days after receiving the Government's demand, the defendant shall serve upon the attorney for the Government a written statement of the names and addresses of any such witnesses. Within seven days after receiving the defendant's written statement, the attorney for the Government shall serve upon the defendant or the defendant's attorney a written statement of the names and addresses of the witnesses, if any, upon whom the Government intends to rely in opposing the defense identified in the notice.

(3) Additional Time. If good cause is shown, the court may allow a party additional time to comply with any obligation imposed by this rule.

(b) Continuing Duty to Disclose. If, prior to or during trial, a party learns of any additional witness whose identity, if known, should have been included in the written statement furnished under subdivision (a)(2) of this rule, that party shall promptly notify in writing the other party or the other party's attorney of the name and address of any such witness.

(c) Failure to Comply. If a party fails to comply with the requirements of this rule, the court may exclude the testimony of any undisclosed witness offered in support of or in opposition to the defense, or enter such other order as it deems just under the circumstances. This rule shall not limit the right of the defendant to testify.

(d) Protective Procedures Unaffected. This rule shall be in addition to and shall not supersede the authority of the court to issue appropriate protective orders, or the authority of the court to order that any pleading be filed under seal.

(e) Inadmissibility of Withdrawn Defense Based Upon Public Authority. Evidence of an intention as to which notice was given under subdivision (a), later withdrawn, is not, in any civil or criminal proceeding, admissible against the person who gave notice of the intention.

Rule 13. Trial Together of Indictments or Informations

The court may order two or more indictments or informations or both to be tried together if the offenses, and the defendants if there is more than one, could have been joined in a single indictment or information. The procedure shall be the same as if the prosecution were under such single indictment or information.

Rule 14. Relief from Prejudicial Joinder

If it appears that a defendant or the government is prejudiced by a joinder of offenses or of defendants in an indictment or information or by such joinder for trial together, the court may order an election or separate trials of counts, grant a severance of defendants or provide whatever other relief justice requires. In ruling on a motion by a defendant for severance the court may order the attorney for the government to deliver to the court for inspection *in camera* any statements or confessions made by the defendants which the government intends to introduce in evidence at the trial.

Rule 15. Depositions

(a) When Taken. Whenever due to exceptional circumstances of the case it is in the interest of justice that the testimony of a prospective witness of a party be taken and preserved for use at trial, the court may upon motion of such party and notice to the parties order that testimony of such witness be taken by deposition and that any designated book, paper, document, record, recording, or other material not privileged, be produced at the same time and place. If a witness is detained pursuant to section 3144 of title 18, United States Code, the court on written motion of the witness and upon notice to the parties may direct that the witness' deposition be taken. After the deposition has been subscribed the court may discharge the witness.

(b) Notice of Taking. The party at whose instance a deposition is to be taken shall give to every party reasonable written notice of the time and place for taking the deposition. The notice shall state the name and address of each person to be examined. On motion of a party upon whom the notice is served, the court for cause shown may extend or shorten the time or change the place for taking the deposition. The officer having custody of a defendant shall be notified of the time and place set for the examination and shall, unless the defendant waives in writing the right to be present, produce the defendant at the examination and keep the defendant in the presence of the witness during the examination, unless, after being warned by the court that disruptive conduct will cause the defendant's removal from the place of the taking of the deposition, the defendant persists in conduct which is such as to justify exclusion from that place. A defendant not in custody shall have the right to be present at the examination upon request subject to such terms as may be fixed by the court, but a failure, absent good cause shown, to appear after notice and tender of expenses in accordance with subdivision (c) of this rule shall constitute a waiver of that right and of any objection to the taking and use of the deposition based upon that right.

(c) Payment of Expenses. Whenever a deposition is taken at the instance of the government, or whenever a deposition is taken at the instance of a defendant who is unable to bear the expenses of the taking of the deposition, the court may direct that the expense of travel and subsistence of the defendant and the defendant's attorney for attendance at the examination and the cost of the transcript of the deposition shall be paid by the government.

(d) How Taken. Subject to such additional conditions as the court shall provide, a deposition shall be taken and filed in the manner provided in civil actions except as otherwise provided in these rules, provided that (1) in no event shall a deposition be taken of a party defendant without that defendant's consent, and (2) the scope and manner of examination and cross-examination shall be such as would be allowed in the trial itself. The government shall make available to the defendant or the defendant's counsel for examination and use at the taking of the deposition any statement of the witness being deposed which is in the possession of the government and to which the defendant would be entitled at the trial.

(e) Use. At the trial or upon any hearing, a part or all of a deposition, so far as otherwise admissible under the rules of evidence, may be used as substantive evidence if the witness is unavailable, as unavailability is defined in Rule 804(a) of the Federal Rules of Evidence, or the witness gives testimony at the trial or hearing inconsistent with that witness' deposition. Any deposition may also be used by any party for the purpose of contradicting or impeaching the testimony of the deponent as a witness. If only a part of a deposition is offered in evidence by a party, an adverse party may require the offering of all of it which is relevant to the part offered and any party may offer other parts.

(f) Objections to Deposition Testimony. Objections to deposition testimony or evidence or parts thereof and the grounds for the objection shall be stated at the time of the taking of the deposition.

(g) Deposition by Agreement Not Precluded. Nothing in this rule shall preclude the taking of a deposition, orally or upon written questions, or the use of a deposition, by agreement of the parties with the consent of the court.

Rule 16. Discovery and Inspection

(a) Governmental Disclosure of Evidence.

(1) Information Subject to Disclosure.

(A) Statement of Defendant. Upon request of a defendant the government must disclose to the defendant and make available for inspection, copying, or photographing: any relevant written or recorded statements made by the defendant, or copies thereof, within the possession, custody, or control of the government, the existence of which is known, or by the exercise of due diligence may become known, to the attorney for the government; that portion of any written record containing the substance of any relevant oral statement made by the defendant whether before or after arrest in response to interrogation by any person then known to the defendant to be a government agent; and recorded testimony of the defendant before a grand jury which relates to the offense charged. The government must also disclose to the defendant the substance of any other relevant oral statement made by the defendant whether before or after arrest in response to interrogation by any person then known by the defendant to be a government agent if the government intends to use that statement at trial. Upon request of a defendant which is an organization such as a corporation, partnership, association or labor union, the government must disclose to the defendant any of the foregoing statements made by a person who the government contends (1) was, at the time of making the statement, so situated as a director, officer, employee, or agent as to have been able legally to bind the defendant in respect to the subject of the statement, or (2) was, at the time of the offense, personally involved in the alleged conduct constituting the offense and so situated as a director, officer, employee, or agent as to have been able legally to bind the defendant in respect to that alleged conduct in which the person was involved.

(B) Defendant's Prior Record. Upon request of the defendant, the government shall furnish to the defendant such copy of the defendant's prior criminal record, if any, as is within the possession, custody, or control of the government, the existence of which is known, or by the exercise of due diligence may become known, to the attorney for the government.

(C) Documents and Tangible Objects. Upon request of the defendant the government shall permit the defendant to inspect and copy or photograph books, papers, documents, photographs, tangible objects, buildings or places, or copies or portions thereof, which are within the possession, custody or control of the government, and which are material to the preparation of the defendant's defense or are intended for use by the government as evidence in chief at the trial, or were obtained from or belong to the defendant.

(D) Reports of Examinations and Tests. Upon request of a defendant the government shall permit the defendant to inspect and copy or photograph any results or reports of physical or mental examinations, and of scientific tests or experiments, or copies thereof, which are within the possession, custody, or control of the government, the existence of which is known, or by the exercise of due diligence may become known, to the attorney for the government, and which are material to the preparation of the defense or are intended for use by the government as evidence in chief at the trial.

(E) Expert witnesses. At the defendant's request, the government shall disclose to the defendant a written summary of testimony the government intends to use under Rules 702, 703, or 705 of the Federal Rules of Evidence during its case in chief at trial. This summary must describe the witnesses' opinions, the bases and the reasons therefor, and the witnesses' qualifications.

(2) Information Not Subject to Disclosure. Except as provided in paragraphs (A), (B), (D), and (E) of subdivision (a)(1), this rule does not authorize the discovery or inspection of reports, memoranda, or other internal government documents made by the attorney for the government or other government agents in connection with the investigation or prosecution of the case. Nor does the rule authorize the discovery or inspection of statements made by government witnesses or prospective government witnesses except as provided in 18 U.S.C. § 3500.

(3) **Grand Jury Transcripts.** Except as provided in Rules 6, 12(i) and 26.2, and subdivision (a)(1)(A) of this rule, these rules do not relate to discovery or inspection of recorded proceedings of a grand jury.

[(4) **Failure to Call Witness.**] (Deleted Dec. 12, 1975)

(b) **The Defendant's Disclosure of Evidence.**

(1) **Information Subject to Disclosure.**

(A) **Documents and Tangible Objects.** If the defendant requests disclosure under subdivision (a)(1)(C) or (D) of this rule, upon compliance with such request by the government, the defendant, on request of the government, shall permit the government to inspect and copy or photograph books, papers, documents, photographs, tangible objects, or copies or portions thereof, which are within the possession, custody, or control of the defendant and which the defendant intends to introduce as evidence in chief at the trial.

(B) **Reports of Examinations and Tests.** If the defendant requests disclosure under subdivision (a)(1)(C) or (D) of this rule, upon compliance with such request by the government, the defendant, on request of the government, shall permit the government to inspect and copy or photograph any results or reports of physical or mental examinations and of scientific tests or experiments made in connection with the particular case, or copies thereof, within the possession or control of the defendant, which the defendant intends to introduce as evidence in chief at the trial or which were prepared by a witness whom the defendant intends to call at the trial when the results or reports relate to that witness' testimony.

(C) **Expert Witnesses.** If the defendant requests disclosure under subdivision (a)(1)(E) of this rule and the government complies, the defendant, at the government's request, must disclose to the government a written summary of testimony the defendant intends to use under Rules 702, 703 and 705 of the Federal Rules of Evidence as evidence at trial. This summary must describe the opinions of the witnesses, the bases and reasons therefor, and the witnesses' qualifications.

(2) **Information Not Subject To Disclosure.** Except as to scientific or medical reports, this subdivision does not authorize the discovery or inspection of reports, memoranda, or other internal defense documents made by the defendant, or the defendant's attorneys or agents in connection with the investigation or defense of the case, or of statements made by the defendant, or by government or defense witnesses, or by prospective government or defense witnesses, to the defendant, the defendant's agents or attorneys.

[(3) **Failure to Call Witness.**] (Deleted Dec. 12, 1975)

(c) Continuing Duty to Disclose. If, prior to or during trial, a party discovers additional evidence or material previously requested or ordered, which is subject to discovery or inspection under this rule, such party shall promptly notify the other party or that other party's attorney or the court of the existence of the additional evidence or material.

(d) Regulation of Discovery.

(1) Protective and Modifying Orders. Upon a sufficient showing the court may at any time order that the discovery or inspection be denied, restricted, or deferred, or make such other order as is appropriate. Upon motion by a party, the court may permit the party to make such showing, in whole or in part, in the form of a written statement to be inspected by the judge alone. If the court enters an order granting relief following such an ex parte showing, the entire text of the party's statement shall be sealed and preserved in the records of the court to be made available to the appellate court in the event of an appeal.

(2) Failure To Comply With a Request. If at any time during the course of the proceedings it is brought to the attention of the court that a party has failed to comply with this rule, the court may order such party to permit the discovery or inspection, grant a continuance, or prohibit the party from introducing evidence not disclosed, or it may enter such other order as it deems just under the circumstances. The court may specify the time, place and manner of making the discovery and inspection and may prescribe such terms and conditions as are just.

(e) Alibi Witnesses. Discovery of alibi witnesses is governed by Rule 12.1.

Rule 17. Subpoena

(a) For Attendance of Witnesses; Form; Issuance. A subpoena shall be issued by the clerk under the seal of the court. It shall state the name of the court and the title, if any, of the proceeding, and shall command each person to whom it is directed to attend and give testimony at the time and place specified therein. The clerk shall issue a subpoena, signed and sealed but otherwise in blank to a party requesting it, who shall fill in the blanks before it is served. A subpoena shall be issued by a United States magistrate judge in a proceeding before that magistrate judge, but it need not be under the seal of the court.

(b) Defendants Unable to Pay. The court shall order at any time that a subpoena be issued for service on a named witness upon an *ex parte* application of a defendant upon a satisfactory showing that the defendant is financially unable to pay the fees of the witness and that the presence of the witness is necessary to an adequate defense. If the court orders the subpoena to be issued the costs incurred by the process and the fees of the witness so subpoenaed shall be paid in the same manner in which similar costs and fees are paid in case of a witness subpoenaed in behalf of the government.

(c) For Production of Documentary Evidence and of Objects. A subpoena may also command the person to whom it is directed to produce the books, papers, documents or other objects designated therein. The court on motion made promptly may quash or modify the subpoena if compliance would be unreasonable or oppressive. The court may direct that books, papers, documents or objects designated in the subpoena be produced before the court at a time prior to the trial or prior to the time when they are to be offered in evidence and may upon their production permit the books, papers, documents or objects or portions thereof to be inspected by the parties and their attorneys.

(d) Service. A subpoena may be served by the marshal, by a deputy marshal or by any other person who is not a party and who is not less than 18 years of age. Service of a subpoena shall be made by delivering a copy thereof to the person named and by tendering to that person the fee for 1 day's attendance and the mileage allowed by law. Fees and mileage need not be tendered to the witness upon service of a subpoena issued in behalf of the United States or an officer or agency thereof.

(e) Place of Service.

(1) In United States. A subpoena requiring the attendance of a witness at a hearing or trial may be served at any place within the United States.

(2) Abroad. A subpoena directed to a witness in a foreign country shall issue under the circumstances and in the manner and be served as provided in Title 28, U.S.C., § 1783.

(f) For Taking Deposition; Place of Examination.

(1) Issuance. An order to take a deposition authorizes the issuance by the clerk of the court for the district in which the deposition is to be taken of subpoenas for the persons named or described therein.

(2) Place. The witness whose deposition is to be taken may be required by subpoena to attend at any place designated by the trial court, taking into account the convenience of the witness and the parties.

(g) Contempt. Failure by any person without adequate excuse to obey a subpoena served upon that person may be deemed a contempt of the court from which the subpoena issued or of the court for the district in which it issued if it was issued by a United States magistrate judge.

(h) Information Not Subject to Subpoena. Statements made by witnesses or prospective witnesses may not be subpoenaed from the government or the defendant under this rule, but shall be subject to production only in accordance with the provisions of Rule 26.2.

Rule 17.1. Pretrial Conference

At any time after the filing of the indictment or information the court upon motion of any party or upon its own motion may order one or more conferences to consider such matters as will promote a fair and expeditious trial. At the conclusion of a conference the court shall prepare and file a memorandum of the matters agreed upon. No admissions made by the defendant or the defendant's attorney at the conference shall be used against the defendant unless the admissions are reduced to writing and signed by the defendant and the defendant's attorney. This rule shall not be invoked in the case of a defendant who is not represented by counsel.

V. VENUE

Rule 18. Place of Prosecution and Trial

Except as otherwise permitted by statute or by these rules, the prosecution shall be had in a district in which the offense was committed. The court shall fix the place of trial within the district with due regard to the convenience of the defendant and the witnesses and the prompt administration of justice.

Rule 19. Rescinded Feb. 28, 1966, eff. July 1, 1966

Rule 20. Transfer From the District for Plea and Sentence

(a) Indictment or Information Pending. A defendant arrested, held, or present in a district other than that in which an indictment or information is pending against that defendant may state in writing a wish to plead guilty or nolo contendere, to waive trial in the district in which the indictment or information is pending, and to consent to disposition of the case in the district in which that defendant was arrested, held, or present, subject to the approval of the United States attorney for each district. Upon receipt of the defendant's statement and of the written approval of the United States attorneys, the clerk of the court in which the indictment or information is pending shall transmit the papers in the proceeding or certified copies thereof to the clerk of the court for the district in which the defendant is arrested, held, or present, and the prosecution shall continue in that district.

(b) Indictment or Information Not Pending. A defendant arrested, held, or present, in a district other than the district in which a complaint is pending against that defendant may state in writing a wish to plead guilty or nolo contendere, to waive venue and trial in the district in which the warrant was issued, and to consent to disposition of the case in the district in which that defendant was arrested, held, or present, subject to the approval of the United States attorney for each district. Upon filing the written waiver of venue in the district in which the defendant is present, the prosecution may proceed as if venue were in such district.

(c) Effect of Not Guilty Plea. If after the proceeding has been transferred pursuant to subdivision (a) or (b) of this rule the defendant pleads not guilty, the clerk shall return the papers to the court in which the prosecution was commenced, and the proceeding shall be restored to the docket of that court. The defendant's statement that the defendant wishes to plead guilty or nolo contendere shall not be used against that defendant.

(d) Juveniles. A juvenile (as defined in 18 U.S.C. § 5031) who is arrested, held, or present in a district other than that in which the juvenile is alleged to have committed an act in violation of a law of the United States not punishable by death or life imprisonment may, after having been advised by counsel and with the approval of the court and the United States attorney for each district, consent to be proceeded against as a juvenile delinquent in the district in which the juvenile is arrested, held, or present. The consent shall be given in writing before the court but only after the court has apprised the juvenile of the juvenile's rights, including the right to be returned to the district in which the juvenile is alleged to have committed the act, and of the consequences of such consent.

Rule 21. Transfer From the District for Trial

(a) **For Prejudice in the District.** The court upon motion of the defendant shall transfer the proceeding as to that defendant to another district whether or not such district is specified in the defendant's motion if the court is satisfied that there exists in the district where the prosecution is pending so great a prejudice against the defendant that the defendant cannot obtain a fair and impartial trial at any place fixed by law for holding court in that district.

(b) **Transfer in Other Cases.** For the convenience of parties and witnesses, and in the interest of justice, the court upon motion of the defendant may transfer the proceeding as to that defendant or any one or more of the counts thereof to another district.

(c) **Proceedings on Transfer.** When a transfer is ordered the clerk shall transmit to the clerk of the court to which the proceeding is transferred all papers in the proceeding or duplicates thereof and any bail taken, and the prosecution shall continue in that district.

Rule 22. Time of Motion to Transfer

A motion to transfer under these rules may be made at or before arraignment or at such other time as the court or these rules may prescribe.

VI. TRIAL

Rule 23. Trial by Jury or by the Court

(a) **Trial by Jury.** Cases required to be tried by jury shall be so tried unless the defendant waives a jury trial in writing with the approval of the court and the consent of the government.

(b) **Jury of Less Than Twelve.** Juries shall be of 12 but at any time before verdict the parties may stipulate in writing with the approval of the court that the jury shall consist of any number less than 12 or that a valid verdict may be returned by a jury of less than 12 should the court find it necessary to excuse one or more jurors for any just cause after trial commences. Even absent such stipulation, if the court finds it necessary to excuse a juror for just cause after the jury has retired to consider its verdict, in the discretion of the court a valid verdict may be returned by the remaining 11 jurors.

(c) **Trial Without a Jury.** In a case tried without a jury the court shall make a general finding and shall in addition, on request made before the general finding, find the facts specially. Such findings may be oral. If an opinion or memorandum of decision is filed, it will be sufficient if the findings of fact appear therein.

Rule 24. Trial Jurors

(a) **Examination.** The court may permit the defendant or the defendant's attorney and the attorney for the government to conduct the examination of prospective jurors or may itself conduct the examination. In the latter event the court shall permit the defendant or the defendant's attorney and the attorney for the government to supplement the examination by such further inquiry as it deems proper or shall itself submit to the prospective jurors such additional questions by the parties or their attorneys as it deems proper.

(b) Peremptory Challenges. If the offense charged is punishable by death, each side is entitled to 20 peremptory challenges. If the offense charged is punishable by imprisonment for more than one year, the government is entitled to 6 peremptory challenges and the defendant or defendants jointly to 10 peremptory challenges. If the offense charged is punishable by imprisonment for not more than one year or by fine or both, each side is entitled to 3 peremptory challenges. If there is more than one defendant, the court may allow the defendants additional peremptory challenges and permit them to be exercised separately or jointly.

(c) Alternate Jurors. The court may direct that not more than 6 jurors in addition to the regular jury be called and impanelled to sit as alternate jurors. Alternate jurors in the order in which they are called shall replace jurors who, prior to the time the jury retires to consider its verdict, become or are found to be unable or disqualified to perform their duties. Alternate jurors shall be drawn in the same manner, shall have the same qualifications, shall be subject to the same examination and challenges, shall take the same oath and shall have the same functions, powers, facilities and privileges as the regular jurors. An alternate juror who does not replace a regular juror shall be discharged after the jury retires to consider its verdict. Each side is entitled to 1 peremptory challenge in addition to those otherwise allowed by law if 1 or 2 alternate jurors are to be impanelled, 2 peremptory challenges if 3 or 4 alternate jurors are to be impanelled, and 3 peremptory challenges if 5 or 6 alternate jurors are to be impanelled. The additional peremptory challenges may be used against an alternate juror only, and the other peremptory challenges allowed by these rules may not be used against an alternate juror.

Rule 25. Judge; Disability

(a) During Trial. If by reason of death, sickness or other disability the judge before whom a jury trial has commenced is unable to proceed with the trial, any other judge regularly sitting in or assigned to the court, upon certifying familiarity with the record of the trial, may proceed with and finish the trial.

(b) After Verdict or Finding of Guilt. If by reason of absence, death, sickness or other disability the judge before whom the defendant has been tried is unable to perform the duties to be performed by the court after a verdict or finding of guilt, any other judge regularly sitting in or assigned to the court may perform those duties; but if that judge is satisfied that a judge who did not preside at the trial cannot perform those duties or that it is appropriate for any other reason, that judge may grant a new trial.

Rule 26. Taking of Testimony

In all trials the testimony of witnesses shall be taken orally in open court, unless otherwise provided by an Act of Congress or by these rules, the Federal Rules of Evidence, or other rules adopted by the Supreme Court.

Rule 26.1. Determination of Foreign Law

A party who intends to raise an issue concerning the law of a foreign country shall give reasonable written notice. The court, in determining foreign law, may consider any relevant material or source, including testimony, whether or not submitted by a party or admissible under the Federal Rules of Evidence. The court's determination shall be treated as a ruling on a question of law.

Rule 26.2. Production of Witness Statements

(a) Motion for Production. After a witness other than the defendant has testified on direct examination, the court, on motion of a party who did not call the witness, shall order the attorney for the government or the defendant and the defendant's attorney, as the case may be, to produce, for the examination and use of the moving party, any statement of the witness that is in their possession and that relates to the subject matter concerning which the witness has testified.

(b) Production of Entire Statement. If the entire contents of the statement relate to the subject matter concerning which the witness has testified, the court shall order that the statement be delivered to the moving party.

(c) Production of Excised Statement. If the other party claims that the statement contains privileged information or matter that does not relate to the subject matter concerning which the witness has testified, the court shall order that it be delivered to the court in camera. Upon inspection, the court shall excise the portions of the statement that are privileged or that do not relate to the subject matter concerning which the witness has testified, and shall order that the statement, with such material excised, be delivered to the moving party. Any portion of the statement that is withheld from the defendant over the defendant's objection must be preserved by the attorney for the government, and, if the defendant appeals a conviction, shall be made available to the appellate court for the purpose of determining the correctness of the decision to excise the portion of the statement.

(d) Recess for Examination of Statement. Upon delivery of the statement to the moving party, the court, upon application of that party, may recess the proceedings so that counsel may examine the statement and prepare to use it in the proceedings.

(e) Sanction for Failure to Produce Statement. If the other party elects not to comply with an order to deliver a statement to the moving party, the court shall order that the testimony of the witness be stricken from the record and that the trial proceed, or, if it is the attorney for the government who elects not to comply, shall declare a mistrial if required by the interest of justice.

(f) Definition. As used in this rule, a "statement" of a witness means:

(1) a written statement made by the witness that is signed or otherwise adopted or approved by the witness;

(2) a substantially verbatim recital of an oral statement made by the witness that is recorded contemporaneously with the making of the oral statement and that is contained in a stenographic, mechanical, electrical, or other recording or a transcription thereof; or

(3) a statement, however taken or recorded, or a transcription thereof, made by the witness to a grand jury.

(g) Scope of Rule. This rule applies at a suppression hearing conducted under Rule 12, at trial under this rule, and to the extent specified:

(1) in Rule 32(f) at sentencing;

(2) in Rule 32.1(c) at a hearing to revoke or modify probation or supervised release;

(3) in Rule 46(i) at a detention hearing; and

(4) in Rule 8 of the Rules Governing Proceedings under 28 U.S.C. § 2255.

Rule 26.3. Mistrial

Before ordering a mistrial, the court shall provide an opportunity for the government and for each defendant to comment on the propriety of the order, including whether each party consents or objects to a mistrial, and to suggest any alternatives.

Rule 27. Proof of Official Record

An official record or an entry therein or the lack of such a record or entry may be proved in the same manner as in civil actions.

Rule 28. Interpreters

The court may appoint an interpreter of its own selection and may fix the reasonable compensation of such interpreter. Such compensation shall be paid out of funds provided by law or by the government, as the court may direct.

Rule 29. Motion for Judgment of Acquittal

(a) Motion Before Submission to Jury. Motions for directed verdict are abolished and motions for judgment of acquittal shall be used in their place. The court on motion of a defendant or of its own motion shall order the entry of judgment of acquittal of one or more offenses charged in the indictment or information after the evidence on either side is closed if the evidence is insufficient to sustain a conviction of such offense or offenses. If a defendant's motion for judgment of acquittal at the close of the evidence offered by the government is not granted, the defendant may offer evidence without having reserved the right.

(b) Reservation of Decision on Motion. The court may reserve decision on a motion for judgment of acquittal, proceed with the trial (where the motion is made before the close of all the evidence), submit the case to the jury and decide the motion either before the jury returns a verdict or after it returns a verdict of guilty or is discharged without having returned a verdict. If the court reserves decision, it must decide the motion on the basis of the evidence at the time the ruling was reserved.

(c) Motion After Discharge of Jury. If the jury returns a verdict of guilty or is discharged without having returned a verdict, a motion for judgment of acquittal may be made or renewed within 7 days after the jury is discharged or within such further time as the court may fix during the 7-day period. If a verdict of guilty is returned the court may on such motion set aside the verdict and enter judgment of acquittal. If no verdict is returned the court may enter judgment of acquittal. It shall not be necessary to the making of such a motion that a similar motion has been made prior to the submission of the case to the jury.

(d) Same: Conditional Ruling on Grant of Motion. If a motion for judgment of acquittal after verdict of guilty under this Rule is granted, the court shall also determine whether any motion for a new trial should be granted if the judgment of acquittal is thereafter vacated or reversed, specifying the grounds for such determination. If the motion for a new trial is granted conditionally, the order thereon does not affect the finality of the judgment. If the motion for a new trial has been granted conditionally and the judgment is reversed on appeal, the new trial shall proceed unless the appellate court has otherwise ordered. If such motion has been denied conditionally, the appellee on appeal may assert error in that denial, and if the judgment is reversed on appeal, subsequent proceedings shall be in accordance with the order of the appellate court.

Rule 29.1. Closing Argument

After the closing of evidence the prosecution shall open the argument. The defense shall be permitted to reply. The prosecution shall then be permitted to reply in rebuttal.

Rule 30. Instructions

At the close of the evidence or at such earlier time during the trial as the court reasonably directs, any party may file written requests that the court instruct the jury on the law as set forth in the requests. At the same time copies of such requests shall be furnished to all parties. The court shall inform counsel of its proposed action upon the requests prior to their arguments to the jury. The court may instruct the jury before or after the arguments are completed or at both times. No party may assign as error any portion of the charge or omission therefrom unless that party objects thereto before the jury retires to consider its verdict, stating distinctly the matter to which that party objects and the grounds of the objection. Opportunity shall be given to make the objection out of the hearing of the jury and, on request of any party, out of the presence of the jury.

Rule 31. Verdict

(a) Return. The verdict shall be unanimous. It shall be returned by the jury to the judge in open court.

(b) Several Defendants. If there are two or more defendants, the jury at any time during its deliberations may return a verdict or verdicts with respect to a defendant or defendants as to whom it has agreed; if the jury cannot agree with respect to all, the defendant or defendants as to whom it does not agree may be tried again.

(c) Conviction of Less Offense. The defendant may be found guilty of an offense necessarily included in the offense charged or of an attempt to commit either the offense charged or an offense necessarily included therein if the attempt is an offense.

(d) Poll of Jury. When a verdict is returned and before it is recorded the jury shall be polled at the request of any party or upon the court's own motion. If upon the poll there is not unanimous concurrence, the jury may be directed to retire for further deliberations or may be discharged.

(e) Criminal Forfeiture. If the indictment or the information alleges that an interest or property is subject to criminal forfeiture, a special verdict shall be returned as to the extent of the interest or property subject to forfeiture, if any.

VII. JUDGMENT

Rule 32. Sentence and Judgment

(a) In General; Time for Sentencing. When a presentence investigation and report are made under subdivision (b)(1), sentence should be imposed without unnecessary delay following completion of the process prescribed by subdivision (b)(6). The time limits prescribed in subdivision (b)(6) may be either shortened or lengthened for good cause.

(b) Presentence Investigation and Report.

(1) When Made. The probation officer must make a presentence investigation and submit a report to the court before the sentence is imposed, unless:

(A) the court finds that the information in the record enables it to exercise its sentencing authority meaningfully under 18 U.S.C. § 3553; and

(B) the court explains this finding on the record.

(2) Presence of Counsel. On request, the defendant's counsel is entitled to notice and a reasonable opportunity to attend any interview of the defendant by a probation officer in the course of a presentence investigation.

(3) Nondisclosure. The report must not be submitted to the court or its contents disclosed to anyone unless the defendant has consented in writing, has pleaded guilty or nolo contendere, or has been found guilty.

(4) Contents of the Presentence Report. The presentence report must contain—

(A) information about the defendant's history and characteristics, including any prior criminal record, financial condition, and any circumstances that, because they affect the defendant's behavior, may be helpful in imposing sentence or in correctional treatment;

(B) the classification of the offense and of the defendant under the categories established by the Sentencing Commission under 28 U.S.C. § 994(a), as the probation officer believes to be applicable to the defendant's case; the kinds of sentence and the sentencing range suggested for such a category of offense committed by such a category of defendant as set forth in the guidelines issued by the Sentencing Commission under 28 U.S.C. § 994(a)(1); and the probation officer's explanation of any factors that may suggest a different sentence—within or without the applicable guideline—that would be more appropriate, given all the circumstances;

(C) a reference to any pertinent policy statement issued by the Sentencing Commission under 28 U.S.C. § 994(a)(2);

(D) verified information, stated in a nonargumentative style, containing an assessment of the financial, social, psychological, and medical impact on any individual against whom the offense has been committed;

(E) in appropriate cases, information about the nature and extent of nonprison programs and resources available for the defendant;

(F) any report and recommendation resulting from a study ordered by the court under 18 U.S.C. § 3552(b); and

(G) any other information required by the court.

(5) Exclusions. The presentence report must exclude:

(A) any diagnostic opinions that, if disclosed, might seriously disrupt a program of rehabilitation;

(B) sources of information obtained upon a promise of confidentiality; or

(C) any other information that, if disclosed, might result in harm, physical or otherwise, to the defendant or other persons.

(6) Disclosure and Objections.

(A) Not less than 35 days before the sentencing hearing—unless the defendant waives this minimum period—the probation officer must furnish the presentence report to the defendant, the defendant's counsel, and the attorney for the Government. The court may, by local rule or in individual cases, direct that the probation officer not disclose the probation officer's recommendation, if any, on the sentence.

(B) Within 14 days after receiving the presentence report, the parties shall communicate in writing to the probation officer, and to each other, any objections to any material information, sentencing classifications, sentencing guideline ranges, and policy statements contained in or omitted from the presentence report. After receiving objections, the probation officer may meet with the defendant, the defendant's counsel, and the attorney for the Government to discuss those objections. The probation officer may also conduct a further investigation and revise the presentence report as appropriate.

(C) Not later than 7 days before the sentencing hearing, the probation officer must submit the presentence report to the court, together with an addendum setting forth any unresolved objections, the grounds for those objections, and the probation officer's comments on the objections. At the same time, the probation officer must furnish the revisions of the presentence report and the addendum to the defendant, the defendant's counsel, and the attorney for the Government.

(D) Except for any unresolved objection under subdivision (b)(6)(B), the court may, at the hearing, accept the presentence report as its findings of fact. For good cause shown, the court may allow a new objection to be raised at any time before imposing sentence.

(c) Sentence.

(1) Sentencing Hearing. At the sentencing hearing, the court must afford counsel for the defendant and for the Government an opportunity to comment on the probation officer's determinations and on other matters relating to the appropriate sentence, and must rule on any unresolved objections to the presentence report. The court may, in its discretion, permit the parties to introduce testimony or other evidence on the objections. For each matter controverted, the court must make either a finding on the allegation or a determination that no finding is necessary because the controverted matter will not be taken into account in, or will not affect, sentencing. A written record of these findings and determinations must be appended to any copy of the presentence report made available to the Bureau of Prisons.

(2) Production of Statements at Sentencing Hearing. Rule 26.2(a)–(d) and (f) applies at a sentencing hearing under this rule. If a party elects not to comply with an order under Rule 26.2(a) to deliver a statement to the movant, the court may not consider the affidavit or testimony of the witness whose statement is withheld.

(3) Imposition of Sentence. Before imposing sentence, the court must:

(A) verify that the defendant and defendant's counsel have read and discussed the presentence report made available under subdivision (b)(6)(A). If the court has received information excluded from the presentence report under subdivision (b)(5) the court—in lieu of making that information available—must summarize it in writing, if the information will be relied on in determining sentence. The court must also give the defendant and the defendant's counsel a reasonable opportunity to comment on that information;

(B) afford defendant's counsel an opportunity to speak on behalf of the defendant;

(C) address the defendant personally and determine whether the defendant wishes to make a statement and to present any information in mitigation of the sentence;

(D) afford the attorney for the Government an opportunity equivalent to that of the defendant's counsel to speak to the court; and

(E) if sentence is to be imposed for a crime of violence or sexual abuse, address the victim personally if the victim is present at the sentencing hearing and determine if the victim wishes to make a statement or present any information in relation to the sentence.

(4) In Camera Proceedings. The court's summary of information under subdivision (c)(3)(A) may be in camera. Upon joint motion by the defendant and by the attorney for the Government, the court may hear in camera the statements—made under subdivision (c)(3)(B), (C), (D), and (E)—by the defendant, the defendant's counsel, the victim, or the attorney for the Government.

(5) Notification of Right to Appeal. After imposing sentence in a case which has gone to trial on a plea of not guilty, the court must advise the defendant of the right to appeal. After imposing sentence in any case, the court must advise the defendant of any right to appeal the sentence, and of the right of a person who is unable to pay the cost of an appeal to apply for leave to appeal in forma pauperis. If the defendant so requests, the clerk of the court must immediately prepare and file a notice of appeal on behalf of the defendant.

(d) Judgment.

(1) In General. A judgment of conviction must set forth the plea, the verdict or findings, the adjudication, and the sentence. If the defendant is found not guilty or for any other reason is entitled to be discharged, judgment must be entered accordingly. The judgment must be signed by the judge and entered by the clerk.

(2) Criminal Forfeiture. When a verdict contains a finding of criminal forfeiture, the judgment must authorize the Attorney General to seize the interest or property subject to forfeiture on terms that the court considers proper.

(e) Plea Withdrawal. If a motion to withdraw a plea of guilty or nolo contendere is made before sentence is imposed, the court may permit the plea to be withdrawn if the defendant shows any fair and just reason. At any later time, a plea may be set aside only on direct appeal or by motion under 28 U.S.C. § 2255.

(f) Definitions. For purposes of this rule—

(1) "victim" means any individual against whom an offense has been committed for which a sentence is to be imposed, but the right of allocution under subdivision (c)(3)(E) may be exercised instead by—

(A) a parent or legal guardian if the victim is below the age of eighteen years or incompetent; or

(B) one or more family members or relatives designated by the court if the victim is deceased or incapacitated;

if such person or persons are present at the sentencing hearing, regardless of whether the victim is present; and

(2) "crime of violence or sexual abuse" means a crime that involved the use or attempted or threatened use of physical force against the person or property of another, or a crime under chapter 109A of title 18, United States Code.

Rule 32.1. Revocation or Modification of Probation or Supervised Release

(a) Revocation of Probation or Supervised Release.

(1) Preliminary Hearing. Whenever a person is held in custody on the ground that the person has violated a condition of probation or supervised release, the person shall be afforded a prompt hearing before any judge, or a United States magistrate who has been given authority pursuant to 28 U.S.C. § 636 to conduct such hearings, in order to determine whether there is probable cause to hold the person for a revocation hearing. The person shall be given

(A) notice of the preliminary hearing and its purpose and of the alleged violation;

(B) an opportunity to appear at the hearing and present evidence in the person's own behalf;

(C) upon request, the opportunity to question witnesses against the person unless, for good cause, the federal magistrate decides that justice does not require the appearance of the witness; and

(D) notice of the person's right to be represented by counsel.

The proceedings shall be recorded stenographically or by an electronic recording device. If probable cause is found to exist, the person shall be held for a revocation hearing. The person may be released pursuant to Rule 46(c) pending the revocation hearing. If probable cause is not found to exist, the proceeding shall be dismissed.

(2) Revocation Hearing. The revocation hearing, unless waived by the person, shall be held within a reasonable time in the district of jurisdiction. The person shall be given

(A) written notice of the alleged violation;

(B) disclosure of the evidence against the person;

(C) an opportunity to appear and to present evidence in the person's own behalf;

(D) the opportunity to question adverse witnesses; and

(E) notice of the person's right to be represented by counsel.

(b) Modification of Probation or Supervised Release. A hearing and assistance of counsel are required before the terms or conditions of probation or supervised release can be modified, unless the relief to be granted to the person on probation or supervised release upon the person's request or the court's own motion is favorable to the person, and the attorney for the government, after having been given notice of the proposed relief and a reasonable opportunity to object, has not objected. An extension of the term of probation or supervised release is not favorable to the person for the purposes of this rule.

(c) Production of Statements.

(1) In General. Rule 26.2(a)–(d) and (f) applies at any hearing under this rule.

(2) Sanctions for Failure to Produce Statement. If a party elects not to comply with an order under Rule 26.2(a) to deliver a statement to the moving party, the court may not consider the testimony of a witness whose statement is withheld.

Rule 33. New Trial

The court on motion of a defendant may grant a new trial to that defendant if required in the interest of justice. If trial was by the court without a jury the court on motion of a defendant for a new trial may vacate the judgment if entered, take additional testimony and direct the entry of a new judgment. A motion for a new trial based on the ground of newly discovered evidence may be made only before or within two years after final judgment, but if an appeal is pending the court may grant the motion only on remand of the case. A motion for a new trial based on any other grounds shall be made within 7 days after verdict or finding of guilty or within such further time as the court may fix during the 7–day period.

Rule 34. Arrest of Judgment

The court on motion of a defendant shall arrest judgment if the indictment or information does not charge an offense or if the court was without jurisdiction of the offense charged. The motion in arrest of judgment shall be made within 7 days after verdict or finding of guilty, or after plea of guilty or *nolo contendere,* or within such further time as the court may fix during the 7–day period.

Rule 35. Correction of Sentence

(a) Correction of a Sentence on Remand. The court shall correct a sentence that is determined on appeal under 18 U.S.C. 3742 to have been imposed in violation of law, to have been imposed as a result of an incorrect application of the sentencing guidelines, or to be unreasonable, upon remand of the case to the court—

(1) for imposition of a sentence in accord with the findings of the court of appeals; or

(2) for further sentencing proceedings if, after such proceedings, the court determines that the original sentence was incorrect.

(b) Reduction of Sentence for Changed Circumstances. The court, on motion of the Government made within one year after the imposition of the sentence, may reduce a sentence to reflect a defendant's subsequent, substantial assistance in the investigation or prosecution of another person who has committed an offense, in accordance with the guidelines and policy statements issued by the Sentencing Commission pursuant to section 994 of title 28, United States Code. The court may consider a government motion to reduce a sentence made one year or more after imposition of the sentence where the defendant's substantial assistance involves information or evidence not known by the defendant until one year or more after imposition of sentence. The court's authority to reduce a sentence under this subsection includes the authority to reduce such sentence to a level below that established by statute as a minimum sentence.

(c) Correction of Sentence by Sentencing Court. The Court, acting within 7 days after the imposition of sentence, may correct a sentence that was imposed as a result of arithmetical, technical, or other clear error.

Rule 36. Clerical Mistakes

Clerical mistakes in judgments, orders or other parts of the record and errors in the record arising from oversight or omission may be corrected by the court at any time and after such notice, if any, as the court orders.

[VIII. APPEAL] (Abrogated Dec. 4, 1967, eff. July 1, 1968)
[Rule 37. Taking Appeal; and Petition for Writ of Certiorari.] (Abrogated Dec. 4, 1967, Eff. July 1, 1968)

Rule 38. Stay of Execution

(a) Death. A sentence of death shall be stayed if an appeal is taken from the conviction or sentence.

(b) Imprisonment. A sentence of imprisonment shall be stayed if an appeal is taken from the conviction or sentence and the defendant is released pending disposition of appeal pursuant to Rule 9(b) of the Federal Rules of Appellate Procedure. If not stayed, the court may recommend to the Attorney General that the defendant be retained at, or transferred to, a place of confinement near the place of trial or the place where an appeal is to be heard, for a period reasonably necessary to permit the defendant to assist in the preparation of an appeal to the court of appeals.

(c) Fine. A sentence to pay a fine or a fine and costs, if an appeal is taken, may be stayed by the district court or by the court of appeals upon such terms as the court deems proper. The court may require the defendant pending appeal to deposit the whole or any part of the fine and costs in the registry of the district court, or to give bond for the payment thereof, or to submit to an examination of assets, and it may make any appropriate order to restrain the defendant from dissipating such defendant's assets.

(d) Probation. A sentence of probation may be stayed if an appeal from the conviction or sentence is taken. If the sentence is stayed, the court shall fix the terms of the stay.

(e) Criminal Forfeiture, Notice to Victims, and Restitution. A sanction imposed as part of the sentence pursuant to 18 U.S.C. 3554, 3555, or 3556 may, if an appeal of the conviction or sentence is taken, be stayed by the district court or by the court of appeals upon such terms as the court finds appropriate. The court may issue such orders as may be reasonably necessary to ensure compliance with the sanction upon disposition of the appeal, including the entering of a restraining order or an injunction or requiring a deposit in whole or in part of the monetary amount involved into the registry of the district court or execution of a performance bond.

(f) Disabilities. A civil or employment disability arising under a Federal statute by reason of the defendant's conviction or sentence, may, if an appeal is taken, be stayed by the district court or by the court of appeals upon such terms as the court finds appropriate. The court may enter a restraining order or an injunction, or take any other action that may be reasonably necessary to protect the interest represented by the disability pending disposition of the appeal.

[Rule 39. Supervision of Appeal.] (Abrogated Dec. 4, 1967, Eff. July 1, 1968)

IX. SUPPLEMENTARY AND SPECIAL PROCEEDINGS

Rule 40. Commitment to Another District

(a) Appearance Before Federal Magistrate Judge. If a person is arrested in a district other than that in which the offense is alleged to have been committed, that person must be taken without unnecessary delay before the nearest available federal magistrate judge. Preliminary proceedings concerning the defendant must be conducted in accordance with Rules 5 and 5.1, except that if no preliminary examination is held because an indictment has been returned or an information filed or because the defendant elects to have the preliminary examination conducted in the district in which the prosecution is pending, the person must be held to answer upon a finding that such person is the person named in the indictment, information or warrant. If held to answer, the defendant shall be held to answer in the district court in which the prosecution is pending—provided that a warrant is issued in that district if the arrest was made without a warrant—upon production of the warrant or a certified copy thereof. The warrant or certified copy may be produced by facsimile transmission.

(b) Statement by Federal Magistrate Judge. In addition to the statements required by Rule 5, the federal magistrate judge shall inform the defendant of the provisions of Rule 20.

(c) Papers. If a defendant is held or discharged, the papers in the proceeding and any bail taken shall be transmitted to the clerk of the district court in which the prosecution is pending.

(d) Arrest of Probationer or Supervised Releasee. If a person is arrested for a violation of probation or supervised release in a district other than the district having jurisdiction, such person must be taken without unnecessary delay before the nearest available federal magistrate judge. The person may be released under Rule 46(c). The federal magistrate judge shall:

(1) Proceed under Rule 32.1 if jurisdiction over the person is transferred to that district;

(2) Hold a prompt preliminary hearing if the alleged violation occurred in that district, and either (i) hold the person to answer in the district court of the district having jurisdiction or (ii) dismiss the proceedings and so notify that court; or

(3) Otherwise order the person held to answer in the district court of the district having jurisdiction upon production of certified copies of the judgment, the warrant, and the application for the warrant, and upon a finding that the person before the magistrate judge is the person named in the warrant.

(e) **Arrest for Failure to Appear.** If a person is arrested on a warrant in a district other than that in which the warrant was issued, and the warrant was issued because of the failure of the person named therein to appear as required pursuant to a subpoena or the terms of that person's release, the person arrested must be taken without unnecessary delay before the nearest available federal magistrate judge. Upon production of the warrant or a certified copy thereof and upon a finding that the person before the magistrate judge is the person named in the warrant, the federal magistrate judge shall hold the person to answer in the district in which the warrant was issued.

(f) **Release or Detention.** If a person was previously detained or conditionally released, pursuant to chapter 207 of title 18, United States Code, in another district where a warrant, information, or indictment issued, the federal magistrate judge shall take into account the decision previously made and the reasons set forth therefor, if any, but will not be bound by that decision. If the federal magistrate judge amends the release or detention decision or alters the conditions of release, the magistrate judge shall set forth the reasons therefore [1] in writing.

Rule 41. Search and Seizure

(a) **Authority to Issue Warrant.** Upon the request of a federal law enforcement officer or an attorney for the government, a search warrant authorized by this rule may be issued (1) by a federal magistrate judge, or a state court of record within the federal district, for a search of property or for a person within the district, (2) by a federal magistrate judge for a search of property or for a person either within or outside the district if the property or person is within the district when the warrant is sought but might move outside the district before the warrant is executed.

(b) **Property or Persons Which May Be Seized With a Warrant.** A warrant may be issued under this rule to search for and seize any (1) property that constitutes evidence of the commission of a criminal offense; or (2) contraband, the fruits of crime, or things otherwise criminally possessed; or (3) property designed or intended for use or which is or has been used as the means of committing a criminal offense; or (4) person for whose arrest there is probable cause, or who is unlawfully restrained.

(c) **Issuance and Contents.**

(1) **Warrant Upon Affidavit.** A warrant other than a warrant upon oral testimony under paragraph (2) of this subdivision shall issue only on an affidavit or affidavits sworn to before the federal magistrate judge or state judge and establishing the grounds for issuing the warrant. If the federal magistrate judge or state judge is satisfied that grounds for the application exist or that there is probable cause to believe that they exist, that magistrate judge or state judge shall issue a warrant identifying the property or person to be seized and naming or describing the person or place to be searched. The finding of probable cause may be based upon hearsay evidence in whole or in part. Before ruling on a request for a warrant the federal magistrate judge or state judge may require the affiant to appear personally and may examine

---
[1] So in original.

under oath the affiant and any witnesses the affiant may produce, provided that such proceeding shall be taken down by a court reporter or recording equipment and made part of the affidavit. The warrant shall be directed to a civil officer of the United States authorized to enforce or assist in enforcing any law thereof or to a person so authorized by the President of the United States. It shall command the officer to search, within a specified period of time not to exceed 10 days, the person or place named for the property or person specified. The warrant shall be served in the daytime, unless the issuing authority, by appropriate provision in the warrant, and for reasonable cause shown, authorizes its execution at times other than daytime. It shall designate a federal magistrate judge to whom it shall be returned.

(2) Warrant Upon Oral Testimony.

(A) General Rule. If the circumstances make it reasonable to dispense, in whole or in part, with a written affidavit, a Federal magistrate judge may issue a warrant based upon sworn testimony communicated by telephone or other appropriate means, including facsimile transmission.

(B) Application. The person who is requesting the warrant shall prepare a document to be known as a duplicate original warrant and shall read such duplicate original warrant, verbatim, to the Federal magistrate judge. The Federal magistrate judge shall enter, verbatim, what is so read to such magistrate judge on a document to be known as the original warrant. The Federal magistrate judge may direct that the warrant be modified.

(C) Issuance. If the Federal magistrate judge is satisfied that the circumstances are such as to make it reasonable to dispense with a written affidavit and that grounds for the application exist or that there is probable cause to believe that they exist, the Federal magistrate judge shall order the issuance of a warrant by directing the person requesting the warrant to sign the Federal magistrate judge's name on the duplicate original warrant. The Federal magistrate judge shall immediately sign the original warrant and enter on the face of the original warrant the exact time when the warrant was ordered to be issued. The finding of probable cause for a warrant upon oral testimony may be based on the same kind of evidence as is sufficient for a warrant upon affidavit.

(D) Recording and Certification of Testimony. When a caller informs the Federal magistrate judge that the purpose of the call is to request a warrant, the Federal magistrate judge shall immediately place under oath each person whose testimony forms a basis of the application and each person applying for that warrant. If a voice recording device is available, the Federal magistrate judge shall record by means of such device all of the call after the caller informs the Federal magistrate judge that the purpose of the call is to request a warrant. Otherwise a stenographic or longhand verbatim record shall be made. If a voice recording device is used or a stenographic record made, the Federal magistrate judge shall have the record transcribed, shall certify the accuracy of the transcription, and shall file a copy of the original record and the transcription with the court. If a longhand verbatim record is made, the Federal magistrate judge shall file a signed copy with the court.

(E) **Contents.** The contents of a warrant upon oral testimony shall be the same as the contents of a warrant upon affidavit.

(F) **Additional Rule for Execution.** The person who executes the warrant shall enter the exact time of execution on the face of the duplicate original warrant.

(G) **Motion to Suppress Precluded.** Absent a finding of bad faith, evidence obtained pursuant to a warrant issued under this paragraph is not subject to a motion to suppress on the ground that the circumstances were not such as to make it reasonable to dispense with a written affidavit.

(d) **Execution and Return with Inventory.** The officer taking property under the warrant shall give to the person from whom or from whose premises the property was taken a copy of the warrant and a receipt for the property taken or shall leave the copy and receipt at the place from which the property was taken. The return shall be made promptly and shall be accompanied by a written inventory of any property taken. The inventory shall be made in the presence of the applicant for the warrant and the person from whose possession or premises the property was taken, if they are present, or in the presence of at least one credible person other than the applicant for the warrant or the person from whose possession or premises the property was taken, and shall be verified by the officer. The federal magistrate judge shall upon request deliver a copy of the inventory to the person from whom or from whose premises the property was taken and to the applicant for the warrant.

(e) **Motion for Return of Property.** A person aggrieved by an unlawful search and seizure or by the deprivation of property may move the district court for the district in which the property was seized for the return of the property on the ground that such person is entitled to lawful possession of the property. The court shall receive evidence on any issue of fact necessary to the decision of the motion. If the motion is granted, the property shall be returned to the movant, although reasonable conditions may be imposed to protect access and use of the property in subsequent proceedings. If a motion for return of property is made or comes on for hearing in the district of trial after an indictment or information is filed, it shall be treated also as a motion to suppress under Rule 12.

(f) **Motion to Suppress.** A motion to suppress evidence may be made in the court of the district of trial as provided in Rule 12.

(g) **Return of Papers to Clerk.** The federal magistrate judge before whom the warrant is returned shall attach to the warrant a copy of the return, inventory and all other papers in connection therewith and shall file them with the clerk of the district court for the district in which the property was seized.

(h) **Scope and Definition.** This rule does not modify any act, inconsistent with it, regulating search, seizure and the issuance and execution of search warrants in circumstances for which special provision is made. The term "property" is used in this rule to include documents, books, papers and any other tangible objects. The term "daytime" is used in this rule to mean the hours from 6:00 a.m. to 10:00 p.m. according to local time. The phrase "federal law enforcement officer" is used in this rule to mean any government agent, other than an attorney for the government as defined in Rule 54(c), who is engaged in the enforcement of the criminal laws and is within any category of officers authorized by the Attorney General to request the issuance of a search warrant.

Rule 42. Criminal Contempt

(a) Summary Disposition. A criminal contempt may be punished summarily if the judge certifies that the judge saw or heard the conduct constituting the contempt and that it was committed in the actual presence of the court. The order of contempt shall recite the facts and shall be signed by the judge and entered of record.

(b) Disposition Upon Notice and Hearing. A criminal contempt except as provided in subdivision (a) of this rule shall be prosecuted on notice. The notice shall state the time and place of hearing, allowing a reasonable time for the preparation of the defense, and shall state the essential facts constituting the criminal contempt charged and describe it as such. The notice shall be given orally by the judge in open court in the presence of the defendant or, on application of the United States attorney or of an attorney appointed by the court for that purpose, by an order to show cause or an order of arrest. The defendant is entitled to a trial by jury in any case in which an act of Congress so provides. The defendant is entitled to admission to bail as provided in these rules. If the contempt charged involves disrespect to or criticism of a judge, that judge is disqualified from presiding at the trial or hearing except with the defendant's consent. Upon a verdict or finding of guilt the court shall enter an order fixing the punishment.

X. GENERAL PROVISIONS

Rule 43. Presence of the Defendant

(a) Presence Required. The defendant shall be present at the arraignment, at the time of the plea, at every stage of the trial including the impaneling of the jury and the return of the verdict, and at the imposition of sentence, except as otherwise provided by this rule.

(b) Continued Presence Not Required. The further progress of the trial to and including the return of the verdict shall not be prevented and the defendant shall be considered to have waived the right to be present whenever a defendant, initially present,

> (1) is voluntarily absent after the trial has commenced (whether or not the defendant has been informed by the court of the obligation to remain during the trial), or

> (2) after being warned by the court that disruptive conduct will cause the removal of the defendant from the courtroom, persists in conduct which is such as to justify exclusion from the courtroom.

(c) Presence Not Required. A defendant need not be present in the following situations:

(1) A corporation may appear by counsel for all purposes.

(2) In prosecutions for offenses punishable by fine or by imprisonment for not more than one year or both, the court, with the written consent of the defendant, may permit arraignment, plea, trial, and imposition of sentence in the defendant's absence.

(3) At a conference or argument upon a question of law.

(4) At a reduction of sentence under Rule 35.

Rule 44. Right to and Assignment of Counsel

(a) Right to Assigned Counsel. Every defendant who is unable to obtain counsel shall be entitled to have counsel assigned to represent that defendant at every stage of the proceedings from initial appearance before the federal magistrate judge or the court through appeal, unless that defendant waives such appointment.

(b) Assignment Procedure. The procedures for implementing the right set out in subdivision (a) shall be those provided by law and by local rules of court established pursuant thereto.

(c) Joint Representation. Whenever two or more defendants have been jointly charged pursuant to Rule 8(b) or have been joined for trial pursuant to Rule 13, and are represented by the same retained or assigned counsel or by retained or assigned counsel who are associated in the practice of law, the court shall promptly inquire with respect to such joint representation and shall personally advise each defendant of the right to the effective assistance of counsel, including separate representation. Unless it appears that there is good cause to believe no conflict of interest is likely to arise, the court shall take such measures as may be appropriate to protect each defendant's right to counsel.

Rule 45. Time

(a) Computation. In computing any period of time the day of the act or event from which the designated period of time begins to run shall not be included. The last day of the period so computed shall be included, unless it is a Saturday, a Sunday, or a legal holiday, or, when the act to be done is the filing of some paper in court, a day on which weather or other conditions have made the office of the clerk of the district court inaccessible, in which event the period runs until the end of the next day which is not one of the aforementioned days. When a period of time prescribed or allowed is less than 11 days, intermediate Saturdays, Sundays and legal holidays shall be excluded in the computation. As used in these rules, "legal holiday" includes New Year's Day, Birthday of Martin Luther King, Jr., Washington's Birthday, Memorial Day, Independence Day, Labor Day, Columbus Day, Veterans Day, Thanksgiving Day, Christmas Day, and any other day appointed as a holiday by the President or the Congress of the United States, or by the state in which the district court is held.

(b) Enlargement. When an act is required or allowed to be done at or within a specified time, the court for cause shown may at any time in its discretion (1) with or without motion or notice, order the period enlarged if request therefor is made before the expiration of the period originally prescribed or as extended by a previous order or (2) upon motion made after the expiration of the specified period permit the act to be done if the failure to act was the result of excusable neglect; but the court may not extend the time for taking any action under Rules 29, 33, 34 and 35, except to the extent and under the conditions stated in them.

[(c) **Unaffected by Expiration of Term.**] (Rescinded Feb. 28, 1966, eff. July 1, 1966.)

(d) **For Motions; Affidavits.** A written motion, other than one which may be heard *ex parte,* and notice of the hearing thereof shall be served not later than 5 days before the time specified for the hearing unless a different period is fixed by rule or order of the court. For cause shown such an order may be made on *ex parte* application. When a motion is supported by affidavit, the affidavit shall be served with the motion; and opposing affidavits may be served not less than 1 day before the hearing unless the court permits them to be served at a later time.

(e) **Additional Time After Service by Mail.** Whenever a party has the right or is required to do an act within a prescribed period after the service of a notice or other paper upon that party and the notice or other paper is served by mail, 3 days shall be added to the prescribed period.

Rule 46. Release From Custody

(a) **Release Prior to Trial.** Eligibility for release prior to trial shall be in accordance with 18 U.S.C. §§ 3142 and 3144.

(b) **Release During Trial.** A person released before trial shall continue on release during trial under the same terms and conditions as were previously imposed unless the court determines that other terms and conditions or termination of release are necessary to assure such person's presence during the trial or to assure that such person's conduct will not obstruct the orderly and expeditious progress of the trial.

(c) **Pending Sentence and Notice of Appeal.** Eligibility for release pending sentence or pending notice of appeal or expiration of the time allowed for filing notice of appeal, shall be in accordance with 18 U.S.C. § 3143. The burden of establishing that the defendant will not flee or pose a danger to any other person or to the community rests with the defendant.

(d) **Justification of Sureties.** Every surety, except a corporate surety which is approved as provided by law, shall justify by affidavit and may be required to describe in the affidavit the property by which the surety proposes to justify and the encumbrances thereon, the number and amount of other bonds and undertakings for bail entered into by the surety and remaining undischarged and all the other liabilities of the surety. No bond shall be approved unless the surety thereon appears to be qualified.

(e) **Forfeiture.**

(1) **Declaration.** If there is a breach of condition of a bond, the district court shall declare a forfeiture of the bail.

(2) Setting Aside. The court may direct that a forfeiture be set aside in whole or in part, upon such conditions as the court may impose, if a person released upon execution of an appearance bond with a surety is subsequently surrendered by the surety into custody or if it otherwise appears that justice does not require the forfeiture.

(3) Enforcement. When a forfeiture has not been set aside, the court shall on motion enter a judgment of default and execution may issue thereon. By entering into a bond the obligors submit to the jurisdiction of the district court and irrevocably appoint the clerk of the court as their agent upon whom any papers affecting their liability may be served. Their liability may be enforced on motion without the necessity of an independent action. The motion and such notice of the motion as the court prescribes may be served on the clerk of the court, who shall forthwith mail copies to the obligors to their last known addresses.

(4) Remission. After entry of such judgment, the court may remit it in whole or in part under the conditions applying to the setting aside of forfeiture in paragraph (2) of this subdivision.

(f) Exoneration. When the condition of the bond has been satisfied or the forfeiture thereof has been set aside or remitted, the court shall exonerate the obligors and release any bail. A surety may be exonerated by a deposit of cash in the amount of the bond or by a timely surrender of the defendant into custody.

(g) Supervision of Detention Pending Trial. The court shall exercise supervision over the detention of defendants and witnesses within the district pending trial for the purpose of eliminating all unnecessary detention. The attorney for the government shall make a biweekly report to the court listing each defendant and witness who has been held in custody pending indictment, arraignment or trial for a period in excess of ten days. As to each witness so listed the attorney for the government shall make a statement of the reasons why such witness should not be released with or without the taking of a deposition pursuant to Rule 15(a). As to each defendant so listed the attorney for the government shall make a statement of the reasons why the defendant is still held in custody.

(h) Forfeiture of Property. Nothing in this rule or in chapter 207 of title 18, United States Code, shall prevent the court from disposing of any charge by entering an order directing forfeiture of property pursuant to 18 U.S.C. 3142(c)(1)(B)(xi) if the value of the property is an amount that would be an appropriate sentence after conviction of the offense charged and if such forfeiture is authorized by statute or regulation.

(i) Production of Statements.

(1) In General. Rule 26.2(a)–(d) and (f) applies at a detention hearing held under 18 U.S.C. § 3144, unless the court, for good cause shown, rules otherwise in a particular case.

(2) Sanctions for Failure to Produce Statement. If a party elects not to comply with an order under Rule 26.2(a) to deliver a statement to the moving party, at the detention hearing the court may not consider the testimony of a witness whose statement is withheld.

Rule 47. Motions

An application to the court for an order shall be by motion. A motion other than one made during a trial or hearing shall be in writing unless the court permits it to be made orally. It shall state the grounds upon which it is made and shall set forth the relief or order sought. It may be supported by affidavit.

Rule 48. Dismissal

(a) By Attorney for Government. The Attorney General or the United States attorney may by leave of court file a dismissal of an indictment, information or complaint and the prosecution shall thereupon terminate. Such a dismissal may not be filed during the trial without the consent of the defendant.

(b) By Court. If there is unnecessary delay in presenting the charge to a grand jury or in filing an information against a defendant who has been held to answer to the district court, or if there is unnecessary delay in bringing a defendant to trial, the court may dismiss the indictment, information or complaint.

Rule 49. Service and Filing of Papers

(a) Service: When Required. Written motions other than those which are heard ex parte, written notices, designations of record on appeal and similar papers shall be served upon each of the parties.

(b) Service: How Made. Whenever under these rules or by an order of the court service is required or permitted to be made upon a party represented by an attorney, the service shall be made upon the attorney unless service upon the party personally is ordered by the court. Service upon the attorney or upon a party shall be made in the manner provided in civil actions.

(c) Notice of Orders. Immediately upon the entry of an order made on a written motion subsequent to arraignment the clerk shall mail to each party a notice thereof and shall make a note in the docket of the mailing. Lack of notice of the entry by the clerk does not affect the time to appeal or relieve or authorize the court to relieve a party for failure to appeal within the time allowed, except as permitted by Rule 4(b) of the Federal Rules of Appellate Procedure.

(d) Filing. Papers required to be served shall be filed with the court. Papers shall be filed in the manner provided in civil actions.

(e) Filing of Dangerous Offender Notice. A filing with the court pursuant to 18 U.S.C. § 3575(a) or 21 U.S.C. § 849(a) shall be made by filing the notice with the clerk of the court. The clerk shall transmit the notice to the chief judge or, if the chief judge is the presiding judge in the case, to another judge or United States magistrate judge in the district, except that in a district having a single judge and no United States magistrate judge, the clerk shall transmit the notice to the court only after the time for disclosure specified in the aforementioned statutes and shall seal the notice as permitted by local rule.

Rule 50. Calendars; Plan for Prompt Disposition

(a) Calendars. The district courts may provide for placing criminal proceedings upon appropriate calendars. Preference shall be given to criminal proceedings as far as practicable.

(b) Plans for Achieving Prompt Disposition of Criminal Cases. To minimize undue delay and to further the prompt disposition of criminal cases, each district court shall conduct a continuing study of the administration of criminal justice in the district court and before United States magistrate judges of the district and shall prepare plans for the prompt disposition of criminal cases in accordance with the provisions of Chapter 208 of Title 18, United States Code.

Rule 51. Exceptions Unnecessary

Exceptions to rulings or orders of the court are unnecessary and for all purposes for which an exception has heretofore been necessary it is sufficient that a party, at the time the ruling or order of the court is made or sought, makes known to the court the action which that party desires the court to take or that party's objection to the action of the court and the grounds therefor; but if a party has no opportunity to object to a ruling or order, the absence of an objection does not thereafter prejudice that party.

Rule 52. Harmless Error and Plain Error

(a) Harmless Error. Any error, defect, irregularity or variance which does not affect substantial rights shall be disregarded.

(b) Plain Error. Plain errors or defects affecting substantial rights may be noticed although they were not brought to the attention of the court.

Rule 53. Regulation of Conduct in the Court Room

The taking of photographs in the court room during the progress of judicial proceedings or radio broadcasting of judicial proceedings from the court room shall not be permitted by the court.

Rule 54. Application and Exception

(a) Courts. These rules apply to all criminal proceedings in the United States District Courts; in the District Court of Guam; in the District Court for the Northern Mariana Islands, except as otherwise provided in articles IV and V of the covenant provided by the Act of March 24, 1976 (90 Stat. 263); in the District Court of the Virgin Islands; and (except as otherwise provided in the Canal Zone Code) in the United States District Court for the District of the Canal Zone; in the United States Courts of Appeals; and in the Supreme Court of the United States; except that the prosecution of offenses in the District Court of the Virgin Islands shall be by indictment or information as otherwise provided by law.

(b) Proceedings.

(1) Removed Proceedings. These rules apply to criminal prosecutions removed to the United States district courts from state courts and govern all procedure after removal, except that dismissal by the attorney for the prosecution shall be governed by state law.

(2) Offenses Outside a District or State. These rules apply to proceedings for offenses committed upon the high seas or elsewhere out of the jurisdiction of any particular state or district, except that such proceedings may be had in any district authorized by 18 U.S.C. § 3238.

(3) Peace Bonds. These rules do not alter the power of judges of the United States or of United States magistrate judges to hold to security of the peace and for good behavior under Revised Statutes, § 4069, 50 U.S.C. § 23, but in such cases the procedure shall conform to these rules so far as they are applicable.

(4) Proceedings Before United States Magistrate Judges. Proceedings involving misdemeanors and other petty offenses are governed by Rule 58.

(5) Other Proceedings. These rules are not applicable to extradition and rendition of fugitives; civil forfeiture of property for violation of a statute of the United States; or the collection of fines and penalties. Except as provided in Rule 20(d) they do not apply to proceedings under 18 U.S.C., Chapter 403—Juvenile Delinquency—so far as they are inconsistent with that chapter. They do not apply to summary trials for offenses against the navigation laws under Revised Statutes §§ 4300–4305, 33 U.S.C. §§ 391–396, or to proceedings involving disputes between seamen under Revised Statutes, §§ 4079–4081, as amended, 22 U.S.C. §§ 256–258, or to proceedings for fishery offenses under the Act of June 28, 1937, c. 392, 50 Stat. 325–327, 16 U.S.C. §§ 772–772i, or to proceedings against a witness in a foreign country under 28 U.S.C. § 1784.

(c) Application of Terms. As used in these rules the following terms have the designated meanings.

"Act of Congress" includes any act of Congress locally applicable to and in force in the District of Columbia, in Puerto Rico, in a territory or in an insular possession.

"Attorney for the government" means the Attorney General, an authorized assistant of the Attorney General, a United States Attorney, an authorized assistant of a United States Attorney, when applicable to cases arising under the laws of Guam the Attorney General of Guam or such other person or persons as may be authorized by the laws of Guam to act therein, and when applicable to cases arising under the laws of the Northern Mariana Islands the Attorney General of the Northern Mariana Islands or any other person or persons as may be authorized by the laws of the Northern Marianas to act therein.

"Civil action" refers to a civil action in a district court.

The words "demurrer," "motion to quash," "plea in abatement," "plea in bar" and "special plea in bar," or words to the same effect, in any act of Congress shall be construed to mean the motion raising a defense or objection provided in Rule 12.

"District court" includes all district courts named in subdivision (a) of this rule.

"Federal magistrate judge" means a United States magistrate judge as defined in 28 U.S.C. §§ 631–639, a judge of the United States or another judge or judicial officer specifically empowered by statute in force in any territory or possession, the Commonwealth of Puerto Rico, or the District of Columbia, to perform a function to which a particular rule relates.

"Judge of the United States" includes a judge of a district court, court of appeals, or the Supreme Court.

"Law" includes statutes and judicial decisions.

"Magistrate judge" includes a United States magistrate as defined in 28 U.S.C. §§ 631–639, a judge of the United States, another judge or judicial officer specifically empowered by statute in force in any territory or possession, the Commonwealth of Puerto Rico, or the District of Columbia, to perform a function to which a particular rule relates, and a state or local judicial officer, authorized by 18 U.S.C. § 3041 to perform the functions prescribed in Rules 3, 4, and 5.

"Oath" includes affirmations.

"Petty offense" is defined in 18 U.S.C. § 19.

"State" includes District of Columbia, Puerto Rico, territory and insular possession.

"United States magistrate judge" means the officer authorized by 28 U.S.C. §§ 631–639.

Rule 55. Records

The clerk of the district court and each United States magistrate judge shall keep records in criminal proceedings in such form as the Director of the Administrative Office of the United States Courts may prescribe. The clerk shall enter in the records each order or judgment of the court and the date such entry is made.

Rule 56. Courts and Clerks

The district court shall be deemed always open for the purpose of filing any proper paper, of issuing and returning process and of making motions and orders. The clerk's office with the clerk or a deputy in attendance shall be open during business hours on all days except Saturdays, Sundays, and legal holidays, but a court may provide by local rule or order that its clerk's office shall be open for specified hours on Saturdays or particular legal holidays other than New Year's Day, Birthday of Martin Luther King, Jr., Washington's Birthday, Memorial Day, Independence Day, Labor Day, Columbus Day, Veterans Day, Thanksgiving Day, and Christmas Day.

Rule 57. Rules by District Courts

Each district court by action of a majority of the judges thereof may from time to time, after giving appropriate public notice and an opportunity to comment, make and amend rules governing its practice not inconsistent with these rules. A local rule so adopted shall take effect upon the date specified by the district court and shall remain in effect unless amended by the district court or abrogated by the judicial council of the circuit in which the district is located. Copies of the rules and amendments so made by any district court shall upon their promulgation be furnished to the judicial council and the Administrative Office of the United States Courts and be made available to the public. In all cases not provided for by rule, the district judges and magistrate judges may regulate their practice in any manner not inconsistent with these rules or those of the district in which they act.

Rule 58. Procedure for Misdemeanors and Other Petty Offenses

(a) **Scope.**

(1) **In General.** This rule governs the procedure and practice for the conduct of proceedings involving misdemeanors and other petty offenses, and for appeals to judges of the district courts in such cases tried by United States magistrate judges.

(2) **Applicability of Other Federal Rules of Criminal Procedure.** In proceedings concerning petty offenses for which no sentence of imprisonment will be imposed the court may follow such provisions of these rules as it deems appropriate, to the extent not inconsistent with this rule. In all other proceedings the other rules govern except as specifically provided in this rule.

(3) **Definition.** The term "petty offenses for which no sentence of imprisonment will be imposed" as used in this rule, means any petty offenses as defined in 18 U.S.C. § 19 as to which the court determines, that, in the event of conviction, no sentence of imprisonment will actually be imposed.

(b) **Pretrial Procedures.**

(1) **Trial Document.** The trial of a misdemeanor may proceed on an indictment, information, or complaint or, in the case of a petty offense, on a citation or violation notice.

(2) **Initial Appearance.** At the defendant's initial appearance on a misdemeanor or other petty offense charge, the court shall inform the defendant of:

(A) the charge, and the maximum possible penalties provided by law, including payment of a special assessment under 18 U.S.C. § 3013, and restitution under 18 U.S.C. § 3663;

(B) the right to retain counsel;

(C) unless the charge is a petty offense for which appointment of counsel is not required, the right to request the assignment of counsel if the defendant is unable to obtain counsel;

(D) the right to remain silent and that any statement made by the defendant may be used against the defendant;

(E) the right to trial, judgment, and sentencing before a judge of the district court, unless the defendant consents to trial, judgment, and sentencing before a magistrate judge;

(F) unless the charge is a petty offense, the right to trial by jury before either a United States magistrate judge or a judge of the district court; and

(G) if the defendant is held in custody and charged with a misdemeanor other than a petty offense, the right to a preliminary examination in accordance with 18 U.S.C. § 3060, and the general circumstances under with the defendant may secure pretrial release.

(3) Consent and Arraignment.

(a) Trial Before a United States Magistrate Judge. If the defendant signs a written consent to be tried before the magistrate judge which specifically waives trial before a judge of the district court, the magistrate judge shall take the defendant's plea. The defendant may plead not guilty, guilty or with the consent of the magistrate judge, nolo contendere.

(b) Failure to Consent. If the defendant does not consent to trial before the magistrate judge, the defendant shall be ordered to appear before a judge of the district court judge for further proceedings on notice.

(c) Additional Procedures Applicable Only to Petty Offenses for Which No Sentence of Imprisonment Will be Imposed. With respect to petty offenses for which no sentence of imprisonment will be imposed, the following additional procedures are applicable:

(1) Plea of Guilty or Nolo Contendere. No plea of guilty or nolo contendere shall be accepted unless the court is satisfied that the defendant understands the nature of the charge and the maximum possible penalties provided by law.

(2) Waiver of Venue for Plea and Sentence. A defendant who is arrested, held, or present in a district other than that in which the indictment, information, complaint, citation or violation notice is pending against that defendant may state in writing a wish to plead guilty or nolo contendere, to waive venue and trial in the district in which the proceeding is pending, and to consent to disposition of the case in the district in which that defendant was arrested, is held, or is present. Unless the defendant thereafter pleads not guilty, the prosecution shall be had as if venue were in such district, and notice of the same shall be given to the magistrate judge in the district where the proceeding was originally commenced. The defendant's statement of a desire to plead guilty or nolo contendere is not admissible against the defendant.

(3) Sentence. The court shall afford the defendant an opportunity to be heard in mitigation. The court shall then immediately proceed to sentence the defendant, except that in the discretion of the court, sentencing may be continued to allow an investigation by the probation service or submission of additional information by either party.

(4) Notification of Right to Appeal After imposing sentence in a case which has gone to trial on a plea of not guilty, the court shall advise the defendant of the defendant's right to appeal including any right to appeal the sentence. There shall be no duty on the court to advise the defendant of any right of appeal after sentence is imposed following a plea of guilty or nolo contendere, except that the court shall advise the defendant of any right to appeal the sentence.

(d) Securing the Defendant's Appearance; Payment in Lieu of Appearance.

(1) Forfeiture of Collateral. When authorized by local rules of the district court, payment of a fixed sum may be accepted in suitable cases in lieu of appearance and as authorizing the termination of the proceedings. Local rules may make provision for increases in fixed sums not to exceed the maximum fine which could be imposed.

(2) Notice to Appear. If a defendant fails to pay a fixed sum, request a hearing, or appear in response to a citation or violation notice, the clerk or a magistrate judge may issue a notice for the defendant to appear before the court on a date certain. The notice may also afford the defendant an additional opportunity to pay a fixed sum in lieu of appearance, and shall be served upon the defendant by mailing a copy to the defendant's last known address.

(3) Summons or Warrant. Upon an indictment or a showing by one of the other documents specified in subdivision (b)(1) of probable cause to believe that an offense has been committed and that the defendant has committed it, the court may issue an arrest warrant or, if no warrant is requested by the attorney for the prosecution, a summons. The showing of probable cause shall be made in writing upon oath or under penalty for perjury, but the affiant need not appear before the court. If the defendant fails to appear before the court in response to a summons, the court may summarily issue a warrant for the defendant's immediate arrest and appearance before the court.

(e) Record. Proceedings under this rule shall be taken down by a reporter or recorded by suitable sound equipment.

(f) New Trial. The provisions of Rule 33 shall apply.

(g) Appeal.

(1) Decision, Order, Judgment or Sentence by a District Judge. An appeal from a decision, order, judgment or conviction or sentence by a judge of the district court shall be taken in accordance with the Federal Rules of Appellate Procedure.

(2) Decision, Order, Judgment or Sentence by a United States Magistrate Judge.

(a) Interlocutory Appeal. A decision or order by a magistrate judge which, if made by a judge of the district court, could be appealed by the government or defendant under any provision of law, shall be subject to an appeal to a judge of the district court provided such appeal is taken within 10 days of the entry of the decision or order. An appeal shall be taken by filing with the clerk of court a statement specifying the decision or order from which an appeal is taken and by serving a copy of the statement upon the adverse party, personally or by mail, and by filing a copy with the magistrate judge.

(b) Appeal From Conviction or Sentence. An appeal from a judgment of conviction or sentence by a magistrate judge to a judge of the district court shall be taken within 10 days after entry of the judgment. An appeal shall be taken by filing with the clerk of court a statement specifying the judgment from which an appeal is taken, and by serving a copy of the statement upon the United States Attorney, personally or by mail, and by filing a copy with the magistrate judge.

(c) Record. The record shall consist of the original papers and exhibits in the case together with any transcript, tape, or other recording of the proceedings and a certified copy of the docket entries which shall be transmitted promptly to the clerk of court. For purposes of the appeal, a copy of the record of such proceedings shall be made available at the expense of the United States to a person who establishes by affidavit the inability to pay or give security therefor, and the expense of such copy shall be paid by the Director of the Administrative Office of the United States Courts.

(d) Scope of Appeal. The defendant shall not be entitled to a trial de novo by a judge of the district court. The scope of the appeal shall be the same as an appeal from a judgment of a district court to a court of appeals.

(3) Stay of Execution; Release Pending Appeal. The provisions of Rule 38 relating to stay of execution shall be applicable to a judgment of conviction or sentence. The defendant may be released pending appeal in accordance with the provisions of law relating to release pending appeal from a judgment of a district court to a court of appeals.

Rule 59. Effective Date

These rules take effect on the day which is 3 months subsequent to the adjournment of the first regular session of the 79th Congress, but if that day is prior to September 1, 1945, then they take effect on September 1, 1945. They govern all criminal proceedings thereafter commenced and so far as just and practicable all proceedings then pending.

Rule 60. Title

These rules may be known and cited as the Federal Rules of Criminal Procedure.

Appendix D

PROPOSED AMENDMENTS TO FEDERAL RULES OF CRIMINAL PROCEDURE

[These amendments were approved by the Supreme Court and submitted to Congress on April 27, 1995; they will take effect on December 1, 1995, unless Congress takes contrary action. New material is underlined and material to be deleted is lined through.]

Rule 5. Initial Appearance Before the Magistrate Judge

(a) **In General.** Except as otherwise provided in this rule, An an officer making an arrest under a warrant issued upon a complaint or any person making an arrest without a warrant shall must take the arrested person without unnecessary delay before the nearest available federal magistrate judge or, in the event that if a federal magistrate judge is not reasonably available, before a state or local judicial officer authorized by 18 U.S.C. § 3041. If a person arrested without a warrant is brought before a magistrate judge, a complaint, satisfying the probable cause requirements of Rule 4(a), must be promptly filed shall be filed forthwith which shall comply with the requirements of Rule 4(a) with respect to the showing of probable cause. When a person, arrested with or without a warrant or given a summons, appears initially before the magistrate judge, the magistrate judge shall must proceed in accordance with the applicable subdivisions of this rule. An officer making an arrest under a warrant issued upon a complaint charging solely a violation of 18 U.S.C. § 1073 need not comply with this rule if the person arrested is transferred without unnecessary delay to the custody of appropriate state or local authorities in the district of arrest and an attorney for the government moves promptly, in the district in which the warrant was issued, to dismiss the complaint.

* * *

Rule 40. Commitment to Another District

(a) **Appearance Before Federal Magistrate Judge.** If a person is arrested in a district other than that in which the offense is alleged to have been committed, that person shall be taken without unnecessary delay before the nearest available federal magistrate judge, in accordance with the provisions of Rule 5. Preliminary proceedings concerning the defendant shall be conducted in accordance with Rules 5 and 5.1, except that if no preliminary examination is held because an indictment has been returned or an information filed or because the defendant elects to have the preliminary examination conducted in the district in which the prosecution is pending, the person shall be held to answer upon a finding that such person is the person named in the indictment, information or warrant. If held to answer, the defendant shall be held to answer in the district court in which the prosecution is pending—provided that a warrant is issued in that district if the arrest was made without a warrant—upon production of the warrant or a certified copy thereof. The warrant or certified copy may be produced by facsimile transmission.

* * *

Rule 43. Presence of the Defendant

(a) Presence Required. The defendant ~~shall~~ <u>must</u> be present at the arraignment, at the time of the plea, at every stage of the trial including the impaneling of the jury and the return of the verdict, and at the imposition of sentence, except as otherwise provided by this rule.

(b) Continued Presence not Required. The further progress of the trial to and including the return of the verdict<u>, and the imposition of sentence</u>, <u>will</u> ~~shall~~ not be prevented and the defendant <u>will</u> ~~shall~~ be considered to have waived the right to be present whenever a defendant, initially present <u>at trial or having pleaded guilty or nolo contendere,</u>

(1) is voluntarily absent after the trial has commenced (whether or not the defendant has been informed by the court of the obligation to remain during the trial), ~~or~~

<u>(2) in a noncapital case, is voluntarily absent at the imposition of sentence, or</u>

~~(2)~~<u>(3)</u> after being warned by the court that disruptive conduct will cause the removal of the defendant from the courtroom, persists in conduct which is such as to justify exclusion from the courtroom.

(c) Presence not Required. A defendant need not be present ~~in the following situations~~:

(1) ~~A corporation may appear by counsel for all purposes.~~ <u>when represented by counsel and the defendant is an organization, as defined in 18 U.S.C. § 18;</u>

(2) ~~In prosecutions for offenses~~ <u>when the offense is</u> punishable by fine or by imprisonment for not more than one year or both, the court, with the written consent of the defendant, may permit arraignment, plea, trial, and imposition of sentence in the defendant's absence~~.~~<u>;</u>

(3) ~~At~~ <u>when the proceeding involves only</u> a conference or ~~argument~~ <u>hearing</u> upon a question of law~~.~~<u>;</u>

<u>(4) when the proceeding is a pretrial session in which the defendant can participate through video teleconferencing and waives the right to be present in court; or</u>

~~(4)~~<u>(5)</u> ~~At~~ <u>when the proceeding involves</u> a <u>correction</u> ~~reduction~~ of sentence under Rule 35.

Rule 49. Service and Filing of Papers

[Subdivision (e) to be deleted.]

Rule 57. Rules by District Courts

(a) In General.

(1) Each district court ~~by action of~~ <u>acting by</u> a majority of ~~the~~ <u>its</u> district ~~the~~ judges ~~thereof~~ may ~~from time to time~~, after giving appropriate public notice and an opportunity to comment, make and amend rules governing its practice ~~not inconsistent these rules~~. <u>A local rule must be consistent with—but not duplicative of—Acts of Congress and rules adopted under 28 U.S.C. § 2072 and must conform to any uniform numbering system prescribed by the Judicial Conference of the United States.</u>

(2) <u>A local rule imposing a requirement of form must not be enforced in a manner that causes a party to lose rights because of a negligent failure to comply with the requirement.</u>

(b) Procedure When There Is no Controlling Law. <u>A judge may regulate practice in any manner consistent with federal law, these rules, and local rules of the district. No sanction or other disadvantage may be imposed for noncompliance with any requirement not in federal law, federal rules, or the local district rules unless the alleged violator has been furnished in the particular case with actual notice of the requirement.</u>

(c) Effective Date and Notice. A local rule so adopted shall take effect upon the date specified by the district court and shall remain in effect unless amended by the district court or abrogated by the judicial council of the circuit in which the district is located. Copies of the rules and amendments so made by any district court ~~shall~~ <u>must</u> upon their promulgation be furnished to the judicial council and the Administrative Office of the United States Courts and ~~shall~~ <u>must</u> be made available to the public. ~~In all cases not provided for by rule, the district judges and magistrate judges may regulate their practice in any manner not inconsistent with these rules or those of the district in which they act.~~

†